The Role of the Member of Parliament Since 1868

The Role of the Member of Parliament Since 1868

From Gentlemen to Players

Michael Rush

OXFORD

UNIVERSITY PRESS

OXFORD

UNIVERSITY PRESS

Great Clarendon Street, Oxford OX2 6DP

Oxford University Press is a department of the University of Oxford.
It furthers the University's objective of excellence in research, scholarship,
and education by publishing worldwide in

Oxford New York

Athens Auckland Bangkok Bogotá Buenos Aires Cape Town
Chennai Dar es Salaam Delhi Florence Hong Kong Istanbul Karachi
Kolkata Kuala Lumpur Madrid Melbourne Mexico City Mumbai Nairobi
Paris São Paulo Shanghai Singapore Taipei Tokyo Toronto Warsaw

and associated companies in Berlin Ibadan

Published in the United States
by Oxford University Press Inc., New York

First published 2001

British Library Cataloguing in Publication Data

Data available

Library of Congress Cataloging in Publication Data
Rush, Michael, 1937–
The role of the member of parliament since 1868: from gentlemen to players/
by Michael Rush.
p. cm.
1. Great Britain. Parliament. House of Commons—History. 2. Legislators—
Great Britain—History. I. Title.
JN673.R85 2001   328.41'072—dc21   2001032878

ISBN 0–19–827577–3

1 3 5 7 9 10 8 6 4 2

Typeset in Stone Sans and Stone Serif by
Cambrian Typesetters, Frimley, Surrey
Printed in Great Britain
on acid-free paper by
T.J. International Ltd.,
Padstow, Cornwall

PREFACE

This book has had a gestation period considerably longer than several generations of elephants. My interest in Parliament began as an undergraduate at the University of Sheffield, grew considerably during my doctoral research into the selection of parliamentary candidates, and became my central research interest soon after I joined the University of Exeter in 1964. The book is thus the culmination of nearly forty years' teaching and research, each informing the other. However, much of my knowledge and understanding of Parliament comes from my long-standing membership of the Study of Parliament Group (SPG), founded in 1964 and consisting of Officers of the two Houses of Parliament and academics with a particular interest in Parliament. This combination of practitioners and academics has been extremely fruitful, as evidenced by the many publications produced under the auspices of the SPG and the evidence given to select committees. In addition, much of my research has involved direct contact with MPs, the practitioners at the heart of this book. I strongly believe that the academic analysis of institutions like Parliament should be embedded in the realities of politics, but academic analysis greatly aids the understanding of those realities. It therefore follows that neither Parliament nor the role of its members can be fully understood without placing both in their historical and political contexts. This is attempted partly by making extensive use of contemporary views of Parliament, both by practitioners and various types of commentators, and by analysing parliamentary activity, both individually and collectively, through Parliament's own records. How successful that effort has been is for the reader to judge.

The book inevitably owes much to many people: to my colleagues at the University of Exeter, especially Victor Wiseman—holder of the Chair of Politics at Exeter from 1963 until his death in 1969—who did much to encourage and extend my interest in Parliament; to the many students who have taken my course on

Parliament, who made and continue to make me think and think again; and to my fellow-members of the SPG, without whom I would know and understand even less than I do. In the end, of course, I remain responsible for any errors, misjudgements and misinterpretations.

Especial thanks, however, are also due to Peter Fletcher, who set up the data-base from which the tables on MPs' backgrounds and political careers are drawn, to Dr Charles Garrity, who helped so much with the *Hansard* indexes, to Dominic Byatt and Amanda Watkins of OUP, who must have wondered at time, if the manuscript would ever materialize, and to Mark Taylor for his splendidly efficient and helpful copy-editing. Above all, I owe an immense debt to my wife, Jean, without whose support and encouragement the gestation period might never have come to an end; it is to her that this book is dedicated.

March 2001
Michael Rush,
Exeter

CONTENTS

TABLES

1

Parliamentary Government

'All ideas seek institutional realisation;
all institutions embody purposes'[1]

Introduction

Between 1865 and 1867 Walter Bagehot wrote the series of articles subsequently published as *The English Constitution*[2] in which he revealed 'the efficient secret'[3] of British politics. This was, of course, the Cabinet, 'a hyphen which joins, a buckle which fastens, the legislative part of the state to the executive part of the state'.[4] It was also in 1867 that Alpheus Todd, the recently-appointed Librarian of the newly-created Parliament of Canada, published the first volume of *On Parliamentary Government in England: its Origins, Development, and Practical Operation*.[5] Both were writing at a crucial juncture in the development of parliamentary government: the modern party system, involving two monolithic parties, each with an extra-parliamentary organization for fighting elections, competing for power, the victor using a cohesive majority in the House of

---

[1] Bernard Crick, *In Defence of Politics*, Penguin Books, London, 1st ed. 1964, 199.

[2] Walter Bagehot, *The English Constitution, Collected Works* (ed. Norman St. John Stevas), 5, *The Economist*, London 1974, 165–409. The original articles appeared in the *Fortnightly Review* between May 1865 and January 1867. A second edition with an introductory section was published in 1872.

[3] *Ibid.*, 210.   [4] *Ibid.*, 212.

[5] The second volume was published in 1869. Todd died in 1884, but a second edition he had been preparing was completed by his son, A. H. Todd, and published by Longman, London: vol. 1 in 1887 and vol. 2 in 1889. In 1840 Alpheus Todd had produced a manual of parliamentary practice, *The Practice and Privileges of the Two Houses of Parliament* for use by the House of Assembly of Upper Canada (Ontario). This was four year before the publication of the first edition of Erskine May's *Treatise on the Law, Privileges, Proceedings and Usage of Parliament* (1844). Todd was clearly familiar with Bagehot, citing him briefly in *Parliamentary Government*.

Commons to carry out a programme of legislation, was beginning to take shape. Neither fully-anticipated the development and impact of such parties, even though both appreciated the significance of party on the operation of parliamentary government. Indeed, Bagehot argued 'party is of its essence'[6] and expressed fears of two possible outcomes of the extension of the vote to skilled working men by the Reform Act of 1867. On the one hand, he feared that the parties would simply crudely seek to outbid each other for the working man's vote and, on the other, that serious class antagonism would result.[7] Writing in the Introduction to the second edition of his book in 1872, Bagehot had the advantage of knowing that in the general election of 1868 more than 99 per cent of the MPs elected were supporters of Gladstone or Disraeli, and he therefore simply speaks of 'both our parties'. Todd had a different concern: he recognized the importance of party, but the fluid party situation after 1846 led him to observe that 'no government can now expect to continue in office by dint of mere party strength. The House of Commons has become more difficult to control . . .'.[8]

Thirty-five years later, in 1902, Moisei Ostrogorski, a Russian scholar, described and analysed in detail these party changes in a massive study comparing party structures in Britain and the United States.[9] In the British case Ostrogorski was particularly interested in the development of the Birmingham Caucus, Joseph Chamberlain's political machine, which, like its American counterpart, he saw as the inevitable model for all political parties in mass democracies. However, Ostrogorski underestimated the ability of parliamentary leaders, and therefore party leaders, in Britain to control their extra-parliamentary organizations, rather than be controlled by them. Even the Labour Party, which in contrast to the Conservative and Liberal Parties, was formed outside Parliament in order to secure the representation of working people, succumbed to the norm of

---

[6] Bagehot, *English Constitution*, 295.
[7] Ibid., Introduction, 173–4.
[8] Todd, *On Parliamentary Government*, 1, 132.
[9] Moisei I. Ostrogorski, *Democracy and the Organisation of Political Parties, Vol. I—England, Vol. II—the United States*, edited and abridged by S. M. Lipset, Quadrangle Books, Chicago, Ill., 1964. Aspects of Ostrogorski's work and theories were published in article form in French in the early 1890s, but his book was published in English.

the leadership controlling the party membership.[10] Nonetheless, the emphasis that Ostrogorski placed on the importance of parties in modern political systems, especially mass democracies, was entirely justified.

This was recognized by Josef Redlich in his monumental study of House of Commons' procedure: 'it it necessary never to lose sight of the actual existence of political parties'.[11] However, Redlich's interest was the internal workings of the House of Commons and he traced in great detail the changes in Commons' procedure from the passing of the Reform Act of 1832. In particular, he showed how government control of the House of Commons, through its timetable and agenda, increased from something close to minimal control to something more akin to absolute control. The means was procedure, the vehicle was party.

In the meantime, the role of party in this process had been traced by Lawrence Lowell, Professor of Political Science at Harvard,[12] who showed that, by the end of the nineteenth century, party voting in the House of Commons was overwhelmingly the norm. This was the final block in the edifice of the modern party system in Britain, but its importance had already been recognized in 1877 by the then Clerk Assistant of the House, Sir Reginald Palgrave, when he wrote, 'It is the discipline enforced by party warfare which enables the Commons to act, not merely efficiently, but at all.'[13]

That three of the five studies mentioned were by observers from outside Britain[14] may be coincidental. But it may have given each

[10] See Robert T. McKenzie, *British Political Parties: The Distribution of Power within the Conservative and Labour Parties,* Heinemann, London, 1955.

[11] Josef Redlich, *The Procedures of the House of Commons* (trans. A. Ernest Steinthal), Constable, London, 1908 (originally published 1905), preface by Sir Courtenay Ilbert, the Clerk of the House of Commons, I, 124n. Redlich also published a history of English local government.

[12] 'The influence of party upon legislatures in England and America', *Annual Report of the American Historical Association,* 1901, 1, 321–542. The data is also published in A. L. Lowell, *The Government of England,* Macmillan, New York, NY, new ed. 1920 (originally published 1908). See also Hugh Berrington, 'Partisanship and dissidence in the nineteenth century House of Commons, *Parliamentary Affairs,* 21, 1967–8, 338–74, which reviews and extends Lowell's data.

[13] Sir Reginald Palgrave, *The House of Commons: Illustrations of its History and Practice,* Macmillan, London, 1878, p. 33. Palgrave was Clerk Assistant 1870–86 and Clerk of the House 1886–1900.

[14] Two were not British and Todd, although born in London, had emigrated to Canada with his parents at the age of 12. He was, of course, a British subject and, probably, like many Canadians of his time, regarded himself as British.

a degree of detachment that contributed significantly to their insights. That said, during the nineteenth century there was no shortage of studies by British scholars and commentators.[15] Of these, perhaps two still attract attention—Bagehot and Dicey, the one because of his focus on the role of the Cabinet and modern arguments about Cabinet versus prime-ministerial government, the other because of his focus on the concept of and modern concerns about parliamentary sovereignty. The interest in Todd and Redlich for this study is their focus on the operation of parliamentary government and, in Ostrogorski and Lowell, for their focus on the significance of party. The aim of the study is to examine how the development of parliamentary government in Britain has affected the role of the Member of Parliament. It is, in part, a study in institutional adaptation: faced with growing demands, how has Parliament, more especially the House of Commons, responded? How has it coped with the growth of government, itself a response to changing ideological perspectives about the intervention of the state in the affairs of society? Changes in the way Parliament operates are bound to affect the role of its members. The focus is almost exclusively on the House of Commons, since, if Parliament remains the locus of any power, that power will reside in the Commons rather than the House of Lords. To achieve this, however, it is necessary to place parliamentary government in its wider context, before returning to the British case.

The Meaning of Parliamentary Government

The origins of parliamentary government lie deep in English history and its development has been long, spasmodic, haphazard and by no means inevitable, the product of evolution rather than revolution. In the context of the history of the British Isles the United Kingdom Parliament is of relatively recent origin, dating from the union of the English and Scottish Parliaments in 1707,

---

[15] Apart from Bagehot, see the 3rd Earl Grey, *Parliamentary Government considered with reference to a Reform of Parliament*, London, 1st ed. 1858; A. V. Dicey, *An Introduction to the Study of the Law of the Constitution*, Macmillan, London, 1st ed. 1885; and Sir William Anson, *The Law and the Constitution*, Clarendon Pres, Oxford, 1st ed. 1886.

extended by the parliamentary union with Ireland in 1800, and subsequently modified by the partition of Ireland in 1920, but the foundations of parliamentary government had already been laid in England. Profound as the social, economic and political conse- quences of the English Revolution were, the Revolution Settlement of 1689 was an adaptation of existing institutions, not the creation of new ones. Only during the English Revolution, notably in the Putney Debates,[16] did those directly engaged in politics discuss publicly and formally whether the country had the most appropri- ate form of government and whether some other form might be more appropriate. To be sure, the Protectorate (1653–9) was a period of institutional experimentation, but, Cromwell's military governors apart, it was experimentation with previously-existing institutions, not an attempt to create totally new ones. What parliamentary government has meant since that time has varied as it has developed and changed. What is important at this juncture is to define parliamentary government in its modern form.

Parliamentary government comprises a set of political arrange- ments in which the executive is constitutionally responsible to and whose personnel are drawn from the legislature. This means, firstly, that the legitimacy or authority of the executive or government rests upon its ability to secure and retain the support of a majority of the members of the legislature. Secondly, it means that the government is responsible or accountable to the legislature for its conduct of affairs. Thirdly, and in order to facilitate that relation- ship, it means that members of the executive are also members of the legislature. This allows, on the one hand, ministers to explain and defend their policies and the administration of them and, on the other, members of the legislature to question ministers directly and discuss policy and administration in their presence. The ulti- mate sanction in the hands of the legislature is to withdraw its support of or confidence in the executive, forcing it to resign or seek a new mandate through an election.

These constitutional arrangements are in direct contrast to those found in presidential-congressional systems, in which the execu- tive, in the person of the president, is constitutionally responsible

---

[16] See A. S. P. Woodhouse (ed.), *Puritanism and Liberty: Being the Army Debates (1647–9)*, J. M. Dent, London, 1938.

not to the legislature but to the people, and in which neither the president nor any member of the executive may simultaneously be a member of the executive and of the legislature. This is, of course, the American model and the Founding Fathers of the United States deliberately incorporated the separation of powers—the constitutional separation of the executive from the legislature—into the United States' Constitution. They did so in the belief that they were correcting the defects of parliamentary government in eighteenth century Britain. In particular, they thought that too much power was concentrated in the hands of the executive—the king and his ministers, who effectively controlled the constitutional source of power, the House of Commons, largely through bribery and corruption. That their understanding of the situation was not entirely accurate is beside the point; their perceptions led them to adopt radically different constitutional arrangements.

Certainly, they were not alone in being concerned about the ability of the government to control the House of Commons. In 1780 the Commons passed one of its most famous motions:

That the influence of the Crown has increased, is increasing and ought to be diminished.   (*Parliamentary History*, 21, 6 April 1780, cc. 340–74.)

What that motion reflected was the concern that George III and his ministers could normally rely on sufficient support in the Commons to remain in office and secure parliamentary approval for their policies. This support was based on a combination of MPs who sat for parliamentary seats directly controlled by the government and its supporters and MPs who were willing to be bribed directly or by the provision of jobs, sinecures, and pensions. What it knowingly ignored was that there was sufficient fluidity in the system—because of independent Members, Members who refused to stay bribed, and shifting alliances—to render government control less than absolute.[17] It reflected more particularly concern about the more active role George III was playing in politics than had been the case with three immediate predecessors, Queen Anne,

[17] See Sir Lewis Namier, *The Structure of Politics at the Accession of George III*, Macmillan, London, 2nd ed. 1958; Sir Lewis Namier and John Brooke, *The History of Parliament: The House of Commons, 1754–1790*, HMSO for the History of Parliament Trust, London, 1964, Vol. I, Introductory Survey; and R.G. Thorne, *The History of Parliament: The House of Commons, 1790–1820*, Secker and Warburg for the History of Parliament Trust, London, 1980, Vol. I, Chapter IV.

George I, and George II. Before the accession of George III in 1760 power had become increasingly concentrated in the hands of the politicians. In effect, George III was trying to turn the clock back, just as James II had sought to do before him. Indeed, there was sufficient concern at the beginning of eighteenth century about the ability of the government to control the House of Commons that Britain came close to adopting a separation of powers in that the Act of Settlement, 1701 forbade Members of Parliament to accept 'offices of profit under the Crown', which included ministerial posts. This was quickly found to be inconvenient by both MPs and ministers and was abandoned, but a vestige remained until 1926 in that some ministers were required to seek the approval of their acceptance of office from their constituents through a by-election.[18]

The model of parliamentary government developed in England and then Britain has been adopted by many other countries, not least those that were part of the British Empire. In varying ways and to a varying extent the model has been developed and adapted: in Germany, for example, the Bundestag may not eject one Chancellor before it is in a position to nominate a successor, a device designed to avoid the instability experienced under the Weimar Republic (1919–33). More recently, Israel separated the election of the prime minister from that of the legislature, but the prime minister remained a member of the Knesset, the members of the government continued to be drawn from it, and the government remained dependent on retaining its confidence. France under the Fifth Republic has gone a step further, creating a hybrid parliamentary-presidential system: the president and the National Assembly are elected separately and ministers may not be members of the legislature, but the government requires majority support in the National Assembly and ministers may participate in its proceedings.

Parliamentary government is not therefore unique to Britain, but, like all sets of political arrangements, it operates in significantly different ways in different countries. Much depends upon

[18] Until the Re-election of Ministers (1919) Amendment Act, 1926 MPs appointed to office between general elections were required to seek re-election through a by-election. This accounted for approximately a fifth of all by-election vacancies between 1832 and 1926.

the circumstances temporally and spatially: in particular, social, economic, and cultural factors, and value systems shape the political system and its operation, but are themselves subject to change. This in turn may result in significant changes in theory and practice, even to the point where practice is or appears to be divorced from theory, so that the latter exists, or appears to exist, in form not substance. Arguably, this is the situation which prevails—or appears to prevail—in the modern British parliamentary system: parties fight elections, win majorities, form governments, use their disciplined majorities to force a programme through the House of Commons, pursuing policies for which they claim to have an electoral mandate, all the while paying lip-service to the norms of parliamentary government by allowing their proposals and policies to be debated, responding to questioning, reporting to Parliament, but always winning the parliamentary votes that matter. All until it is time for another election, when, of course, the governing party may lose, in which case its victorious rival merely begins a new cycle in the same process.

Such a description smacks at worst of caricature, at best of exaggeration, but it is a recognizable one, widely accepted and probably reflected in the widespread cynicism expressed about politics and politicians. What evidence is there to sustain such a view? Three examples provide strong, prime facie support. First, in each parliamentary session or year almost all government legislation is passed and that which is not usually fails because of government's legislative timetable has got too crowded; in contrast, legislative proposals introduced by backbenchers or Private Members, whether government supporters or not, mostly fail to pass. Secondly, most votes in the House of Commons are on party lines; dissent in the division lobbies has increased since the late sixties, but it remains limited. And, thirdly, governments are rarely forced out of office by losing the confidence of the House of Commons; most changes of government result from defeat at a general election.

The broad picture this evidence paints is an accurate one: a government with a cohesive majority normally does get its way. Whatever constitutional theory may say about Parliament controlling the executive, the reality is that, for the most part, the executive controls Parliament. However, there is a more complex and subtle picture to be drawn and that is part of the task of this study. For instance, crucial to the government's control of Parliament is party. Conservative governments have controlled the House of Commons in the sense of having a party majority three times since 1945—1951–64, 1970–4, and 1979–97. Similarly, Labour governments have controlled the Commons four times since 1945—1945–1, 1964–70, 1974–6, and since 1997. However, these majorities were the product of each party's ability to win sufficient electoral support in the country to win a majority of seats in the Commons, although in no case did that support amount to, let alone exceed more than 50 per cent of those who voted. Had a system of proportional representation been in operation or were it adopted for future elections, *single-party* majority government would become the exception rather than the rule. Of course, some form of coalition government might well emerge and a stable coalition, sustained by a clear and cohesive majority would be as much in control of the House of Commons as a single-party majority government. Failure to secure a majority at a general election—or losing such a majority through by-elections—and seeking to form and sustain a minority government, dependent sometimes on the *ad hoc* support, sometimes on the agreed support of other parties, severely reduces government control of the Commons, as the minority Labour governments of February–October 1974 and 1976–9 found. Much depends on the parliamentary arithmetic: in 1976–9 the Callaghan government was safe from ejection from office unless all non-Labour MPs voted against it or, of course, unless it lost the support of its own Members. It thus sustained a large number of defeats, but none on a vote of confidence, until, that is, the last one. The term 'cohesive' becomes crucial here: a significant fall in party cohesion reduces the ability of any government, single-party or coalition, majority or minority, to control the House of Commons, as the experience of the Major government illustrates. In spite winning what was initially regarded as a comfortable working majority of twenty-one in the 1992 general election, the 1992–7 Conservative government ran into increasing difficulty with its own backbench supporters, particularly over Europe. The governing party's cohesion was undermined and, through a combination of by-election losses and defections, found its majority gradually whittled away. Yet, forty years earlier, Churchill's post-war government of 1951–5 survived without difficulty on a majority of sixteen, later seventeen, after a by-election victory.

In the period after 1832, however, MPs were less 'reliable' and no government could be sure of winning all its votes. Between 1846, following the repeal of the Corn Laws, and 1868, when the modern two-party system could be said to have emerged, matters 'worsened'. They worsened because the party system was in a state of flux, a realignment was in process, leading to Conservative and Liberal Parties that were recognizably modern. They had built up extra-parliamentary organizations, they offered themselves as alternative governments, and, in the House of Commons, MPs voted increasingly with their parties. Neither was the monolithic party characteristic of modern political parties, but both were moving rapidly in that direction.

Was this inevitable? It is easy with hindsight to say it was, but hindsight needs to be treated with care; it can be a reliable servant but an unreliable master. The extension of the franchise made the setting up of far more extensive extra-parliamentary party organization necessary: support from a mass electorate could not be won by the methods and resources available to individuals, nor through the rudimentary party machinery that previously existed. Party organization also laid the basis for party cohesion: loyalty to the party inside and outside Parliament could be and was demanded at the risk of being cast out into the political wilderness. These forces shaped the development of modern party structures. This was Ostrogorski's point in respect of both Britain and the United States, but it was not only the Conservative and Liberal Parties in Britain that were affected—so also were the Irish Nationalists. Under Charles Stewart Parnell they became a highly-disciplined, highly-organized party inside Parliament, but their electoral base was significantly different. Irish Nationalist support was nationally-based—or within the context of the United Kingdom, regionally-based—and heavily, though not exclusively, religiously-based. Yet the Irish Nationalist Party was unlike religiously-based parties in a number of continental-European countries: it sought to defend Catholics in Ireland rather than the interests of the Catholic faith generally; its objective was essentially nationalist, not religious. The Irish Nationalist objective was Home Rule—the restoration of the Irish Parliament, self-government through the reintroduction of parliamentary government to Ireland. What sort of party system would have eventually emerged in Ireland had Home Rule been achieved is a matter of speculation, but it would not have been the party system that emerged after the partition of Ireland in 1920, based largely on the protagonists in the Irish Civil War.

There was, of course, a regional and religious dimension to the electoral support of the Conservative and Liberal Parties, notwithstanding the impact of electoral bribery and corruption before 1885. However, this reflected traditional socio-economic ties, the old division between Whigs and Tories, which included important ideological differences, and, increasingly, the occupational divide between manual and non-manual workers. The nature and extent of this support fostered the development of two monolithic parties, first Conservative and Liberal, then Conservative and Labour. In this it was assisted, but not caused, by the first-past-the-post or simple plurality electoral system. The major impact of the latter has been to produce single-party majority governments as the norm. The relationship between parliamentary government and the party system is crucial, but the party system is a crucial factor in any form of representative government and modern parliamentary government is representative government.

Parliamentary Government and Representative Government

Modern representative government is normally seen as a form of democracy, that is systems of government that seek to involve the consent of and control by the governed. Representative government seeks to achieve this by having the attitudes and interests of the governed taken into account in the making and implementation of policy through bodies of individuals or representatives elected by them for that purpose. Modern democracy, in the form of liberal-democracy, is also commonly associated with the existence of various safeguards, such as freedom of speech and association, equality before the law, and, in some value systems, social and economic rights, such as a right to education, housing, food and work, provided, if necessary, by the state.[19]

---

[19] See Barry Holden, *The Nature of Democracy*, Nelson, London, 1974 and David Held, *Models of Democracy*, Polity Press, Cambridge, 2nd ed., 1996.

Historically, however, representative government has taken what would be regarded as non-democratic forms judged by modern democratic values, in which representation was based not on equality, as expressed in the phrase 'one person, one vote, one value', but upon interests, particularly property. Owners of property were perceived as having a stake in society, which those without property lacked. The latter, it was argued in defence of the *status quo*, did not need direct representation in any case, since they were the beneficiaries of 'virtual' or indirect representation through the existing representatives, an argument subsequently applied to women before they had the vote.

Nonetheless, in both the historical and contemporary conceptions of representative government, the question of whether those elected to bodies like the House of Commons were representatives or delegates has always loomed large.[20] The representative in this context is someone who claims freedom of action in deciding what is best in the interests of those he or she represents; the delegate is someone acting on the instructions of those he or she represents— two distinct meanings of the term 'represent'. Notwithstanding periodic attempts by electors to issue instructions or exact pledges from Members of Parliament and parties to enforce discipline by demanding the signing of pledges or clear commitments to abide by party rules, the balance in Britain has always been clearly in favour of the representative rather than the delegate. Thus, in his *Commentaries on the Laws of England*, published in 1765, Blackstone states:

Every Member, though chosen by one particular district, when elected and returned serves for the whole realm. For the end of his coming thither is not particular, but general; not barely to the advantage of his constituents, but the *common* wealth . . . And therefore he is not bound, like a deputy in the United Provinces [of the Netherlands], to consult with, or take the advice of his constituents upon any particular point, unless he himself thinks proper so to do.   (Sir William Blackstone, *Commentaries on the Laws of England*, London, 1765, I, 159).

This clearly reflects the view of Sir William Yonge, MP expressed in the House of Commons in 1745:

---

[20] See A. H. Birch, *Representative and Responsible Government*, Allen and Unwin, London, 1964, 13–17.

Everyone knows that, by our constitution, after a gentleman is chosen, he is the representative, or if you please, the attorney of the people of England, and as such is at full freedom to act as he thinks best for the people of England in general. He may receive, he may ask, he may even follow the advice of his particular constituents; but he is not obliged, nor ought he, to follow their advice, if he thinks it inconsistent with the general interest of his country.   (Quoted by Strathearn Gordon, *Our Parliament*, Cassell for the Hansard Society, London, 6th ed., 1964, 45.)

However, much the most well-known and frequently repeated statement of the appropriate MP-constituent relationship is that of Edmund Burke, so much so that it gives rise to the concept of the Burkean MP:

... it ought to be the happiness and glory of a representative to live in the strictest union, the closest correspondence, and most unreserved communication with his constituents. Their wishes ought to have great weight with him, their opinion high respect, their business his unremitted attention. It is his duty to sacrifice his repose, his pleasures, his satisfaction, to theirs, and, above all, even, and in all cases, to prefer their interest to his own. But, his unbiased opinion, his mature judgement, his enlightened conscience, he ought not to sacrifice to you, to any man, to any set of men living ... Your representative owes you, not his industry only, but his judgement; and he betrays, instead of serving you, if he sacrifices it to your opinion. ...

To deliver an opinion is the right of all men; that of constituents is a weighty and respectable opinion, which a representative ought always rejoice to hear; and which he ought always most seriously to consider. But authoritative instructions; mandates issued, which the Member is bound blindly to obey, to vote and argue for, though contrary to the clearest conviction of his judgement and conscience—these are things utterly unknown to the laws of the land, and which arise from a fundamental mistake of the whole order and tenor of our Constitution.

Parliament is not a Congress of ambassadors from different and hostile interests; which interests each must maintain, as an agent, and advocate, against other agents and advocates; but Parliament is a deliberative assembly of one nation, with one interest, that of the whole; where, not local purposes, not local prejudices, ought to guide, but the general good, resulting from the general reason of the whole. You choose a Member indeed: but when you have chosen him, he is not the Member for Bristol, but he is a Member of Parliament.   (Edmund Burke, 'Letter to the Electors of Bristol', *Works*, George Bell, London, 1883, I, 446–7).[21]

[21] See also David Judge, 'Representation in Westminster in the 1990s: the ghost of Edmund Burke', *Journal of Legislative Studies*, 5, 1999, 12–34.

Whenever modern MPs are faced with demands from constituents that they act in this way or that or are threatened by the local parties with deselection because they have publicly opposed or criticized party policy, they invariably summon the ghost of Edmund Burke to their aid. However, it is often forgotten that when Burke thus addressed the electors of Bristol there were cases of constituents instructing Members and Members willing to accept instructions. It is important, therefore, to examine briefly what happens in practice.

It has long been the practice for parliamentary candidates, certainly the vast majority who are elected, to offer themselves with party labels attached to their names and, once elected to accept their party's whip in the House of Commons. This raises three questions. First, if the Member changes or abandons his or her party allegiance between elections, should he or she resign and seek re-election in a by-election under the new party label or, if appropriate, as an independent candidate? In practice, this is not the general rule:[22] Members crossing the floor of the have mostly resisted demands for their resignation and implicitly or explicitly adopted a Burkean defence—by changing allegiance they have acted, in their judgement, in the best interests of *all* their constituents, not merely those who voted for them, whatever they may think.

The second question is whether a local party is entitled to deselect an MP who has publicly criticized or opposed party policy, whether in Parliament or the country at large. There is no shortage of examples of local parties refusing to adopt rebellious MPs.[23] Indeed, all parties have mechanisms for such action, although the grounds for action may include other reasons for dissatisfaction, such as a Member who has allegedly neglected their constituency.

[22] See David Butler and Gareth Butler, *Twentieth Century British Political Facts, 1900–2000*, Macmillan, London, 2000, 245–9. The cases of Dick Taverne, Labour MP for Lincoln from 1962 to 1972, when he resigned and won a by–election in 1973 under the label Democratic Labour, and Bruce Douglas-Mann, Labour MP for Kensington N. from 1970 to February 1974 and Mitcham and Morden from February 1974 to 1981, when he resigned but lost a by-election in 1982 as an Independent SDP candidate, are exceptions to the general rule.

[23] See Butler and Butler, *British Political Facts*, 251–2; Michael Rush, *The Selection of Parliamentary Candidates*, Nelson, London, 1969, 54–5 and 161–3; and Alison Young, *The Reselection of MPs*, Heinemann, London, 1983.

The logic of the rebellious MP situation is that local parties choose candidates in the belief that they share the same party aims and policies and that local parties are therefore entitled to reject an MP who no longer shares their aims and policies. The reality is more complex: quite apart from the MP, the local party or the party nationally may have shifted its stance, either particularly or generally; the disagreement may have been over a particular policy or generally; and the act of rebellion may be a single instance or a series of instances. The logic remains, however, and the incidence of MPs being rejected by their local parties, even if they are seen as examples of an anti-Burkean position, does not undermine the prevailing view of the MP as a representative. Burke himself acknowledged the right of his electors to reject him and the logic of his position extends to party:

He should not blame his [his constituents] if they did reject him; the event would afford a very useful example, on the one hand, of a senator inflexibly adhering to his opinion against interest and against popularity; and, on the other, of constituents exercising their undoubted right of rejection; not on corrupt motives, but from their persuasion, that whom they had chosen had acted against the judgement and interest of those he represented.   (*Parliamentary History*, T. C. Hansard, London, 1814, Proceedings in the House of Commons on the Irish Trade Bills, 2 April 1778, c. 1123.)

It would, of course, be naïve and factually inaccurate not to acknowledge that disputes between MPs and their local parties cannot have a personal dimension, but that disturbs the logic of the relationship only a little.

The third question is similar to the second: do national parties depart from the Burkean norm if they withdraw the whip from one of their MPs or refuse to recognize the candidature of an MP at a subsequent election? It is similar to the second question because the same logic applies: if the party's parliamentary leadership is dissatisfied with an MP's support of the party in the House of Commons, then it is entitled to withdraw the whip; and if the national party leadership confers recognition on a candidate— whether that individual is an MP or not, it may withdraw that recognition if is dissatisfied with the candidate's attitudes or behaviour. Historically, however, there has been a further dimension in that the Irish Nationalists required their MPs and, in its early days, the Labour Party required its candidates to resign if they failed to sign a pledge of support which included a promise to resign if they failed to observe the pledge.[24] Labour MPs are still expected to observe the standing orders of the Parliamentary Labour Party (PLP), although there has long been a clause permitting abstention on issues of conscience. Withdrawal or threatened withdrawal of the whip may, of course, be seen—and is certainly often intended— as a means of coercion, but unless its use is widespread or it can be established that the fear of loss of the whip is what makes MPs vote with their parties, then, again, it does little to undermine the norm of the MP as a representative. Neither, in fact, is the case—see Ch. 7 below.

What of *instructions* from constituents or others? Writing in his memoirs. Sir Alfred Pease (Liberal MP for York 1885–92 and for Cleveland 1895–1902) remarks, 'Even a Radical like John Bright declared that it was a duty to stand like a "tiger" in the path of people when they are wrong.'[25] Instructions from constituents have invariably been resisted by MPs. Thus, in 1880, in response to letters from their local party seeking to instruct them, the two Liberal MPs for Hull made their position absolutely clear:

I feel it due to myself at once to intimate to you, so far as I am concerned, it will be unnecessary for your association to issue mandates until it learns to adopt a tone which any gentleman has a right to expect (Charles Norwood, MP for Hull 1866–85);

and

There is no inducement for me to be in Parliament unless I have the sympathy and confidence of my supporters; and I beg you will convey to the Liberal Association my sense of undesirable relations which would exist between us if my conduct is to be criticized and my course of action dictated in such a spirit (Charles Wilson, MP for Hull 1874–85 and Hull West 1885–1905)   (Cited in G. H. Jennings, *An Anecdotal History of the British Parliament*, Appleton & Co., New York, 1881, 394.)

Similarly, Sir Edward Clarke (Conservative MP for Plymouth, 1880–1900 and the City of London, January–June 1906), relates in 1884:

---

[24] See William B. Gwyn, *Democracy and the Cost of Politics in Britain*, Athlone Press, London, 1962, 143—5; and Conor Cruise O'Brien, *Parnell and His Party, 1880–90*, Clarendon Press, Oxford, 1957, 140–3.

[25] Sir Alfred Pease, *Elections and Recollectons*, John Murray, London, 1932, 11.

I received a letter signed by a member of my constituency urging me to vote against the Deceased Wife's Sister Bill, or at all events to refrain from voting or speaking in its favour. I at once replied that my conduct in Parliament must be guided entirely by my own convictions, and I prepared, and . . . delivered a speech in support of the Bill . . .   (Sir Edward Clarke, *The Story of My Life*, John Murray, London, 1918, 232–3.)

The rejection of instructions also applies to individuals other than the Member's constituents, leading one Conservative candidate in 1918 to affix a printed slip to questionnaires eliciting his views and support on various issues. The slip stated:

These replies are intended to indicate the views I hold at the present time; but they are not to be regarded as binding on me in the future, and they are not to interfere with my complete freedom to vote as I may think right at the time and under the then existing circumstances whenever such matters come up for consideration. (Lord Hemmingford (Sir Denis Herbert), *Backbencher and Chairman: Some Parliamentary Reminiscences*, John Murray, London, 1946, p. 12).[26]

This is essentially the view of the House of Commons itself, as expressed in a resolution passed in 1947, which declares:

. . . that is inconsistent with the dignity of the House, with the duty of a member to his constituents, and with the maintenance of the privilege of freedom of speech, for any Member of this House to enter into any contractual agreement with an outside body controlling or limiting the Member's complete independence and freedom of action in Parliament or stipulating that he shall act in any way as the representative of such outside body in regard to any matters to be transacted in Parliament; the duty of a Member being to his constituents and to the nation as a whole, rather than to any particular section thereof.   (HC Debs., 440, 15 July 1947, c.365.)

This case arose because W. J. Brown—then Independent MP for Rugby, but formerly Labour MP for Wolverhampton West, 1929–31—alleged that the Civil Service Clerical Association, of which he was an official and which supported him financially, had sought to influence his behaviour in Parliament by threatening to withdraw its financial support. No breach of privilege was found, but the Privileges Committee sought to clarify the position by

---

[26] Hemmingford was Conservative MP for Watford, 1918–43.

recommending that the House of Commons pass a resolution.[27] The 1947 resolution simply formalized what had long been the practice. It did not, of course, prevent MPs from advocating or supporting the views of individuals or organizations with whom they had a pecuniary or similar relationship, although paid advocacy was banned in 1995, when the 1947 resolution was amended, following the first report of the then Nolan Committee on Standards in Public Life.[28]

Whatever complexities there may be about the theory of representative government, its practice is more complex. This is well summarized by Hannah Pitkin in her study of representation:

> . . . representing . . . means acting in the interest of the represented, in a manner responsive to them. The representative must act independently; his action must involve discretion and judgement; he must be the one who acts. The represented must also be (conceived as) capable of independent action and judgement. Not merely being taken care of. And, despite the resulting potential for conflict between representative and represented about what is to be done, that conflict must not normally take place. The representative must act in such a way that there is no conflict, or if it occurs an explanation is called for. He must not be found persistently at odds with the wishes of the represented without good reason in terms of their interest, without a good explanation of why their wishes are not in accord with their interest.   (Hannah Pitkin, *The Concept of Representation*, University of California Press, Berkeley, CA, 1967, 209–10).[29]

Pitkin argues that 'Representative government is not defined by particular actions at a particular moment, but by long term systematic arrangements—by institutions and the way in which they function' and acknowledges that this creates a 'duality and tension between purpose and institutionalisation.'[30] And that needs to be borne in mind, whether historically or contemporaneously, in

---

[27] See HC 118, 1946–47.

[28] See HC Debs., 265, 6 November 1995, c. 661 and Michael Rush, 'The Law relating to Members' Conduct' in Dawn Oliver and Gavin Drewry (eds.), *The Law and Parliament*, Butterworths, London, 1998, 105–24.

[29] John Stuart Mill expressed an essentially similar view in 1861, arguing in general 'actual pledges should not be required'. But that electors 'are entitled to a full knowledge of the political opinions and sentiments of the candidate' and are 'not only entitled, but often bound, to reject one who differs from them in the few articles which are the foundation of their political belief' (J. S. Mill, *Representative Government*, Everyman's Library ed., J. M. Dent, London, 1910, 323.

[30] Pitkin, *Representation*, 234 and 235.

considering the position of the Member of Parliament as a representative and therefore in considering the relationship between
Member and constituency, Member and party, and the very role of
the MP.

Parliamentary Government and Responsible Government

Parliamentary government is also characterized as responsible
government in that the government needs to secure and retain the
confidence and support of a majority in the House of Commons.
The ultimate form of this constitutional doctrine is that the
Commons may withdraw its confidence and bring about a change
of government, but in practice this is a rare occurrence. It last
happened in 1979, when the minority Labour government led by
James Callaghan was forced into a general election, but it is worth
noting that the government lost by a single vote and that one
Labour MP was too ill to vote. Had he been able to vote, the
government would have survived because in the event of a tie the
Speaker is obliged to vote in favour of the *status quo*. It is necessary
to go as far back as 1924 to find a government being forced to
resign in this way, although it happened twice that year. The first
time, however, was when, after the Conservatives had lost their
overall majority in the general election of 1923, the Prime Minister,
Stanley Baldwin, decided to wait until Parliament met, since no
party had an overall majority. In the event, the first minority
Labour government was formed, but later in 1924 it too resigned
after an adverse vote, following the withdrawal of Liberal support.
And before 1924? 1895, when the Liberal government led by Lord
Rosebery courted defeat and allowed itself to be outvoted on a
minor matter. The resignation of Neville Chamberlain's government in 1940, following a substantial reduction in its normal
majority, could also be properly cited, but it merely reinforces the
fact that the ultimate form of ministerial responsibility seldom
happens. Its constitutional significance is that it *can* happen.

The concept of responsible government is, in practice, of greater
consequence in setting the parameters of the day-to-day relationship between the government and Parliament, particularly the

House of Commons. It is, however, like much of the British constitution, based on constitutional convention, not law, so that it is
ultimately a matter of opinion and, no matter how well-founded
that opinion, the courts cannot enforce any convention. The
doctrine of ministerial responsibility lays down that the government is answerable to Parliament for policy and its administration,
but this has two dimensions: first, the government has an obligation to explain its policies and their administration of them to
Parliament and, second, that it has an obligation to accept responsibility for policy and its administration. This in turn takes two
forms—collective and individual ministerial responsibility.
Collective responsibility means that the government as a whole is
responsible to Parliament and may therefore be forced to resign or
call an election if it cannot retain the confidence of the House of
Commons. At a more mundane level it means that ministers are
bound by collective responsibility and, while not obliged always to
express public support for or agreement with government policy,
must not express public disagreement. In the event of the latter, the
prime minister has the right to dismiss the minister or ministers
concerned.[31] Such dismissals are rare,[32] but resignations on the
grounds of collective responsibility—that is, where a minister feels
unable to accept agreed government policy—are more common.[33]

Individual ministerial responsibility places on ministers a duty
to explain and defend their policy and administration of their
departments in and to Parliament, and to take the blame for any
failures in either. This means that, even where errors are the fault
of civil servants rather than ministers, ministers remain constitutionally responsible for them. As in the case of collective responsibility, the ultimate penalty is resignation, but resignations on the
grounds of individual ministerial responsibility are much rarer
than those resulting from collective responsibility. In a seminal
article, S. E. Finer showed that, between 1855 and 1955, there were

[31] In practice, collective responsibility extends to parliamentary private secretaries
(PPSs) i.e. MPs who act as unpaid aides to ministers, a position widely seen as the
first step on the ministerial ladder. Collective responsibility is also applied by the
Leader of the Opposition to members of the Opposition frontbench; and fifteen
members of the opposition frontbench were dismissed between 1968 and 1997.
[32] Only two ministers have been dismissed on the grounds of collective responsibility since 1945, but twenty PPSs were dismissed between 1945 and 1997.
[33] There were thirty-five such ministerial resignations between 1945 and 1997.

only twenty resignations on the grounds of individual ministerial responsibility—an average of one every five years or 0.20 per year;[34] between 1956 and 1997 there were eleven such resignations—an average of one every four years or 0.27 per year.[35] It is not, however, difficult to produce examples of policy or administrative failure which did not result in ministerial resignations, but which might have been thought serious enough to do so. The explanation lies in a variety of factors, such as a time lag between the occurrence of the error and its discovery, so that a different minister or even a new government is in office, the discreet 'reshuffle' of ministerial posts, or a judicious but subsequent retirement from office. In addition, there are errors and failures that do not merit resignation and an explanation, combined with steps to put the matter right or see that it does not happen again, may be more appropriate. Whatever the merits of a particular case, resignation is the exception rather than the general rule in the application of individual ministerial responsibility.

Taken together collective and individual ministerial responsibility have a more important role in that the doctrine of ministerial responsibility is the basis on which Parliament in general, and the House of Commons in particular, can claim to hold the government to account. It thus underpins most debates, most committee work, all parliamentary Questions, and the representations that MPs make on behalf of their constituents. In short, it is the basis for Parliament's scrutiny role—keeping a check on the government and the civil service, on policy and administration.

Parliamentary Government and the Role of the Member of Parliament

Parliamentary government imposes three major roles on MPs: a partisan role—supporting the party under whose label he or she was elected, particularly as a supporter of the government or the

[34] S. E. Finer, 'The individual responsibility of ministers', *Public Administration*, 34, 1956, 377–96.
[35] However, three of these resignations occurred at the same time —over the invasion of the Falkland Islands by Argentina in 1982. If these are counted as one case, the average is 0.22 per year.

official opposition; a constituency role—looking after the collective and individual interests of those they represent; and a scrutiny role—acting as a parliamentary watchdog not on behalf of their constituents in particular but of the people in general, the ultimate Burkean role of acting in 'one interest, that of the whole'. These are not mutually exclusive roles: all MPs perform them, but they vary over time and from Member to Member and may, indeed, produce role conflict. In addition, of course, some MPs—a growing number over the last century—become ministers or members of the opposition frontbench. For both the partisan role continues unabated, indeed more strongly, for ministers are bound by collective responsibility and opposition frontbenchers by political solidarity in the guise of collective responsibility. Although a limited degree of informal flexibility sometimes allows ministers or opposition frontbenchers to escape the demands of party, public dissent courts dismissal. Ministers and frontbenchers also continue to have a constituency role, although they often fulfil it in a less public way than backbenchers. By definition ministers cannot and do not have a scrutiny role in Parliament, but for the official opposition it is a major role and hardly less important for other parties in opposition to the government. This book, however, is primarily concerned with backbench MPs, although it remains important to place backbenchers in the wider context of a political career, including ambition for and the achievement of ministerial office. It is also worth mentioning that most ministers serve as backbenchers before achieving office and not a few resume a backbench role after leaving office.

Other studies have sought to delineate the role or roles of the Member of Parliament. One of the most important is Donald Searing's *Westminster's World*.[36] Initially, he divides MPs into two major groupings according to whether they fulfil backbench or leadership roles. Backbench roles are 'preferential roles', of which there are four key types:

... each framed by one of Parliament's institutional tasks: checking the executive (Policy Advocates); monitoring institutional structures (Parliament Men); making ministers (Ministerial Aspirants); and redressing

---

[36] Donald D. Searing, *Westminster's World: Understanding Political Roles*, Harvard University Press, Cambridge, MA., 1994.

grievances (Constituency Members). Backbenchers make their roles with a view to making themselves useful in the established framework of rules that they find at Westminster. They pass over some of these roles, adopt others, and then interpret and modify them to suit their preferences. They certainly do make their own roles, but they make them in and for Westminster's world.   (Searing, *Westminster's World*, 16).[37]

TABLE 1.1. *Searing's 'preferential roles' for backbenchers (1970s)*

Role	Conservative	Labour	All MPs
Policy advocate	44.3	35.8	40.7
Ministerial aspirant	22.7	27.8	24.6
Constituency MPs	21.0	29.8	25.4
Parliament men	11.9	6.6	9.3
Total	100.0	99.9	100.0
n	176	151	334

Leadership roles, in contrast, are what Searing terms 'positional roles', that is the position requires the 'performance of many specific duties and responsibilities, whereas preferences roles require the performance of few specified duties and responsibilities.'[38] Thus, for

preference roles the process is usually one of 'role choice', in which the opportunities become conditions that structure desires and beliefs, which, in their turn, influence the choices that politicians make among alternative roles. For position roles, the process is more likely to be one of 'recruitment', in which the same sorts of opportunities become criteria that gatekeepers use to select recruits. Here role choice becomes mainly a matter of accepting or rejecting their offers.   (Searing, *Westminster's World*, 374.)

The 'opportunities' to which Searing refers relate to a combination of constituency and personal characteristics.

Leadership roles are also subdivided into categories—PPS, whip, junior minister, and minister.[39] Of course, individual MPs choose leadership roles in the sense that they aspire to ministerial office,

[37] For more details on Searing's backbench roles see *ibid.*, Part I.
[38] Ibid., 12.
[39] See ibid., Part II.

but once they acquire such positions it is the position that largely determines how the role is carried out. It is not clear exactly where opposition frontbenchers fit into Searing's scheme of things, being part ministerial aspirant and part leadership roles. Nonetheless, the richness of his data enables him to underpin the complex range of roles he delineates. By definition this presents no problem with positional roles, but the preferential roles of backbenchers are more problematic. This is not because they cannot be shown to exist, because they do, but rather because Searing makes insufficient allowance for a multiplicity of roles, both over time and, more importantly, at any one time. That backbenchers make choices is not in dispute, but those role choices are not just the product of constituency and personal characteristics, important as these undoubtedly are. They are, as Searing himself points out, shaped by Westminster's world.

The modern MP has little choice but to fulfil a partisan role and little choice but to fulfil a constituency role—Westminster demands it. His or her choice is greatest when it comes to the scrutiny role: parties make demands, constituents make demands that must to a significant extent be heeded, but no one insists that the backbench MP performs the scrutiny function, whatever the political and constitutional theorists may say. That Searing's categories reflect the attitudes of MPs and what they do is not in question, but it is legitimate to ask, what else do they do? The role of the MP is not a single but a multiple one. Similarly, that MPs concentrate on or prefer some aspects of their role more than others and may be accurately described as primarily a policy advocate, ministerial aspirant, Parliament 'man', or constituency Member is reasonable enough, but these are not mutually exclusive roles and may vary for the individual MP over time. What happens to the ministerial aspirant whose aspirations are not realized? What happens to the ex-minister who returns to the backbenches? More importantly, what has happened to the partisan, constituency, and scrutiny roles over time? Putting these three roles in their parliamentary context and seeking to trace to what extent, if at all, they have changed since the middle of the nineteenth century is the task of this book.

2

The Political Context

The Ideological Context

Labour's triumph in 1997 was due in no small measure to the fact that the party had undergone a significant ideological shift since its defeat in 1983. The Labour manifesto for that election, famously described by Gerald Kaufman as 'the longest suicide note in history', was itself a product of an ideological shift from right to left that the party had undergone since losing office in 1979.[1] Ideological shifts by parties are, of course, by no means unusual: the Conservatives shifted to the right under Margaret Thatcher and both the Conservative and Labour Parties shifted towards the political centre in the 1950s. Each of these ideological shifts has its own significance, but each also illustrates that differing ideological positions are an important part of the context of British politics.

Although party allegiances, whether in the form of electoral support or party membership or party activists—including MPs— cannot simply be explained by ideological differences, they form an important part of that explanation. Family tradition, deference, and religion have all played their part, but ideology in the sense of a prevailing set of ideas and values or conflicting sets of ideas and values has been ever present. The Reformation was, of course, a clash of religious ideas, but it was also an ideological conflict and nowhere more than in England. Thus, by the time the English Civil War began in 1642, the ideological differences between the King and his opponents in Parliament went much further than a narrow

[1] See David Butler and Dennis Kavanagh, *The British General Election of 1983*, Macmillan, London, 1984, Chaps. 5, 12, and 13; David Butler and Dennis Kavanagh, *The British General Election of 1987*, Macmillan, 1988, Chaps. 4, 11 and 12; Ivor Crewe and Anthony King, SDP: *The Birth, Life and Death of the Social Democratic Party*, Oxford University Press, Oxford, 1995.

argument over religion, important as that was. There was a fundamental disagreement about the distribution of power and how society should be organized. This is further illustrated by the
subsequent conflict between the new rulers and the Levellers and
Diggers, who had a much more radical view of how society should
be organized. The conflict between Whigs and Tories centred
around different views of the role of the monarch and of religion,
which, although subsequently caricatured by the Whig interpretation of history, were serious and significantly different views about
how society should be ordered.

As part of the political context within which Parliament operates
ideology can be seen in two different dimensions. First, ideology
needs to be seen as part of broader ideas and sets of ideas which
underpin the way that politicians and others see the society in
which they live, whether they want to change it and, if so, in what
ways. Second, it needs to be seen in a narrower sense as part of the
daily language of politics and political conflict, as part of the way
in which the politicians articulate their opinions, proposals, and
policies. This second view, however, is contained within and
shaped by the first. Neither is immutable and historically both have
been subject to immense change.

Modern British history has been dominated by two opposing
traditions, the libertarian and the collectivist, and it is a complex
mixture of libertarianism and collectivism that ideologically underpins British politics. In his massive and comprehensive study, *The
British Political Tradition*,[2] W. H. Greenleaf argues that between
these two 'there is a contention or interplay . . . that makes our
politics what it is.'[3] Libertarianism, he suggests, has four strands:

1. . . . a stress on the basic importance of individuality, that is, on
   the rights of the individual and his freedom from both social
   supervision and arbitrary political control.[4]
2. . . . the role of government or cognate authority must, in principle be limited. It may not properly interfere in (or at least
   permanently eliminate) this sphere of individuality; indeed it
   exists to sustain it.[5]

    [2] W. H. Greenleaf, *The British Political Tradition*, 4 volumes, Routledge/Methuen,
London 1983–7.
    [3] Greenleaf, *Political Tradition*, 1, *The Rise of Collectivism*, 14.
    [4] Ibid., 15.   [5] Ibid., 17.

3. . . . any high concentration of power is likely to be dangerous to this sacrosanct zone of individual choice and activity.[6]
4. . . . libertarianism demands . . . the Rule of Law . . . which sets limits to the legitimate acts of government.[7]

Against this, collectivism involves:

1. . . . a concern with the public good . . . [which] . . . brings to the fore . . . the interests of the community which are regarded as primary claims morally superior to any individual demands.[8]
2. . . . the creation of uniform conditions of both equality and security as a means of preventing or mitigating . . . [social] . . . suffering.[9]
3. . . . to secure these goals action on the part of public authority is essential . . . subordinating individual claims to social need . . . not as an incidental but as a permanent feature of political action.[10]

It seems but a short step from delineating these two positions to the ideology commonly associated with particular political parties, from libertarianism to conservatism and liberalism, and collectivism to socialism and communism. However, Greenleaf goes on to say: 'Nothing could be more misleading. Each partisan doctrine is ambivalent, a kind of "living oxymoron" reflecting a range of libertarian and collectivist attitudes. Moreover, as a matter of historical fact, supporters of Conservative and Liberalism have contributed more to the actual development of collectivism . . . than have the exponents of socialism, in the Labour Party or out of it.'[11] To be sure, the Conservative and Liberal Parties lean more towards libertarianism and the Labour Party towards collectivism, but none has an exclusive claim to either and the interplay between and within each of the parties is a continuing and vital part of their operation and reflected in the policies they propose and pursue. Moreover, the balance between the libertarian and collectivist strands is not unchanging but shifting, with greater emphasis on one or the other at different times, in the short-term and the long-term.

Historically, it is possible to argue that the libertarian is epitomized by the economic doctrine of *laissez-faire* and that the collectivist by

---

[6] Ibid., 17.   [7] Ibid., 19.   [8] Ibid., 20.
[9] Ibid., 21.   [10] Ibid., 22.   [11] Ibid., 28.

ever-increasing government or state intervention in the affairs of society, especially but not exclusively in the economic sphere. The reality is infinitely more complex. That there was a widespread belief in the nineteenth century and earlier that government intervention should be kept to a minimum is clear enough, but this did not preclude significant intervention to deal with particular problems that went beyond the Victorian constitutional ideal of maintaining 'peace, order, and good government'. The repeal of the Corn Laws and the sweeping away of other protectionist legislation is often seen as the triumph of *laissez-faire*, but in the same decade Parliament was passing legislation to regulate public health, factory conditions, and the operation of railways.[12] Such intervention was not new, however: the poor law had been reformed in 1834 and municipal government in 1835; the first Factory Act was passed in 1802, early banking reforms had taken place in the 1820s; the first government grant for education was made in 1833 and in 1839 the Privy Council appointed a Committee on Education. Nor should these be seen simply as isolated reactions to particular problems: many of their proposers and supporters argued that improvements in public health and working conditions and the creation of a literate and better-educated population were desirable in their own right. Even railway regulation, which might be seen as a narrow response to safety concerns—after all, one of the earliest railway casualties, in 1830, was no less a person than William Huskisson, then President of the Board of Trade—is no exception, since railways were seen as a 'public good'.[13]

What can and should be acknowledged is that historically there has been a massive shift towards collectivism, but it is a shift much tempered by the libertarian point of view, so that the ideological positions of the political parties at any one time can only be explained in both collectivist and libertarian terms. Thus the development of the local government system, of state education, of the transport and communications infrastructure, of the welfare state, and of the state direction of the economy can be explained in collectivist terms, but each is permeated by libertarian concerns,

[12] See. William C. Lubenow, *The Politics of Government Growth: Early Victorian Attitudes Towards State Intervention, 1833–1848*, David and Charles, Newton Abbot, 1971.
[13] See ibid., 107–9.

with an emphasis on the rights of the individual and the redressing of grievances, with a need for limitations upon government, and with a need to call governments to account. The effect on government has been profound: on the one hand, it has resulted in an enormous, pervasive growth in government; on the other, it has transformed the party system, the bureaucracy, the role of Parliament and, therefore, of the individual Member of Parliament.

The Growth of Government

It is a truism that in the nineteenth and twentieth centuries government was a growth industry. That growth, however, has been the product of both collectivist and libertarian ideas. An increasing belief in the collectivist view that the needs of society should come before those of the individual, made the growth of government inevitable. Only the state, directly or indirectly, could create the means to fulfil societal needs, but the libertarian stress on the individual added to the growth of government by seeking to protect the individual from the state, on the one hand, and the free market, on the other. To realize the aims of collectivism demanded stronger and more pervasive political institutions in the form of a more powerful executive, a more efficient legislature, a larger and more efficient administrative apparatus, and a stronger and more highly-organized party system. Meeting libertarian concerns demanded more law, not less; more checking mechanisms, not fewer; more rights, not fewer; and greater vigilance, not less.

There is no difficulty in demonstrating the growth of government—arguably it is self-evident. Certainly, it is dramatically illustrated by a small piece of research conducted on behalf of the Kilbrandon Commission on the Constitution, which reported in 1973. The Commission was told that an analysis of the parliamentary Questions asked in one month in 1970 showed that between 80 and 90 per cent could not have been asked in 1900 because they were not matters of government responsibility.[14] Very soon after that, with the election in 1906 of a radical, reforming Liberal

---

[14] Royal Commission on the Constitution (the Kilbrandon Commission), *Report*, Cmnd., 5640, October 1973, 76.

government and under the impact of the First World War, many more of those Questions would have been answered by ministers, but that should not be taken to mean that there was no significant growth of government before 1900. On the contrary, it was the growth of government in the nineteenth century that led Sir Frederick Maitland, an eminent constitutional historian, to remark in 1888 that Britain was a 'much-governed nation'.[15]

However, a proper understanding of the impact of the growth of government on Parliament requires a multifaceted approach to what was a complex and haphazard process and no single approach will suffice. For example, in 1830 the government comprised forty-seven ministers, of whom thirteen were members of the Cabinet; in 1900 the figures were sixty and nineteen, not a dramatic difference. Indeed, in 1840 the number of ministers was sixty and remained just under sixty for the rest of century.[16] Tony Blair's first Cabinet in 1997 had twenty-two members. The Cabinet has never been larger than twenty-four and, War Cabinets apart, the smallest Cabinet this century was the sixteen-member Cabinet formed by Churchill in 1951. But the 1997 Blair government had no fewer than 112 members in total and it is in posts outside the Cabinet that the increase in the executive has been most dramatic and significant.

This ministerial expansion was, not surprisingly, accompanied by a bureaucratic expansion—see Table 2.1: in 1832 there were some 21,000 non-industrial civil servants—that is, bureaucrats—by the middle of the nineteenth century the number had risen to 39,000, by 1902 to 50,000, and by 1914 to 70,000. It was, however, the impact of government activities during the First World War that had the most dramatic effect, and by 1918 the number of non-industrial civil servants was three times that of 1914. Although

[15] F. W. Maitland, *The Constitutional History of England: A Course of Lectures Delivered by F. W. Maitland in 1887 and 1888*, Cambridge University Press, 1st ed. 1908, reprinted 1948, 501. Maitland was referring specifically to the growth of subordinate or secondary legislation, but his remarks had a wider implication and are worth quoting in full: 'Year by year the subordinate governing is becoming more and more important. The new movement set in with the Reform Bill of 1832: it has gone far already and assuredly will go further. We are becoming a much governed nation, governed by all manner of councils and boards and officers, central and local, high and low, exercising the powers which have been committed to them by modern statutes.'
[16] See Table 5.9 below.

TABLE 2.1. *The growth of the non-industrial civil service, 1832–1998 ('000s)*

Year	No. of non-indust. civil serv.	Year	No. of non-indust. civil serv.
1832	21	1939	165
1851	39	1944	505
1902	50	1950	433
1910	55	1960	380
1914	70	1970	493
1918	221	1980	542
1920	161	1990	495
1930	111	1998	430

Note: Until the Post Office became a public corporation in 1970, its staff was counted as non-industrial civil servants. For comparative purposes Post Office staff have been excluded from the figures in the table. In 1890 the Post Office had no fewer than 108,000 employees and by 1914 over 200,000 (Howard Robinson, *The British Post Office: A History*, Greenwood Press, Westport, CN, 1970. Originally published by Princeton University Press, 1948).

Sources: 1902–70: *Civil Service Statistics*, HMSO, London, 1970, 14, Table 1; 1980–98: *Civil Service Statistics* for the year concerned; earlier years: Chris Cook and Brendan Keith, *British Historical Facts, 1830-1900*, Macmillan, London 1975, 150.

there was then a period of contraction during the interwar period, the Second World War brought an even greater expansion from which the subsequent retreat was proportionately limited. Periods of Conservative rule were usually marked by a reduction in the size of the bureaucracy, notably during the 1930s and Margaret Thatcher's premiership from 1979 to 1990. Although the reductions of the Thatcher years were part of 'the rolling back of the state', they were only a limited part of that process, which owed more to the privatization of public corporations and the introduction of competitive tendering and internal markets. The downward trend since 1979 has been largely achieved by 'efficiency gains', rather than a decline in governmental responsibilities.

What was also crucial was the transformation of the civil service into a modern bureaucracy. This involved fundamental changes in structure and recruitment. The catalyst in this process was the Northcote–Trevelyan Report of 1854, which laid the foundations for a permanent, politically-neutral civil service, recruited on merit through open competition.[17] Change came only gradually: a Civil Service Commission to recruit civil servants was set up in 1855, but not until 1870 were most posts filled by open competition; a start on the structural changes recommended by Northcote–Trevelyan was not made until 1876 and not fully-implemented until 1920; and, similarly, the creation of a unified civil service involving the transfer of individuals between departments was not completed until 1919. Significantly, although the pre-Northcote–Trevelyan civil service was recruited largely by patronage and nepotism, it had become largely permanent and politically-neutral. This was because it was personal rather than party patronage. The result was that an American-style 'spoils system' in which the holders of civil service posts changed with a change of government did not develop.

The growth of the civil service, however, also illustrates the nature and the extent of governmental expansion. As Geoffrey Fry points out:

The role of state in eighteenth century Britain was largely confined to law and order, national defence, the conduct of foreign policy, the promotion of trade and some attempt at imperial management, various local functions (chiefly, poor relief), and the collection of revenue to sustain these activities. (Geoffrey K. Fry, *The Growth of Government: the Development of Ideas about the Role of the State and the Machinery and Functions of Government in Britain since 1780*, Frank Cass, London, 1979, 92.)

This continued into the early years of the nineteenth century and is confirmed by a listing of the government departments in existence in 1830: the Admiralty, the Attorney-General's Office, the Foreign Office, the Home Office, the Board of Control (for India)— forerunner of the India Office, established in 1858—the Irish Office, the Privy Council Office, the Mint—part of the Treasury after 1850—the Post Office, the Board of Trade, the Treasury, and the War and Colonial Office—separated in 1854. During the nineteenth century other departments—often misleadingly called

---

[17] See Henry Parris, *Constitutional Bureaucracy*, Allen and Unwin, London 1969; W. J. M. Mackenzie and J. W. Grove, *Central Administration in Britain*, Longman, 1957, ch. 1; and Gavin Drewry and Tony Butcher, *The Civil Service Today*, Basil Blackwell, Oxford, 2nd ed. 1991, ch. 1.

boards—were set up, resulting from the expansion of government into new areas: the Poor Law Board (1847), the Board of Works and Public Buildings (1851), the Local Government Board (1871), the Scottish Office (1885), the Board of Agriculture (1889—preceded by a committee of the Privy Council from 1883), and the Board of Education (1899—preceded by a committee of the Privy Council from 1839). However, such listings do not reveal the full extent of government intervention. The Poor Law system of workhouses, for instance, dates from 1834, but was operated by Poor Law Commissioners from then until 1847. The first Factory Act regulating conditions of employment was passed as early as 1802, the first education grant from central government was made in 1833, and the first Public Health Act was passed in 1848. In areas such as transport, railways and canals became subject to considerable regulation by the Board of Trade and legislation was passed establishing highway districts to develop and maintain roads. The Public Health Act of 1848 set up a General Board of Health, whose responsibilities were later transferred to the Privy Council and the Local Government Board, which had the power to create local boards of health. Similarly, following the passage of the Education Act, 1870, which introduced compulsory elementary education, local school boards were established.

Central government thus tended to establish the parameters of intervention, but gave responsibility for implementation to locally-based bodies, subject to a degree of national oversight, usually falling short of establishing a particular department for the purpose. This in turn formed the basis for a comprehensive local government system, replacing administration through local justices and lord lieutenants, starting with the Municipal Corporations Act in 1835 and culminating in the creation of county councils and urban and district councils towards the end of the nineteenth century. The massive growth of the central government in terms of functional departments and a massively-expanded civil service occurred in the first two decades of the twentieth century, following rather than accompanying the growth of government intervention in the nineteenth. The election of the Liberal government of 1906 accelerated this process, so that before the outbreak of the First World War the civil service had already increased from some 50,000 in 1902 to 70,000 in 1914—an increase of 40 per cent. The First World War served only to increase the degree of intervention and the rate at which departments and civil servants proliferated.

What emerges from all this is a process of governmental growth that was complex, haphazard, and piecemeal. It is, moreover, a process which continued throughout the twentieth century, notwithstanding the Thatcherite 'rolling back of the state' and the privatization of many public utilities and services. At the beginning of the twenty-first century government intervention in the form of the direct provision of various services and welfare benefits, the regulation of others provided by the private sector and of the lives of individual citizens remains massive and pervasive.

The growth of government found expression in Parliament in the volume of legislative output (see Table 2.2). The number of Acts of Parliament has actually declined, but the volume, as measured in pages of legislation per act and per year, has increased massively. Thus, from less than 3 pages per act or 237 pages per year in the 1831–2 Parliament, it has increased to nearly 50 pages per act or approaching 3,000 pages per year in the 1992–7 Parliament. Indeed, in the last normal-length session of the latter the total exceeded 3,000. This, however, is not all, since these figures are far exceeded by those for secondary or delegated legislation, that is rules and regulations issued by government departments and other bodies under powers conferred by Act of Parliament.

The practice of giving a person or persons in authority the power to issue detailed regulations can be traced back to at least the reign of Henry VIII and was not uncommon in the eighteenth century, but it became increasingly important in the nineteenth as governmental activity expanded. By 1900, statutory instruments, the most common form of delegated legislation, numbered nearly a thousand; before the end of the twentieth century that number had more than tripled and constituted more than 10,000 pages of legislation per year.[18]

Table 2.2 is evidence enough that Parliament, more especially the House of Commons, somehow managed to cope with this exponential increase in the amount of legislation passed; how it coped is

[18] On the development of delegated legislation see Cecil Carr, 'Delegated Legislation', in Lord Campion (ed.), *Parliament: A Survey*, Allen and Unwin, London, 1952, 232–51.

TABLE 2.2. *Legislative output: Public Acts and statutory instruments, 1831–1997*

Parl.	Mean no. of acts/yr	Mean no. of pp./act	Mean no. of pp./yr	No. of SIs (sel yrs.)	Parl.	Mean no. of acts/yr	Mean no. of pp./act	Mean no. of pp./yr	No. of SIs (sel yrs.)
1831–32	85	2.8	237		1959–64	71	10.5	747	2,495 (1960)
1833–35	105	3.2	337		1966–70	78	15.8	1,229	2,044 (1970)
1868–74	103	5.0	514		1970–74	70	16.7	1,178	
1900–06	37	2.3	85	995 (1900)	1974–79	74	15.6	1,151	
1906–10	59	4.2	249	1,368 (1910)	1979–83	64	19.5	1,250	2,051 (1980)
1924–29	62	8.6	527	1,262 (1929)	1992–97	57	47.7	2,732	3,327 (1994)
1945–50	70	13.8	968	2,144 (1950)					

Notes: 'pp' indicates the number of printed pages per Act, and the numbers of pages are adjusted to take account of different page sizes so that the figures represent the current A4 page size; 'SI' indicates 'Statutory Instrument'.

Sources: The data on public acts are taken from the annual volumes of Acts of Parliament. Except for 1994, the data on SIs is taken from David Butler and Gareth Butler, *Twentieth Century British Political Facts, 1900–2000*, Macmillan, London, 2000, 217.

largely the subject of Chapter 3. However, no amount of procedural or organizational change would have been sufficient without the development of disciplined, cohesive political parties in Parliament and in the country at large. It is parties and the party system which, to a significant degree, make Parliament what it is and determine how it operates. In short, parties are the engines of Parliament.

The Party Context

The Origins and Development of the Party System

> . . . every boy and every girl
> That's born into the world alive,
> Is either a little Liberal, or
> Else a little Conservative.
>
> (W. S. Gilbert, *Iolanthe*, Act II)

Britain is widely regarded as being the exemplar of a two-party system—Conservative v. Liberal, later Conservative v. Labour. Indeed, if the Whig interpretation of history is to be believed, there has been a two-party system since before the Glorious Revolution of 1688, with Tories on the one side and Whigs on the other.[19] Whatever may have happened in the late seventeenth century, however, Sir Lewis Namier and his colleagues argued that the Tory-Whig dichotomy lapsed into factionalism in the middle of the eighteenth, and that two-partyism did not re-emerge until the late eighteenth and early nineteenth centuries. Thus Namier argued that there were 'three broad divisions based on type not on party'.[20] These three groupings were 'followers of the court and administration', the 'independent country gentlemen', and the 'political factions contesting for power'. However, because the old party names were current they gave the appearance of a two-party system. Namier acknowledged the existence and importance of 'personal parties'—these were the followers of particular individuals, such as

---

[19] See Thomas Babington (Lord) Macaulay, *History of England from the Accession of James II*, Longman, Brown, Green and Longmans, London, 3rd ed., 1849; G. M. Trevelyan, *History of England*, Longman, London 1926; and Herbert Butterfield, *The Whig Interpretation of History*, G. Bell, London, 1931.

[20] Sir Lewis Namier, *Crossroads of Power: Essays on Eighteenth Century England*, Hamish Hamilton, London, 1962, 220.

the Elder Pitt, Grenville, Bedford, and Rockingham, but they were more akin to factions than parties, constituting rival groups for office. Shifting alliances created what Namier termed 'ins' and 'outs', with those in office having the advantage of the support of the 'placemen', those sitting for constituencies controlled by the Treasury or in receipt of government patronage, but always needing additional support from the third type, the independent country gentlemen.

Critics of Namier do not dispute the existence of these types or groupings, but they strongly question Namier's claim of the absence of party. Certainly, the period of Whig domination from 1714 to 1761, especially under Walpole as first minister from 1720 to 1742, was one when the two 'old parties' clearly existed, even though the same system of placemen and patronage was its essential foundation. What happened subsequently is that the growth of factions within both the Tory and Whig parties, particularly after the fall of Walpole in 1742, was reinforced with the accession in 1760 of George III, because he was determined to play a more active role in politics than either of his immediate predecessors. The king disliked parties and wanted much greater freedom of choice in choosing his ministers, especially the prime minister. To that extent he wished to 'turn back the clock', but not to the extent that he sought to emulate William III, who was his own prime minister. As a result, the term 'Tory' and 'Whig' were used more discreetly by the politicians, but this hardly amounted to the disappearance of the 'old' parties. As Brian Hill has noted:

Some of the weaknesses in Namier's basic contention on the unimportance of parties were inherent in his own writing. He conceded Whig and Tory *names and creeds* 'which covered enduring types moulded by deeply ingrained differences in temperament and outlook' and, even more importantly, admitted that 'in a good many constituencies the names of Whig and Tory still corresponded to real divisions'. How names could survive in Parliament, and 'real divisions' continue in those constituencies without meaning or significance was never fully explained.   (B. W. Hill, *British Parliamentary Parties 1742–1832: From the Fall of Walpole to the First Reform Act*, Allen and Unwin, London, 1985, 5, original italics).[21]

---

[21] Citations from Namier, *Crossroads of Power*, 229 and 230. See also B. W. Hill, *The Growth of Parliamentary Parties 1689–1742*, Allen and Unwin, London, 1976.

If the politics of the period before 1761, when the Whig domination came to an end, was complex, as it most certainly was, then politics after that date was almost infinitely more so. Factionalism predated Whigs and Tories, but it became increasingly significant after the fall of Walpole and was a key characteristic of British politics in the second half of the eighteenth century. However, the factions were largely elements within parties, although this did not preclude coalitions, such as the Fox–North coalition of 1783. Hill concludes that

. . . though the parties existed under difficult conditions . . . the Tories and Whigs of the eighteenth century laid the foundations of the later fully-fledged party system. The survival of both parties under their original names after a century and a half, in spite of numerous attempts to extirpate or ignore them, indicates that they served a need too important to be denied. Their continuation was neither an accident nor an illusion. (Hill, *British Parliamentary Parties*, 235)

The concept of a two-party system is not so much one of numbers as of characteristics. Clearly, no political system with a wide range of parties, none of which ever secures an absolute majority of seats in the legislature is likely to be described other than as a multi-party system. In such cases, of course, it may be entirely appropriate to speak of major and minor parties, although these terms lack precision. However, it is not unusual to find legislatures in which three or more parties are represented, nonetheless, properly being described as a two-party system, simply because, however many parties may be represented, two parties hold the overwhelming majority of seats. This is a necessary but not sufficient condition for defining a two-party system; other, more stringent tests need to be applied. These are the largest, combined proportion of candidates standing for any two parties, the combined electoral support for those parties, the combined proportion of seats they win in the legislature, and, crucially, which party forms the government.

Applying these criteria to the general election of 1997 shows that 34.6 per cent of the candidates standing were either Conservative or Labour, 73.6 per cent of the votes were for these two parties, that they won 88.4 per cent of the seats, and, of course, that Labour formed the government. The proportion of Conservative and Labour candidates looks less than overwhelming and it is necessary to go back to 1987 to find more than half the candidates being drawn from the two major parties.[22] This not only reflects the growth of the nationalist parties in Scotland and Wales but, more importantly, the proliferation of candidates standing for other parties, such as the Referendum Party, the UK Independence Party, and the Natural Law Party, none of which succeeded in securing the election of a single MP.[23] However, the proportion of candidates standing for the two major parties is the least important of the four criteria suggested. Even though the proportion of votes cast for the two parties fell below three-quarters, it still resulted in nearly nine out of ten MPs being either Conservative or Labour. What picture emerges if these criteria are applied to the period since 1832?

TABLE 2.3. *Two-party domination, 1832–1997*

Election period	Two major parties: % of candidates.	Two major parties: % of votes cast.	Two major parties: % of MPs elected.
1832–68	98.1	98.8	98.3
1874–1910	88.1	93.7	86.1
1918–35	71.4	77.1	85.4
1945–70	76.4	91.3	97.9
1974–97	49.1	74.8	93.0

Notes: The figures for each of the periods consist of the combined percentages of candidates nominated, votes cast, and MPs elected for the two largest parties in each election. For all elections between 1832 and 1918 the two largest parties were the Conservatives and Liberals. In the elections of 1922 and 1923, however, there were more Liberal than Labour *candidates*, although the Labour Party secured the election of more MPs and a larger proportion of the votes cast. Since 1924 the two largest parties have been Conservative and Labour.

Sources: F. W. S. Craig, *British Electoral Facts, 1832-1987*, Parliamentary Research Services, Dartmouth, Political Research Services, Chichester, 1989, Tables 1.41–1.43; and *The Times House of Commons*, Times Books, London, 1992 and 1997.

[22] In fact, in the general elections of both 1979 and 1983 the proportion fell below 50%, at 48.3 and 49.1% respectively.

[23] It is worth noting, however, that the UKIP did win three seats in the European Parliament election of 1999, benefiting from the PR closed party list system used for the first time in an election in the UK.

Taken at face value the figures in Table 2.3 provide strong evidence for arguing that Britain has had a two-party system from at least 1832, even though there were some periods when it was less dominant, notably between 1918 and 1935 and to a lesser extent since 1974. Moreover, for almost the whole of the period since 1832 governments have been formed by one or other of two major parties; coalitions have been rare, fulfilling Disraeli's dictum of 1852 that 'England does not love coalitions'. All this presents little or no problem after 1868, since from that date there were clearly-defined Conservative and Liberal Parties which dominated British politics until the Liberals were supplanted by Labour after the First World War, although care needs to be taken in assessing the levels of party cohesion in the House of Commons from 1868 to the end of the nineteenth century. The problem arises with the period 1832–68, especially between 1846 and 1868.[24] In broad terms Table 2.3 accurately reflects the existence of two parties after 1832, initially Whigs and Tories, later Liberals and Conservatives, but it does not reflect the looser sense of party that existed for much of the nineteenth century compared with today. Nor does the Table reflect the gradual process of party realignment that took place after 1832 and which was not complete until 1868, with the clear emergence of the Conservative and Liberal Parties. Indeed, it can be powerfully argued that the process of realignment was not complete until after 1886, when a substantial number of 'Whigs' allied themselves with the Conservatives as Liberal Unionists, although this was complicated by the simultaneous secession of Joseph Chamberlain and his Radical supporters to the Liberal Unionists.

In practice, the overwhelming majority of MPs identified themselves and were identified by their electorates with one of the two major parties, but both parties had moderate and more extreme wings. The looser sense of party manifested itself in the way MPs described themselves in *Dod's Parliamentary Companion*, which has been published annually since 1832 and provides short biographies of all Members of Parliament. Various party labels were used, often modified by appropriate adjectives—'a moderate Reformer', 'an

[24] See Robert Stewart, *Party and Politics, 1832–1852*, Macmillan, London, 1989; and Angus Hawkins, *Parliament, Party and the Art of Politics in Britain, 1855–59*, Macmillan, London 1987.

advanced Liberal', 'a moderate Conservative', 'of decidedly Liberal opinions', 'a staunch Liberal', 'of moderate Whig principles', 'of Whig principles', 'inclining to Conservatism', 'a radical Reformer', as well as the more straightforward 'Whig', 'Tory', 'Liberal' and 'Conservative', 'Radical', 'Liberal-Conservative', and 'Protectionist'. Some proclaimed their support for particular party leaders—'a Conservative supporter of Lord Derby', 'a firm supporter of Mr Disraeli', and 'a hearty supporter of Mr Gladstone'. It was even more common to declare support for or against particular policies, such as free trade or protection, a further extension of the franchise, or the disestablishment of the Irish church. One Conservative described himself as 'a Conservative, in favour of "safe and progressive" improvement and of "sound economy but not unwise retrenchment" '.[25] What was crucial was that these were not necessarily empty declarations. They could be and were carried into the division lobbies, so that governments could not be certain that their legislation would survive unscathed or, in some cases, even survive at all, and, from time to time, the fate of the government itself hung in the balance. As was the case before 1832, governments were most under threat not from their opponents but from their supporters, whose backing could not be taken for granted.

Apart from a brief interlude between December 1834 and April 1835, the Whig governments of Grey and Melbourne survived from 1833 to 1841 precisely because they retained sufficient backing from their supporters. Melbourne, however, became increasing vulnerable through losses at by-elections and general elections and a falling away of support, until his government lost a vote of confidence in 1841 and then the consequent general election. Sir Robert Peel's Conservative government similarly survived, until he split his party by repealing the Corn Laws in 1846. This created a situation in which it became more difficult to form and sustain governments—the Conservatives, because the Peelite Free Traders were unwilling to support their nominal party; and the Whigs because they were vulnerable to the growing number of Radicals, who had played a major part in the repeal of the Corn Laws, but who also

[25] Examples culled from Michael Stenton and Stephen Lees (eds.), *Who's Who of British Members of Parliament: A Biographical Dictionary*, Vol. I, 1832–85, Harvester Press, Hassocks. Sussex, 1976.

demanded other changes that the Whigs were less happy to concede. The period between 1846 and 1868, in fact, saw only three short-lived Conservative governments, the two Derby administrations of 1852 and 1858–9 and the Derby–Disraeli government of 1866–8. Thus Whig-Liberal governments dominated this period, but their survival rested on the support of varying combinations of Peelites, Radicals, and, to a lesser extent, Irish support.

Between 1846 and 1868, when Gladstone formed his first administration, there were no fewer than eight different governments, but it would inaccurate to describe this as a period of political instability in the sense that there were frequent changes of government. On the contrary, Lord John Russell's government of 1846–52, Aberdeen's coalition of 1852–5, and Palmerston's two governments of 1855–8 and 1859–65 are evidence of relative stability. Each of these governments fell because of defeats in the House of Commons; all but Russell's government of 1847–52 had majority support in the Commons, but that support was more fragile and less certain than post-1868 governments enjoyed. Even after 1868, governments found it necessary to make legislative concessions to their supporters, but they could normally expect to survive between general elections and this expectation increased as party cohesion increased.

From 1832 to 1846, then, a two-party system clearly existed: a looser, less cohesive system than its modern successor, but a two-party system nonetheless. The overwhelming majority of MPs were drawn from the Tory/Conservative and Whig/Liberal parties, whatever factions may have existed within each. Even between 1846 and 1868, only these two parties were capable of forming a government and the only true coalition was Aberdeen's Peelite-Liberal government. Where 1846–68 differed from 1832–46 was that the party system was in a state of flux. The Peelite wing of the Conservative Party gradually detached itself and joined the Whigs and Radicals to form the Liberal Party, but it was not until 1859 that Gladstone, by then the leading Peelite, finally abandoned his Liberal-Conservative label and stood in an election as a Liberal. By 1868 the realignment was complete and, as party cohesion strengthened, so did the two-party system. The growth of the Irish Nationalists weakened it only to the extent that it reduced the two-party proportions of candidates, votes and MPs and rendered the

Liberal governments of 1892–5 and 1910–15 dependent on nationalist support in the Commons, but the Nationalists had little choice—only the Liberals were committed to Home Rule.[26] Only the Conservative and Liberal Parties could form governments and there was no serious thought of coalition until the wartime coalition of 1915.

Between 1918 and 1935 a further party realignment took place, with the Liberals being supplanted by the Labour Party as the alternative to the Conservatives. The two-party system had reasserted itself and did not come under serious challenge again until the 1970s, when, first the growth of support for the nationalist parties in Scotland and Wales and then a serious split in the Labour resulted in the setting up of Social Democratic Party (SDP) in 1981. The SDP's proclaimed objective was 'to break the mould' of British politics, to bring about a further realignment of parties. That did not happen, but in an electoral alliance with the Liberal Party it mounted a serious challenge to Labour.[27] In the general election of 1983 the Liberal-SDP Alliance came within 2.2 per cent of Labour in votes—25.4 against Labour's 27.6 per cent—though winning only twenty-three seats to Labour's 209. However, at the next general election, in 1987, the Alliance's vote declined to 22.5 per cent, although it suffered only a net loss of one in seats, but Labour had already begun to shift its ideological position, a process which was reinforced by the loss of yet another election in 1992. The Alliance collapsed when a majority of the members of the SDP and the Liberal Party decided to merge to form the Liberal Democratic Party: the SDP had failed to break the mould, but it had had a profound impact on the Labour Party, helping lay the foundations for Labour's massive victory in 1997. In spite of the Conservatives' worst electoral defeat since 1832 in terms of votes and since 1906 in terms of seats and the doubling of the Liberal Democrat MPs—the best Liberal result since 1931—the two-party system survives.

[26] Of course, the impact of the Irish Nationalists on parliamentary organization and procedure was more profound, but, if anything, that reinforced the two-party system by strengthening the grip of the government and the official opposition on the House of Commons.
[27] See Crewe and King, *SDP*.

The Growth of Party Organization

As long as libertarian views predominated the need to transform
the party system and Parliament was limited, but, as collectivism
became more important, the more necessary it became to adapt
both to its demands. Yet it was initially a libertarian development,
though not necessarily by intent, that was to begin the transformation of the party system. This was the extension of the franchise,
beginning with the Reform Act of 1832. Elections before 1832 were
notoriously corrupt and a major facilitation factor was the size of
individual electorates: in 1830 only 3.5 per cent (7) of the 202
English boroughs had more than 5,000 electors and as many as
37.1 per cent (75) had a hundred or fewer. In the forty English
counties the largest electorate was Yorkshire, with 20,000 voters,
but two-thirds (67.5 per cent) had fewer than 5,000; only two
Welsh counties had 2,000 voters and one Welsh borough more
than a 1,000; and the largest Scottish county electorate was 200,
the largest Scottish burgh electorate 125.[28] Population growth and
a further extension of the franchise in 1867 had made corruption a
much more expensive business, but 1832 had little impact on
corruption. Although the electorate increased nearly 50 per cent
between 1831 and 1832, the numerical increase was only from
435,000 to 653,000 and individual electorates remained small.[29]

The extension of the franchise was not basically libertarian by
intent; on the contrary, apart from correcting the worst of the
anomalies created by socio-economic changes arising out of the
industrial revolution, it was widely seen by contemporaries as a
means of preserving the hegemony of the landed and the wealthy;
but it was also a recognition of the growing importance of the
middle classes and it set an important precedent. By extending the
franchise the 1832 Act implicitly conceded the case for future
extensions to those that could claim a definable economic contri-
bution to, and therefore stake in, society. Furthermore, although
the franchise remained firmly linked to property, it was just as

[28] Chris Cook and John Stevenson, *British Political Facts, 1760–1830*, Macmillan,
London, 1980, 54–9.
[29] The mean UK constituency electorate was 784 in 1831, 1,230 in 1833, 3,717 in
1869, and 8,470 in 1886 (calculated from figures in Chris Cook and Brendan Keith,
British Political Facts, 1830–1900, Macmillan, London, 1975, 116–17).

clearly linked to the individual, so that the libertarian case for universal male and then universal adult suffrage became easier to argue. There were those before 1832, such as Bentham, who argued for universal adult suffrage, but the full force of the libertarian argument for the franchise to be linked to the individual had to await Bentham's utilitarian successor, John Stuart Mill.[30]

The significance of the Reform Act of 1832 for party organization lay not in the details of the extension of the franchise, but in the specific requirement that a register of electors in each constituency be compiled and registers required constituency organization. The latter was not, however, a new phenomenon: election committees and election agents, mostly local lawyers, were common before 1832. So also was the practice of canvassing voters, although a major purpose was often to allow a would-be candidate to judge whether a constituency was winnable before committing himself to a contest.[31] However, the need to register voters stimulated the formation of registration societies and, more crucially, constituency or local party organization. Indeed, the small electorates in many constituencies were an added incentive in what could be closely-fought contests. Inside Parliament there already existed a degree of party organization: the Tories had a chief whip in the House of Commons from 1802 until 1832, though not appointing a successor until 1835; the Whig/Liberals had a chief whip from 1830. But the parties now began to extend their organizational activities beyond Westminster, with the Conservatives appointing a national party agent in 1832 to co-ordinate electoral registration and the Liberals similarly in the 1840s. In addition, London clubs provided an important physical focus for party activity—the Carlton, founded in 1832 by those who opposed the Reform Bill, for Tories and Conservatives; Brooks's, originally founded in 1798, and the

[30] See Jeremy Bentham, 'First Principles Preparatory to Constitutional Code', [1830] in Collected Works of Jeremy Bentham, ed. Philip Schofield, Clarendon Press, Oxford, 1989, 96–100. Bentham was in favour of women's suffrage in principle, but against in practice because the 'contents and confusion produced by the proposal of this improvement would entirely engross the public mind, and throw improvements, in all other shapes, to a distance.'(100). See also John Stuart Mill, Representative Government, Everyman's Library ed., J. M. Dent, London, 1910 (originally published 1859), 290–2.

[31] See Frank O'Gorman, Voters, Patrons and Parties: the Unreformed Electorate of Hanoverian England, 1734–1832, Clarendon Press, Oxford, 1989, 67–105.

Reform, founded in 1834 when Brooks's refused to admit any more members, for the Whigs and Liberals. It was only a matter of time before the various local party organizations were brought together under a national party organization, leading to the first Conservative Party annual conference in 1867 and the first meeting of the National Liberal Federation in 1877.

This burgeoning of extra-parliamentary party organization was made all the more necessary by the continued growth of the electorate. By 1866, with no further extension of the franchise, it had risen to more than a million and the Reform Act of 1867 increased that electorate by 88 per cent, to nearly two million.[32] Corruption remained widespread, but it was no longer possible to fight elections without organization at the local level and that organization was overwhelmingly party rather than personal. Even in the nineteenth century few candidates won seats independently of a party label and party organization. Moreover, party leaders increasingly made appeals to the electorate nationally, facilitated by the massive improvement in transport brought about by railway development and a national press made much more widely accessible by the abolition of paper duty in 1861.

Within Parliament the parties became more highly organized and more and more cohesive, so that governments not only survived from one election to the next, but also could increasingly guarantee the delivery of a programme of policies year on year. Government business took precedence and government legislation seldom failed to reach the statute book. Governments rarely lost office through loss of parliamentary support; electoral fortunes determined whether parties moved from government to opposition and vice versa. The seeds of this system, however, were sown earlier in the nineteenth century and by 1868 had already borne significant fruit: two large, well-organized parties confronted each other in Parliament and the country; single-party, majority government became the rule, and executive dominance increasingly became the norm. Ostrogorski's belief that the caucus—the extra-parliamentary organization—would come to dominate the parliamentary organization was not fulfilled.

---

[32] Cook and Keith, *Political Facts, 1830–1900*, 116.

Indeed, as Robert McKenzie argued in *British Political Parties*,[33] the parliamentary leadership and the party leadership remained synonymous and power within the parties was concentrated in its hands. The main reason for this was that the route to political power and office lay through Parliament: power was won and office secured by winning a majority of seats in the House of Commons and it was therefore control of Parliament that was the crucial factor. The older parties had their origins in Parliament and only subsequently created extra-parliamentary organizations, but the Labour Party had its origins outside Parliament and it might have been expected that its extra-parliamentary organization would be the locus of power. That was certainly the position under successive Labour Party constitutions, but, as McKenzie pointed out, the institutional demands of parliamentary government quickly led to Labour conforming to the norms established by its older rivals—power was largely concentrated in the party leadership in Parliament. Whatever other impact the Labour Party has had on British politics, it has not fundamentally altered the norms of parliamentary government.

The Development of Party Cohesion

It is the discipline enforced by party warfare which enables the Commons to act, not merely efficiently, but at all.   (Sir Reginald Palgrave, *The House of Commons: Illustrations of its History and Practices*, Macmillan, London, 1878, Vol. 2, 33.)

Edmund Burke provided a powerful argument for party cohesion when, in 1770, he defined a party as 'a body of men united for promoting by their joint endeavours the national interest, upon some particular principle upon which they are all agreed'.[34] The promotion of such joint endeavours is not impossible in the absence of party, but they are much more likely to be realized with rather than without parties. As early as 1848 Disraeli argued '. . . you can have no parliamentary government if you have no party

[33] Robert T. McKenzie, *British Political Parties: The Distribution of Power within the Conservative and Labour Parties*, Heinemann, London, 1st ed. 1955.
[34] Edmund Burke, 'Thoughts on the Present Discontents', *The Works of Edmund Burke*, George Bell, London, 1883, Vol. 1, 375.

government'.[35] The idea of a Parliament consisting entirely of independent Members, untrammelled by party ties, was scornfully dismissed by Lord Salisbury in the mid-nineteenth century: 'Independent Members are Members upon whom nobody can depend',[36] a sentiment also expressed by Burke.[37]

The importance of party was reinforced by the extension of the franchise: not only was party necessary to form and maintain a government and its programme in Parliament, but it was necessary to secure sufficient elected support to win a majority of seats in the House of Commons to realize that objective. Small wonder that political leaders placed such a stress on party and therefore on the need for party cohesion. The idea of securing the support of like-minded MPs for particular proposals from the government is hardly new. Edward Porritt, in his massive study of the House of Commons before 1832, notes that 'whips' or written appeals 'underscored by as many as six lines, were sent to the King's friends in the House of Commons as early as 1621.'[38] Similarly, the idea of 'pairing'—the practice of allowing the absence of MPs from opposite sides or parties to be absent, thus cancelling out their votes and preserving the government's majority—can be traced back to 1730.[39]

The data in Table 2.4 clearly show the increasing dominance of party in the House of Commons in the nineteenth century, notwithstanding the fall in party voting in the middle of the century. As early as 1836, just under the half the divisions were subject to party whipping, even though the proportion of two-party votes, in which the Conservatives and Liberals were on opposite sides, was at the most a third. By the end of the century nine out of ten divisions were whipped, well over three-quarters were

[35] HC Debs., 101, 30 August 1848, c. 706. This same view was more famously put in a speech in Manchester in April 1872: '. . . without party, parliamentary government is impossible'. (Anthony Jay (ed.), *The Oxford Dictionary of Political Quotations*, Oxford University Press, Oxford, 1996, 119).

[36] Quoted in Andrew Roberts, *Salisbury: Victorian Titan*, Weidenfeld and Nicolson, London, 1999, 60.

[37] See Alpheus Todd, *On Parliamentary Government in England*, Longman, London, 2nd ed., 1889, Vol. 2, 414.

[38] Edward Porritt, *The Unreformed House of Commons: Parliamentary Representation before 1832*, Cambridge University Press, 1909, Vol. 1, 509.

[39] Romney Sedgwick, *History of Parliament: The House of Commons 1715–1754*, HMSO (for History of Parliament Trust), London, 1970, Vol. 2, 3.

TABLE 2.4. *The growth of party cohesion, 1836-1903*

Year	Whipped divisions %	Two-party votes %	Party votes %
1836	49	34 (23)	48
1850	69	18 (16)	43
1860	67	5 (6)	26
1871	82	38 (35)	66
1881	85	49 (47)	62
1883	n.a.	35 (n.a.)	n.a.
1890	n.a.	65 (n.a.)	n.a.
1894	88	84 (76)	84
1899	91	75 (68)	91
1903	n.a.	86 (n.a.)	n.a.

Notes: 1. Two-party votes are divisions in which nine out of ten Conservatives and Liberals each voted with their parties on opposite sides. There are limited differences between Berrington and Lowell. Lowell's figures are shown in brackets. 2. Party votes are two-party votes *plus* divisions in which nine out of ten members of one party cast a party vote and the other party did not.

Sources: Hugh B. Berrington, 'Partisanship and dissidence in the nineteenth century House of Commons', *Parliamentary Affairs*, 21, 1967–8, 388–74 and A. Lawrence Lowell, *The Government of England*, Macmillan, New York, NY, 1926 (originally published 1908), ch. 35.

two-party votes, and nine out of ten party votes. It was not a smooth transition, however: whereas the proportion of whipped divisions steadily increased, reaching four-fifths by 1871, the number of two-party and party votes declined after 1836, falling dramatically to 5 and 26 per cent respectively in 1860. This reflected the party realignment that took place between 1846 and 1868, rather than the decline in party as such. As Lowell remarks: 'During the middle period of the century it was not uncommon for a Cabinet to be saved from defeat at the hands of its own followers by the help of its opponents.'[40] There was also a decline in two-party voting during Gladstone's second ministry (1880–5), as the figures for 1883 demonstrate, but this was the result of dissent by

---

[40] Lowell, *The Government of England*, 80.

Radicals within the Liberal Party and collusion between the government and opposition frontbenches in opposing Radical proposals. The development of party cohesion may have been less than smooth, but the increasing proportion of whipped divisions reflects a determination to achieve that cohesion, which became almost complete following the further party realignment consequent upon the breakaway of the Liberal Unionists over Home Rule in 1886.

Remarkably little academic attention has been paid to party cohesion after 1900,[41] until Philip Norton produced a series of studies on dissent. Cohesion was taken as a given, a fact of parliamentary life and behaviour: party voting had become the norm to the extent that there was no point in producing systematic and detailed statistics to prove it. Norton, in fact, approaches cohesion from a diametrically opposite viewpoint: Lowell and Berrington are interested in establishing how many MPs were voting for their parties; Norton is interested in how many MPs are *not* voting for their parties.[42] The growth of dissent from the late 1960s is, of course, an important feature of recent parliamentary behaviour, but it has not seriously disturbed the norm of party voting, so characteristic of the modern House of Commons.

Conclusion

Contextually, by 1900 all was in place: British politics was dominated by two, ideologically-divided parties; collectivist demands, significantly tempered by libertarian concerns, had resulted in an expansion of government, and the state now intervened in areas which were beyond the ideological pale a hundred years before; the governmental machine had expanded accordingly, with an

[41] See, for example, Geoffrey Hosking and Anthony King, 'Radicals and Whigs: the British Liberal Party 1906–1914', in William O. Ayedelotte (ed.), *The History of Parliamentary Behaviour*, Princeton University Press, Princeton, NJ, 1977, 136–56.

[42] See Philip Norton, *Dissension in the House of Commons, 1945–74*, Macmillan, London, 1975; *Conservative Dissidents: Dissidence within the Parliamentary Conservative Party, 1970–74*, Temple Smith, London, 1978; *Dissidence in the House of Commons, 1974–79*, Clarendon Press, Oxford, 1980; and Philip Cowley and Philip Norton, 'Rebels and rebellions: Conservative MPs in the 1992 Parliament', *The British Journal of Politics and International Relations*, 1, 1999, 84–105.

increase in the number ministers and civil servants; and the House of Commons, the key part of the legislative machine, was controlled by party. Parliament, however, especially the Commons, also needed to adapt its procedures and working practices, as will be related in Chapter 3.

3

The Adaptation of Parliament

Recognizing the Problem

The growth in the legislative output of Parliament in the nine-teenth and twentieth centuries—see Table 2.2—was the product of the growth of government, itself the product of the increasing acceptance of collectivist ideas. It is, however, an error to assume that before 1832 Parliament was a relatively inactive body in legislative terms. In his study of the House of Commons from 1688 to 1832, published in 1843, Charles Townsend produced statistics that clearly illustrated that Parliament was far from idle:

TABLE 3.1. *Number of public and private Acts of Parliament, 1688–1820*

Reign	No. of public acts	Mean no. per year	No. of private acts	Mean no. per year
William III (1689–1702)	343	26	466	36
Anne (1702–14)	338	28	605	50
George I (1714–27)	377	29	381	29
George II (1727–60)	1,477	45	1,244	38
George III (1760–1820)	9,980	166	5,257	88

Source: Charles Townsend, *History of the House of Commons: From the Convention Parliament of 1688 to the Passing of the Reform Bill in 1832*, Henry Colburn, London, 1843, Vol. 2, 379–80.

Townsend goes on the quote from a pamphlet describing the situation in the 1820s:

Parliament is now overwhelmed with business: twenty-five committees of the House may be found sitting on the same day. Thirty committees on private business have met in a single day, nineteen having been fixed to meet in one room . . .!

In the sessions between 1822 and 1828 inclusive 2,100 Acts of Parliament received the royal assent. The king sends these measures into the world in bevies of 80 and even 100 at a time. The number of public petitions printed has averaged 1,400 in the session. There are piles upon piles of reports.

From the Colonial Department alone, in 1825, were laid on the table papers amounting to 5,000 pages. The printed papers of a session, entirely exclusive of the bills printed, the votes of the two Houses, and Journals, exceed twenty-five full-sized and closely-printed folio volumes. (Townsend, *History of the House of Commons*, Vol 2, 380–1.)

A substantial amount of the business that Parliament had to deal with consisted of private legislation, that is bills applying to limited geographical areas or named persons. The former, known as local acts, were and are used to authorize local developments, such as railways, canals, and harbours; the latter, known as personal acts, are used to deal with matters such as difficulties arising out legacies and estates or to permit marriage between persons not eligible to marry under the prevailing law. Personal bills are now few in number, but until 1857 a divorce could only be obtained by the passage of a private bill through Parliament. These were and are distinct from public Acts of Parliament, which apply to the country and population as a whole.

Private legislation was of particular importance in facilitating the industrial revolution, since most of the legislation necessary to develop railways and canals and, later, various municipal utilities, such as the supply of gas and water, needed specific parliamentary approval. During the nineteenth century the number of private acts of Parliament passed each parliamentary session considerably exceeded the number of public acts, especially as the latter declined in number to between sixty and seventy a session, even though they increased in length—see Table 2.2. This continued into the twentieth century and it was not until after the First World War that the number of private acts was regularly less than the number of public acts.

Parliament dealt with this burden of private legislation principally through committees, but public legislation was dealt with almost exclusively on the floor of the two Houses. Any increase in public legislation, therefore, was likely to increase the burden on Parliament as a whole. Before 1830, however, the government made only limited legislative demands on Parliament. Redlich cites the first Lord Halifax as saying, in about 1855, 'When I was first in Parliament, twenty-seven years ago, the functions of government were chiefly executive. Changes in our laws were proposed by individual Members, and carried, not as party questions, by their combined action on both sides.'[1] The government was, of course, responsible for financial legislation, but not much more, and public income and expenditure were limited in size and scope. However, as governments began to intervene more in the affairs of society and initiate legislation, the nature of the problem changed. Furthermore, the uncertainties created by the realignment of parties in the middle of the nineteenth century served only to exacerbate the problem.

Writing originally in 1867 Todd remarks in the preface to his book: 'The great and increasing defect in all parliamentary governments, whether provincial or imperial, is the weakness of executive authority.'[2] Subsequently, Todd cites the 3rd Earl Grey:

Our constitution brings the whole conduct of government under the control of the House of Commons; unless therefore ministers, as its leaders, are enabled to exercise in the Chamber an authority that cannot easily be shaken, to command a majority on all ordinary occasions, it is obvious that the policy of the government must fall under the direction of a fluctuating majority of the House; and their measures will necessarily be ruled by popular passion and feeling, instead of by reason and prudence.   (Earl Grey, *Parliamentary Government*, London, rev. ed. 1864 (originally published 1858), cited by Todd, *On Parliamentary Government*, Vol. 1, 32.)

The problem was recognized Gladstone, when Prime Minister in 1874, although his concern was rather more prosaic and his solution lay outside Parliament, in a direction already taken by successive governments in the nineteenth century:

[1] Josef Redlich, *The Procedure of the House of Commons*, trans. A. Ernest Steinthal, Constable, London, 1908 (originally published 1905), Vol. 1, 122.
[2] Alpheus Todd, *On Parliamentary Government in England: Its Origins, Development and Operation*, Longman, London, 2nd ed. (ed., A. H. Todd), 1887, Vol. 1, xii).

... the duties of Parliament have reached a point where they seem, for the present, to defy all efforts to overtake them. I think we ought not only to admit, but to welcome, every improvement in the organisation of local and subordinate authority which, under the unquestioned control of Parliament, would tend to lighten its labours and to expedite public business. (Gladstone, Speech, 23 June 1874, cited by Todd, *On Parliamentary Government*, Vol. 1, 478.)

Clearly, some of the burden on Parliament could be relieved by giving responsibility to local authorities, whether in the form of borough councils and, later, district and county councils, or specialized bodies, such as school boards, sanitary districts, or highway authorities. But this would do little to relieve Parliament of its legislative burden, nor of its growing scrutiny burden, a matter that alarmed the then Clerk Assistant of the House, Sir Reginald Palgrave. He noted that in 1857 the number of parliamentary Questions on the Commons' order paper was 451, in 1867 it was 912 and in 1877 1,343. Palgrave calculated that if Questions continued to increase at this rate they would occupy about a quarter of the parliamentary session by 1897. He further calculated that, if the various motions tabled by MPs similarly increased and were also taken into account, the Commons would have to sit an additional nine weeks a year all told.[3] This was when the House normally sat for twenty-four weeks a year. Palgrave's calculations did not anticipate the practice of giving written answers to most Questions, which was not introduced until 1902, nor the modern practice of tabling motions as a means of expressing Members' opinions, rather than matters actually to be debated, but he had good reason to be concerned.

Before 1832 the House of Commons was not only unreformed in its role as an elected and representative body, it was also unreformed in regard to its procedures and practices. The procedural initiative lay largely in the hands of individual Members and governments had little control over parliamentary time. Such time as was allocated to the government could easily be usurped by backbench Members moving motions, particularly for the adjournment of the House, which had to be debated. With the benefit of hindsight, Redlich, commenting on the situation in 1832 observed:

[3] Sir Reginald Palgrave, *The House of Commons: Illustrations of its History and Practices*, Macmillan, London, 1878, Vol. 2, 40.

The traditional prolixity of the procedure of the House, and the uncertainty as to the completion of its tasks caused by every Member having complete freedom of initiative, were serious hindrances in conducting the business of the state, which could not fail to be recognised by the House itself with increasing clearness.   (Redlich, *Procedure of the House of Commons,* Vol. 1, 71.)

Redlich was correct in his first observation, but less so in his second: as 'the business of the state' increased governments found the House of Commons a less and less efficient legislative machine, but this produced an inevitable conflict between the government and backbenchers. Indeed, it can be argued that this was wider in nature and that, as the official opposition increasingly saw itself and was seen as an alternative government, the conflict was to become one of frontbenchers versus backbenchers. That, of course, is an oversimplification, since the roles of government and opposition and government and opposition backbenchers are complex and equivocal.

Governments are intent on implementing their policies; oppositions are intent on exposing those policies to as much scrutiny and criticism as possible and, where they disagree, preventing their implementation. Governments therefore favour procedures that expedite and facilitate the passing of legislation and minimize scrutiny and criticism; oppositions favour procedures that slow down the legislative process and maximize scrutiny and criticism. But oppositions hope to become governments and governments anticipate becoming oppositions; their interests are therefore not mutually exclusive. Similarly, with the growth of party cohesion, backbenchers focused increasingly on their role as supporters of the government or the opposition and all that that implied procedurally. Although this ignores the predilections of individual backbenchers' different perspectives of the backbench role, especially at different stages of a parliamentary career, it serves only to increase the complexity of attitudes towards procedural change.

Addressing the Problem

The procedures of Parliament rest on the twin pillars of practice and standing orders, but practice is much the more ancient of the two; standing orders are a relatively modern phenomenon. Medieval Parliaments developed rules and working practices which, like English common law, were based on precedents and were adapted as parliamentary practice or usage. Thus rules governing the order of business and of debate were developed. One of the most fruitful periods was between 1547 and 1610, from the accession of Edward VI to the early years of the reign of James I. This followed Henry VIII's use of Parliament to legitimize the English Reformation and was a period when Parliament, especially the House of Commons, was becoming increasingly assertive. The practice of having three readings for bills became more formalized, the procedure of the form and method of putting questions to be debated and voted upon was settled, and the rules governing order in debate were laid down. At the beginning of the period the Commons began to record its proceedings formally in a House of Commons Journal and towards the end of the period committees of the whole House— the Committee of Supply and the Committee of Ways and Means— were established to deal with financial matters.

Apart from the formal records in the Journal, a number of Clerks of the House produced manuals of parliamentary procedure— Henry Elsynge in the seventeenth century, John Hatsell in the eighteenth and, most famously, Thomas Erskine May in his *Treatise on the Law, Privileges, Proceedings and Usage of Parliament*, first published in 1844.[4] The very fact that Hatsell's manual was entitled *Precedents of Proceedings in the House of Commons* epitomizes the nature of parliamentary procedure before 1832.

Crucially and not surprisingly, as the conflict between king and Parliament became more intense, so the pace of procedural development quickened, but it also created the essence of parliamentary practice, as a former Clerk of the House, Lord Campion, points out:

The character of practice is well-marked. It was leisurely, ceremonious, cumbersome; it was individualistic, giving wide scope to the initiative of

---

[4] Henry Elsynge, Clerk of the House 1640–9, edited his father's treatise on procedure, *The Manner of Holding Parliaments in England* (reprinted by Irish University Press, Dublin, 1972); John Hatsell, *Precedents of Proceedings in the House of Commons* (originally published in 1776), London, 1781; and Thomas Erskine May, *Treatise on the Law, Privileges, Proceedings and Usage of Parliament*, Charles Knight, London, 1844. See also Thomas Erskine May, *Remarks and Suggestions with a View to Facilitating the Despatch of Public Business in Parliament*, James Ridgway, London, 1849.

Members and affording no special facilities to the government; it was designed to protect the rights of minorities in debate and to encourage opposition to the executive. Since the formative period of practice lay during the first half of the seventeenth century, when the majority of the House [of Commons] was in chronic opposition to the government of Charles I, it acquired the characteristics of 'the procedure of an opposition'; and it retained these characteristics permanently, in spite of the fact that by the middle of the eighteenth century the establishment of the Cabinet system had turned the majority of the House from opponents to supporters of the government. (Gilbert Campion, 'Parliamentary Procedure, Old and New', in Lord Campion (ed.), *Parliament: A Survey*, Allen and Unwin, London, 1952, 142.)

Campion goes on to remark that, even though their responsibilities were limited, '. . . it is hard to see how ministers (who had to compete for time with ordinary Members and were always liable to find their business forestalled by one of a multitude of technical forms), made any progress with government business.'[5]

There was also another dimension, as Redlich points out, in citing Spencer Walpole on the impact of the 1832 Reform Act on Parliament:

The whole character and conduct of Parliament had been modified by the Reform Act. The reformed House of Commons was largely recruited by a class of persons who had found no place in the unreformed House. The fashionable young gentlemen, who had been nominated as representatives of rotten boroughs, had been replaced by earnest men chosen by the populous places enfranchised by the Reform Act . . . They insisted on receiving a public hearing for their own views; and on obtaining comprehensive information on the many subjects of the day in which they, and those who sent them to Parliament, were interested. Their determination in these respects produced two results. Parliamentary debates were lengthened to an enormous and, as some people thought, to an inordinate degree; parliamentary papers were multiplied to an extent which probably no one, who has not had occasion to consult them regularly, has realised. (Spencer Walpole, *History of England*, London, 1878–86, Vol. 4, 340–1, cited Redlich, *Procedure of the House of Commons*, Vol. 1, 81–2).[6]

---

[5] Campion, Parliamentary Procedure, 143.
[6] Walpole goes on to point out that, in the eight years up to and including 1832, parliamentary papers comprised 252 volumes, compared with 400 volumes in the eight years after 1832.

In contrast to practice, standing orders are written rules specifically passed by a motion of the either of the two Houses of Parliament, thus becoming a resolution of the House, which lay down procedures to deal with particular circumstances or situations, such as the order of business, the conduct of debates, the handling of different types of business, the conduct of Members, and so on. Standing orders take precedence over practice, but are, to varying degrees, open to interpretation by the Speaker, whose rulings create further precedents, thus adding to practice. It was essentially through the development of standing orders on public business that the House of Commons addressed the problem of the growth of government.

TABLE 3.2. *The development of the standing orders of the House of Commons, 1810–1990*

Year	No. of standing orders on private business	No. of standing orders on public business
1810	72	7
1830	147	6
1850	205	11
1870	245	70
1890	249	97
1910	259	95
1930	279	95
1950	249	112
1970	248	122 (1971)
1990	248 (1991)	146

Source: HC Papers, standing orders for the years concerned.

Precisely because so much legislation was private rather than public, standing orders on the former were greater in number and far more elaborate, so that in 1800 the number of standing orders on private business exceeded those on public by a ratio of 10 to 1. Even by the middle of the nineteenth century there were still only eleven standing orders on public business and the ratio of private to public had actually increased to more than 18 to 1. By 1870, however, the number of standing orders on public business had increased dramatically to seventy and by the end of the century to ninety-seven. Thereafter standing orders on public business provided the framework for the work of the House.

The Adaptation Process

The House of Commons has long claimed a number of privileges[7] or rights designed to protect it from interference by forces outside Parliament, notably but not only the monarch historically. These privileges are recognized by the courts and the most important and well-known is that of freedom of speech in all parliamentary proceedings. Another important privilege, however, is that of 'exclusive cognisance of proceedings', that is the right to regulate its own proceedings and operation. This means that the House of Commons must approve any changes in procedure. It also means that the major vehicle for examining and recommending formal proposals for procedural change are committees of the House, usually a Select Committee on Procedure, but sometimes select committees set up to examine a specific aspect or area of procedure.

Redlich points out that between 1832 and the original publication of his book in 1905 no fewer than fourteen committees were appointed to consider the procedures of the House of Commons. Of these Redlich argues that ten were of significance—those of 1837, 1848, 1854, 1861, 1869—a joint committee with the House of Lords—1871, 1878, 1886, 1888, and 1890, to which should be added that of 1906, as Sir Courtenay Ilbert notes in his preface to the 1908 English edition of Redlich.[8] The impact of these committees was not necessarily that their reports always led directly to change, but that, by their frequency and by their wide-ranging investigations, they demonstrate a growing awareness of the need for change and of the nature of the changes needed. Thus, where they did not produce change, they were nonetheless a stimulus to change at a later date.

The initiative in setting up these committees was usually that of the government, not least because governments had a vested interest in procedural change, but governments were not always able to

---

[7] See Erskine May, *Parliamentary Practice*, 22nd ed. edited by Sir Donald Limon and W. R. McKay. Butterworths, London, 1997, chs. 5–11.

[8] See Redlich, *Procedure of the House of Commons.*, Vol. 1, chs. 1–4, and Supplementary Chapter by Sir Courtenay Ilbert, Vol. 3, 202–23.

carry the House with them and backbenchers sometimes strenu-
ously and successfully resisted changes in procedure or secured
significant modifications to proposals. As party cohesion strengthened, however, governments were increasingly able to force
through changes, but not without criticism or resistance.
Governments also sometimes took the initiative without first
appointing a select committee, notably in 1881 in the face of severe
obstructive tactics by Irish Nationalist MPs and in 1902, when the
then prime minister introduced what became dubbed 'Mr Balfour's
parliamentary railway timetable'.

By 1907, when the Liberal government elected in 1906 had acted
upon the recommendations of the Procedure Committee it had set
up soon after taking office, the procedures of the House of
Commons had been transformed so that the government effectively controlled the parliamentary agenda and could, through its
majority, virtually guarantee the passage of its legislative
programme. The 1906 Liberal government and, later, Labour
governments had problems with the House of Lords, but the ability of a Conservative-dominated upper house to frustrate the will of
a Liberal- or Labour-controlled Commons was severely curtailed by
the Parliament Act of 1911. Once the 1907 changes were in place,
therefore, any subsequent procedural changes were almost entirely
detailed rather than fundamental in nature, tightening the government's grip, improving the *productive* efficiency of the House of
Commons as a legislative machine. This is reflected in the pattern
of procedural committees after 1907. Although the number of
procedural committees set up between 1907 and 1945–6 was similar to that of the previous seventy-five years—on average one every
five years—most focused on narrower aspects of procedure than
their predecessors and refined the existing rules, rather than seeking any major tightening of the government's grip. There were two
major exceptions. The first was the two Select Committees on
Procedure (Public Business) of 1930–1 and 1931–2, which straddled
the general election of 1931 and produced essentially similar
reports, concerning the House of Commons' ability—or lack of it—
to scrutinize government policy effectively. The second exception
was the Procedure Committee report of 1945–6, which did
contribute significantly to the government's ability to manage its
legislative programme.

However, between 1946 and 1956–7 no procedural committees were appointed, other than the Select Committee on Delegated Legislation in 1952–3, whose report was concerned with the detailed scrutiny of secondary legislation. The pace then began to quicken and between 1956 and 1997 a Select Committee on Procedure was appointed in all but six years and in three of the latter other procedural committees on particular aspects of procedure were appointed. In addition, specialized procedural committees were also appointed in 1962–3, 1971–2, 1986–7, 1987–8 and 1991–2 and from 1983–4 the Procedure Committee became permanent, set up under standing orders. Finally, one of the first actions of the Labour government elected in 1997 was to establish a Select Committee on Modernization. It has mostly focused on detail rather than fundamental changes in procedure, but in 2000 it brought forward recommendations which further strengthened the government's legislative grip by effectively ending all-night sittings and requiring all government bills to be subject to timetabling or programme motions. The government then used its massive post-1997 majority to ensure their implementation, against strong opposition from the Conservatives and Liberal Democrats.

Nonetheless, the period since 1956 has seen a shift in focus: the concern with increasing the government's ability to secure the passage of its legislative programme has continued with, for example, changes in financial procedure and the introduction of second reading committees, as well as the changes in 2000, but the main emphasis has been on improving the ability of the House of Commons to scrutinize government policy and administration. That development, however, belongs to a different part of the story and will be examined in more detail in Chapter 7.

The adaptation of the Commons' procedures to cope with the growing burden of parliamentary business, especially the legislative burden, can be divided into four areas—increasing the amount of parliamentary time available, increasing the proportion of parliamentary time when government business takes precedence, controlling the use of time so that decisions on government business can be made rather than indefinitely delayed, and using committees to spread the burden and enable the House to cope with more business, particularly legislation.

TABLE 3.3. *Mean number of sitting days in the House of Commons, 1832–1997*

Period	Mean no. of sitting day per calendar year
1832–68	125
1868–1906	126
1906–45	149
1945–97	164

Source: Chris Cook and Brendan Keith, *British Political Facts, 1830–1900*, Macmillan, London, 1975, 100–3; David Butler and Gareth Butler, *Twentieth Century British Political Facts 1900–2000*, Macmillan, London, 2000, 191–3.

Increasing Parliamentary Time

Increasing the amount of parliamentary time available by increasing the number of sitting days was the most obvious solution to coping with the growth in parliamentary business and, as Table 3.3 shows, there has been an increase in sitting days per year. In practice, there has been some fluctuation, usually related to how active governments have been and therefore how demanding of parliamentary time. Thus in the 1830s the Commons met on average for 144 days a year, but in the less active Parliaments of 1859–68 the average was as low as 116. Similarly, the turbulent Commons for 1880–5 averaged 142 sitting days, whereas the less active Commons of 1895–1906 met for 125 days a year. However, the contrast between the nineteenth and the twentieth centuries is much greater, with nearly 150 days a year between 1906 and 1945 and a further increase to 164 between 1945 and 1997. Moreover, between 1979 and 1992 the Commons averaged 167 days per year, although this fell back to 160 a year in the 1992–7 Parliament.

Changes in the length of the average sitting day have been far less marked, influenced in part by the increasing control that governments had over parliamentary time and therefore the parliamentary day. Thus, between 1832 and 1868 the Commons met for about eight hours a day; between 1868 and 1906 this increased to between eight and nine hours; but after 1906 it fell back to eight, only to increase again to between eight and nine hours after 1945. Increasing the amount of time available undoubtedly helped, but such time was of limited use so long as government control of it was limited.

Government Time

Until the early part of the nineteenth century government business did not take precedence on particular days when Parliament was sitting. Government business had to compete with business brought forward by backbench Members. Furthermore, any business, including the government's, could be interrupted and disrupted at the whim of one or more backbenchers. In practice, there was a good deal of give and take. As Campion notes, the ultimate weapon of denying the government supply—the granting of money was threatened, but seldom deployed.[9]

In the early nineteenth century it became the practice for one or two days to be set aside for government business, but this was a matter of practice, not a standing order. By 1832 government business took precedence on two days a week, but this was not made a standing order until 1846. In 1852 the number of government days was increased to three, but government business was still subject to interruption by private Members and the government did not secure firm control of the order paper or agenda until 1878. The final dominance of government business over backbench business was not achieved until the introduction of Balfour's reforms of 1902, from which time backbench business took precedence on only one day a week. Thus, from a situation in which there was no parliamentary time it could call its own, government business came to take overwhelming precedence.

Controlling Parliamentary Time

Having precedence was clearly of great importance to governments, but controlling the time in which it had precedence was a different matter altogether. Before and after 1832 it was clearly

---

[9] Campion, Parliamentary Procedure, 144.

useful for the government to have two days in which its business took precedence, but this did nothing to reduce the ability of back-bench MPs to delay that business once it was before the House. Two significant examples will suffice. The first is that of public petitions, which, under the existing procedure took precedence over any other business and could be and were used by MPs to secure debates on matters they wanted discussed and to obstruct business they opposed. This would have been less of a problem were it not that petitions increased in number from a mere 298 in 1785 to 10,394 in 1833 and, with fluctuations, continued to rise throughout the nineteenth century, only tailing off in the early 1900s.[10] Between 1833 and 1839, however, debates on petitions were first curtailed, then abolished, although they continued to be a significant expression of public opinion. The abolition of debates on petitions was incorporated in standing orders in 1842. The second example is that of dilatory motions, which, if passed, postpone further discussion of the immediate business before the House. The most common dilatory motion is that to adjourn the sitting, whether of the whole House or one of its committees. Such motions could be and often were debated, but, gradually, in the course of the nineteenth century most dilatory motions were made subject to an immediate vote without debate, all through the adoption of specific standing orders.

A similar process occurred with stages through which bills had to pass. Although the practice of putting public bills through five stages—three readings, a committee stage and a report stage—had long been established, before 1848 this involved no fewer than eighteen occasions when the House had to vote and on each occasion the motion could be debated. Furthermore, this applied only to the three readings and takes no account of amendments to a bill that might be tabled during the committee and report stages. These eighteen occasions, when the question before the House could be debated, were reduced to two between 1848 and 1854 and, from 1856, only verbal amendments intended to clarify the intentions of a bill were permitted at third reading.

[10] Strathearn Gordon, *Our Parliament*, Cassell for the Hansard Society, London, 6th rev. and enlarged ed., 1964, 213, Appendix 7 (II). In 1893–4 the number of petitions was 33,742; by 1913 it had dwindled to 600.

These changes considerably strengthened the hand of the government, but ultimately there was no means of ensuring that a debate could be brought to a close. This meant that the pressure on the Commons remained considerable. It is no exaggeration to say that the House of Commons operated through a process of legislative exhaustion, well-summarized by a partisan but not entirely inaccurate observation by Lord George Hamilton (Conservative MP for Middlesex 1868–85, and Middlesex (Ealing) 1885–1906) on Gladstone's first ministry (1868–74):

Gladstone apparently was made of iron, and he remorselessly used his powers of endurance in compelling the House of Commons to sit until any hour in the morning, provided that by doing so he could advance the legislation of his government. (Lord George Hamilton, *Parliamentary Reminiscences and Reflections 1868 to 1885*, John Murray, London, 1916, 45–6.)

The House depended much more than its does now on the goodwill of its members and in particular on their willingness to eschew systematic obstruction. Obstruction will, of course, always be associated with the Irish Nationalists, under the leadership of Charles Stewart Parnell, during the Parliament of 1880–5 and, to those with a closer interest in parliamentary history, with the four members of the so-called 'Fourth Party'—Lord Randolph Churchill, John Gorst, Sir Henry Drummond-Wolff, and the young Arthur Balfour in the same Parliament. Obstruction by the Irish Nationalists was the immediate cause of the introduction of closure—the arbitrary ending of a debate provided it is supported by at least a hundred Members. But obstruction was not a new phenomenon and examples of its use by one or more Members can be traced back to at least the time of Edmund Burke and, indeed, to Burke himself.

In 1771 Burke forced twenty-three divisions over proceedings taken against newspapers for publishing accounts of debates of the House.[11] Redlich, in fact, suggests that the first recorded use of deliberate obstruction occurred in 1641, when supporters of Charles I sought to prevent the passing of the Grand Remonstrance, a listing of the alleged illegal actions of the king, and goes on to cite other cases in 1806, 1831, 1833, and 1843,

---

[11] Redlich, *Procedure of the House of Commons*, Vol. 1, 138–9, n.2.

remarking apropos the later Irish obstruction, 'It will be seen that there had been no lack of warnings of the danger of obstruction in the House of Commons.'[12] Elsewhere Redlich cites the case of Lord Brougham in 1816, using the procedure on public petitions to oppose the continuation of income tax.[13] Other instances occurred in the 1868–74 Parliament over the abolition of the purchase of army commissions in 1871,[14] over successive attempts to introduce the secret ballot for parliamentary elections between 1870 and 1872 when the Ballot Act was finally passed,[15] and, more generally, by a number of Conservative MPs, the most well-known of whom was James Lowther (MP for York 1865–80, North Lincolnshire 1881–5, and the Isle of Thanet 1888–1904). So effective an obstructionist was Lowther that he was credited by some contemporaries as being the originator, or at least the co-originator, of obstruction.[16] Lowther's rival claimant was the Irish Nationalist, Joseph Biggar (MP for Cavan 1874–85 and West Cavan 1885–90), who was also an active obstructionist before the 1880–5 Parliament. But Lowther, Biggar, and others who joined them, marked the beginning of more frequent and systematic obstruction. Nonetheless, it would appear that systematic Irish obstruction was not anticipated by Gladstone: during the 1868–74 Parliament he was asked, in relation to the activities of Lowther and his friends, 'whether or not this practice, if extended, would not upset all the traditions and usages of the House of Commons', and replied, 'Oh, they are gentlemen; they will never go to that length'.[17] There is no reason to believe that his view of the Irish Members was any different.

For the Irish Nationalists, however, this was totally irrelevant: they had no such inhibitions; the objective was to force the issue of Home Rule onto and up the political agenda. It was, in fact, one of the earlier Liberal Home Rulers, Joseph Ronayne (MP for Cork City 1872–6), who made this abundantly clear in 1874: 'We will never make any impression on the House until we interfere in

---

[12] Ibid.   [13] Ibid., 76, n.1.
[14] Sir Alexander Mackintosh, *Echoes of Big Ben: A Journalist's Parliamentary Diary (1881–1940)*, Jarrolds, London, 1946, 15.
[15] Stanley Hyland, *Curiosities from Parliament*, Allan Wingate, London, 1955, 191.
[16] See Hamilton, *Parliamentary Reminiscences*, 46; and Herbert (Viscount) Gladstone, *After Thirty Years*, Macmillan, London, 1928, 179.
[17] Hamilton, *Parliamentary Reminiscences*, 46.

English business ... Let us interfere in English legislation; let us show them that if we are not strong enough to get our own work done, we are strong enough to prevent them getting theirs.'[18] On the day in 1875 that Parnell first took his seat, Joe Biggar was obstructing the passage of the Irish Coercion Bill,[19] but Isaac Butt (Conservative MP for Harwich 1852, Protectionist and then Liberal-Conservative MP for Youghal 1852–65, and Home Rule MP for Limerick City 1871–9), leader of the Home Rulers, did not approve of such tactics and Irish obstruction did not reach its zenith until after Parnell succeeded him in May 1880 as leader of what was now the Irish Nationalist Party, following Butt's death in 1879. Even before then Parnell and Biggar showed what could be achieved by a small number of MPs, knowledgeable about procedure and determined to engage in obstruction. Parnell and his followers came into their own when Gladstone sought first to solve the Irish problem by negotiation, then by coercion, until he was finally persuaded that the only solution was Home Rule.[20]

However, as already noted, the Irish Nationalists were not the only systematic obstructionists at work in the 1880–5 Parliament. Lord Randolph Churchill and his three colleagues in the 'Fourth Party' became increasingly dissatisfied with what they regarded as the pusillanimous leadership of Sir Stafford Northcote, who led the Conservative opposition in the Commons after the election defeat of 1880. The Irish developed obstruction into a formidable parliamentary weapon; the Fourth Party developed it into an art form.[21] What the Fourth Party demonstrated was that, even in the absence of the Irish Nationalists, some means by which the government could control its own time and, almost certainly, parliamentary time more generally had become a necessity.

That necessity was met, initially at least, by the introduction of

[18] Barry O'Brien, *The Life and Times of Charles Stewart Parnell*, Smith, Elder and Co., London, 1898, Vol. 1, 93.

[19] Redlich, *Procedure of the House of Commons*, Vol. 1, 138.

[20] See ibid., ch. 2; T. P. O'Connor, *Gladstone's House of Commons*, Ward Downey, London, 1885; F. H. O'Donnell, *A History of the Irish Parliamentary Party*, Longman Green, London, 1910; Conor Cruise O'Brien, *Parnell and His Party, 1880–90*, Clarendon Press, Oxford, 1957; and Robert Kee, *The Laurel and the Ivy: the Story of Charles Stewart Parnell and Irish Nationalism*, Penguin, London, 1994 (first published by Hamish Hamilton 1993).

[21] See H. E. Gorst, *The Fourth Party*, Smith, Elder and Co., London, 1906; and O'Connor, *Gladstone's House of Commons.*, 2, 8, 60–1, 73–83, and 262–4.

closure. It is worth noting that, as early as 1848, the then Speaker, Charles Shaw Lefevre, urged the adoption of closure, a plea he repeated in evidence to a Procedure Committee in 1854, stating, in Redlich's words, 'that it was an expedient to which the House would some day or other be obliged to resort.'[22] Irish obstruction was the immediate but not the long-term cause of the introduction of closure; its introduction sooner or later was an inevitable consequence of the growth of government. It actually came about as a result of what became known as 'the Speaker's coup d'état' on 1st February 1881, when Mr Speaker Brand, on his own initiative, ended a $41^{1}/_{2}$ hour debate on the Irish Coercion Bill. The government then brought forward proposals for the introduction of closure as part of standing orders, accompanied by other measures, notably the exclusion of Members who defied the rulings of the Speaker. These proposals invoked much bitterness, not just on the part of the Irish Members: the introduction of the closure rule in particular was denounced as an alien device and scornfully described by Lord Randolph Churchill and others as 'clôture'. In fact, the closure rule was not very effective and led the Speaker to propose a timetable for the stages of bills declared urgent – a device to which another alien term, the 'guillotine', was aptly given. A new and more workable closure rule was introduced in 1887 and the guillotine became a permanent feature of Commons' procedure.[23]

At first, governments used these new weapons in their armoury sparingly, but in due course they became a regular part of the operation of the Commons, even though the opposition would—and still does—cry 'gag' whenever such timetable motions are imposed, rather than negotiated. The government's control of parliamentary time culminated in the adoption of Balfour's 'parliamentary railway timetable' in 1902, which, notwithstanding refinements since, constitutes the procedural basis for government control of the parliamentary agenda and its domination of parliamentary business.

The Use of Legislative Committees

There was one further change to be put in place: the use of committees to facilitate the simultaneous passage of more than one bill at

---

[22] Redlich, *Procedure of the House of Commons*, Vol. 1, 95.
[23] See ibid., ch. 3.

a time. Committees have long been used by the House of
Commons to deal with particular types of business—one of the
oldest is the Privileges Committee (now Standards and Privileges),
that dates back to the seventeenth century. During the nineteenth
century select committees—committees set up and chosen to carry
out a particular task—were widely used to enquire into various
policy issues, sometimes with a view to producing draft legislation.[24] Although there were precedents for bills being referred to
committees after second reading as early as the sixteenth century,[25]
their regular use is a much more recent development. During his
time as a member of the Clerk's Department and subsequently as
Clerk, Erskine May—in 1854, 1871 and 1878—urged the adoption
of committees for the committee stage of bills[26] and Speaker
Denison also supported their introduction in 1861.[27] However, it
was not until 1883 that two such standing committees were established. Even then, their initial use was desultory: they took the
committee stage of four bills in 1883, three in 1884, followed by a
hiatus in their appointment until 1888. From then until 1906 the
two standing committees were appointed, but never dealt with
more than eight bills in a single session. The Liberal government
elected in 1906 showed a much greater enthusiasm for standing
committees, however, referring fifteen government bills to the two
committees in 1906 and, following a Procedure Committee report
that session, increased the number of standing committees to four.
Between 1907 and 1914—excluding the truncated session of
1910—an average of twelve government bills per session were
referred to them.

The 1907 changes also introduced a standing order that stated
that bills would be referred to a standing committee unless the
house ordered otherwise, in which case the committee stage would
be taken on the floor of the House. However, although standing
committees had the advantage of allowing up to four bills—including, of course, Private Members' bills—to be dealt with simultaneously, they had the disadvantage, from the government's point of

---

[24] See Todd, *On Parliamentary Government,* Vol. 1, 428–39.
[25] Sir Courtenay Ilbert, Supplementary Chapter to Redlich, *Procedure of the House
of Commons*, Vol. 3, 208.
[26] See Redlich, *Procedure of the House of Commons,*Vol. 1, 91, 107, and 117.
[27] Ibid., 101.

view, of not being subject to the guillotine. In short, the government ultimately had less control over standing committees than over proceedings on the floor of the House. This made governments somewhat reluctant to refer most government bills to standing committees. In addition, a convention quickly developed that the committee stage of bills of constitutional importance would normally be taken in the whole House and, understandably, short, non-controversial bills were and are also taken on the floor.

Nonetheless, the standing committees provided greater flexibility in dealing with the government's legislative programme and this was increased in 1909 by the introduction of the selection of amendments to be considered by the chair of the committee, following consultation with those concerned, a process known as 'the kangaroo'. The position of the chair in this regard was strengthened in 1919 by allowing the chair to select amendments without giving reasons. Also in 1919 the number of standing committees was increased to six. The final piece of the jigsaw was put in place in 1947, when the guillotine was introduced for standing committee proceedings and the number of committees was increased to as many as might be necessary. As a consequence between seven and nine standing committees are now appointed each session. One deals exclusively with Private Members' bills and the remaining committees usually take the committee stage of some 60 per cent of government bills.

Conclusion

With the development and regular use of standing committees, the four major developments in parliamentary procedure needed to enable the House of Commons to cope with the growth of government were all in place – an increase in parliamentary time, precedence given to government business, the extension of government control over its own time and over the parliamentary agenda generally, and the use of committees to spread the legislative burden. In addition, from 1906 Parliament adopted the practice of spreading sittings throughout the year, rather than concentrating them between January/February and July/August.

There was one other change that facilitated the acceptance of these changes and that was the role of the Speaker. Arthur Onslow, Speaker from 1728 to 1761, is regarded as the prototype of the modern Speaker—politically-neutral, the defender of minorities, and the arbiter in all matters procedural. Speakers before and, indeed, to a lesser extent after Onslow had strong associations with the government. After 1832, however, the precedent set by Onslow increasingly became the norm and, as Campion notes, 'After the election of Shaw Lefevre, Speaker from 1839 to 1857, the principle has been observed that the Speaker is not only impartial but abstains from anything which could cause the slightest suspicion of partisanship.'[28]

All these developments were in place by the early part of the twentieth century; what followed were refinements of these procedures and practices, not further fundamental reform. What Redlich called 'the reform of the antiquated procedures' was complete; what was to become necessary was a redressing of the balance between the executive and the legislature. Whether it has been achieved, however, is the subject of another chapter in the development of Parliament and therefore the role of the Member of Parliament.

A Footnote on the Role of the House of Lords[29]

From the time they became separate Houses of Parliament in the fourteenth century, the House of Lords and the House of Commons have been procedurally and, to a large extent, organizationally separate. The modern Lords and Commons share some services, such as computer, telephone, and security services, but others, such as the provision of office accommodation and refreshment services are separate, and each has its own library and information service. On procedural matters the two Houses are entirely separate in that

[28] Campion, *Parliamentary Procedure*, 51. See also Philip Laundy, *The Office of Speaker*, Cassell, London, 1964; and Philip Marsden, *The Officers of the Commons 1363–1965*, Barrie and Rockcliff, London, 1966, ch. 4.

[29] See Donald Shell, *The House of Lords*, Harvester-Wheatsheaf, Hemel Hampstead, 2nd ed. 1992; Donald Shell and David Beamish (eds.), *The House of Lords at Work: A Study of the 1988–89 Session*, Clarendon Press, Oxford, 1993; P. A. Bromhead, *The House of Lords and Contemporary Politics*, Routledge and Kegan Paul, London, 1958; Bernard Crick, *The Reform of Parliament: The Crisis of British Government*, Weidenfeld and Nicolson, London, 2nd rev. ed. 1968, chs. 5 and 6; and Michael Wheeler-Booth, 'The House of Lords', in J. A. G. Griffith and Michael Ryle, *Parliament: Functions, Practices and Procedures*, Sweet and Maxwell, London, 1989.

each decides its own procedures, although these are basically similar and any differences are of a detailed rather than a fundamental nature. Bills in both Houses, for instance, go through the same stages, although the upper house mostly takes the committee stage on the floor of the House, rather than using separate committees. Some of the differences, however, though detailed, are important and the most important is that there is no form of closure in the House of Lords. Essentially, the government must get its legislation through by persuasion rather than *force majeure*. Indeed, the latter is rarely if ever an option. Only the Conservatives have ever had a clear majority in the House of Lords and, although it has always been Liberal and Labour governments that have had the greatest problems with the upper house, recent Conservative governments have regularly found the upper house a thorn in their side. In Parliaments in the 1980s and 1990s the Conservatives have always been the largest single party, but not to the extent of a guaranteed, absolute majority. This situation was complicated by the fact that, until the removal of most of the hereditary peers in 1999, there was an absolute Conservative majority among the membership as a whole, but not among regular attenders. To complicate matters further, it was always possible for the Conservatives to summon 'the backwoodsmen'—the irregular attenders taking the Conservative whip—to secure an absolute majority in a particular vote, but, by definition, this was not a regular option. Moreover, to understand the position of the House of Lords a further dimension needs to be explained.

In spite of the pressures on the House of Commons produced by the growth of government, the House of Lords has always been under much less pressure, essentially because the constitutional and therefore political supremacy of the Commons over the Lords had long been recognized. That is not to say that there have not been serious clashes, but a distinction needs to be drawn between clashes over particular pieces of legislation, in which the will of the Lords has quite often prevailed, and clashes over the broader supremacy of the lower house, in which the Commons has always prevailed, though not without a struggle. The most serious clash, of course, was that of 1909–11, which culminated in the passing of the Parliament Act of 1911, removing the power of the Lords over financial business and limiting the veto of the upper house over other legislation. The two-year veto introduced in 1911 was reduced to one year by the

Parliament Act of 1949, but a more important development was the 'Salisbury convention' after Labour's massive election victory in 1945. This was an informal undertaking not to reject outright legislative proposals that had been in Labour's election manifesto, although reserving the right of detailed amendment. In practice, much as Labour governments resented the House of Lords, this arrangement worked well, not preventing but channelling and containing conflict.

In the meantime, the advent of life peerages in 1958 helped the upper house develop a clearer and more active role as a revising chamber that would challenge government legislation but seldom reject it outright. Ironically, this provided governments of all parties a means of amending their own legislation after often-inadequate discussion in the Commons because of the pressure of time. Without the need to devote a considerable amount of time to financial business and the recognition of the ultimate supremacy of the Commons, the House of Lords has not needed to develop the more elaborate and stringent procedures adopted by the Commons. This is further and crucially assisted by the less partisan atmosphere of the Lords. Thus, while the House of Commons was developing and elaborating its procedures by extending standing orders, the upper house was developing its procedures more slowly and remained and remains governed more by practice than formal rules. Not surprisingly, given its complexity, the two Houses have not dissimilar numbers of standing orders on private business—217 for the Lords and 248 for the Commons—but there is a marked difference in their respective numbers of standing orders on public business—84 for the Lords and 163 for the Commons.[30]

The preamble of the Parliament Act, 1911 unambiguously states that the curbing of the power of the House of Lords was the first of two stages of reform, the second of which would create a second chamber 'constituted on a popular instead of hereditary basis'. In spite of the First World War, that second stage appeared to be well on the way with the appointment in 1917 of a commission, which duly reported the following year,[31] but no action followed and further

---

[30] HL 15, 1994–5 and HC 7, 1998–9. See also *A Brief Guide to the Procedures and Practices of the House of Lords* and *The Companion to the Standing Orders* (HL 9, 1994–5).

[31] *Report of the Conference on the Reform of the Second Chamber* (the Bryce Commission), Cd. 9038, 1918.

attempts at reform in 1948 and 1968 also foundered. It was not until Labour won its huge 179-seat majority in 1997, that Lords' reform was again high on the political agenda. Political observers nearly ninety years after the 1911 Act could be forgiven for a sense of *déjà vu*, when the Labour government announced that its reform of the Lords was take place in two stages, the first involving the removal of the hereditary members of the upper house, the second the creation of a modern, 'more democratic' second chamber. The first stage was indeed accomplished by the House of Lords Act, 1999, which removed all but ninety-two hereditary members of the Lords—the ninety-two being part of a compromise deal to facilitate the passage of the bill. However, the government firmly rejected a wholly or substantially-elected second chamber, as did the royal commission it appointed to advise on a reformed upper house.[32] In addition the Prime Minister, Tony Blair, has used his powers of patronage to give the Labour Party virtual parity with the Conservatives in the Lords, but has deliberately eschewed the opportunity to secure an overall Labour majority. The Liberal Democrat and crossbench peers therefore hold the balance of power in the upper house.

Thus, from early 2000 the House of Lords has been a 'transitional' house, awaiting, as its predecessor did after 1911, further reform. This transitional house, however, has not only continued to perform the functions of its unreformed predecessor, but has also continued to act in an essentially similar fashion in showing a willingness to amend government legislation, even occasionally rejecting government bills. This has led the Labour government to invoke the Parliament Acts on two occasions to override the Lords' veto.[33] Indeed, while still adhering to the Salisbury Convention, the transitional House of Lords appears to have been emboldened by what it sees as its greater legitimacy, now that almost all the hereditaries have been removed.

---

[32] Royal Commission on the House of Lords, *A House for the Future* (the Wakeham Report), Cm. 4534, January 2000.

[33] The European Elections Act, 1999 and the Sexual Offences (Amendment) Act, 2000. The previous Conservative government had used the Parliament Acts once, to secure the passage of the War Crimes Act, 1991, but at the time this was only the fourth act to be passed in this way, the others being the Welsh Church Act, 1913, the Government of Ireland Act, 1914, and the Parliament Act, 1949.

4

The Socio-Economic Transformation of the House of Commons

Introduction

An inevitable consequence of the societal changes that were both a cause and consequence of the growth of government was that, in due course, these were reflected in the socio-economic composition of the House of Commons.[1] In particular, during the nineteenth century industrial, commercial, and financial interests were increasingly represented in the Commons and, in the first half of the twentieth century, this was extended to working class interests.

The composition of the House of Commons is determined by a process of supply and demand, the supply of those eligible and aspiring to membership of the Commons and the demands of the political parties and of the electorate. Supply and demand are, in turn, much influenced by what the literature on political recruitment calls 'opportunity structures'—the formal and informal processes and institutions that influence the recruitment process. These include the legal requirements imposed on candidates—usually in the form of various restrictions or limitations on the eligibility to stand for election or to be a member of the legislature—the financial constraints on candidates and members of the legislature, the processes by which parties choose candidates, and the electoral process. Supply and demand are also affected by longer-term trends in the party system, but these result largely from wider changes in society, including attitudinal and ideological

---

[1] They also produced significant changes in the composition of the House of Lords, with the growth of a 'new' aristocracy whose wealth was based not on land but on industry, commerce, and finance, even though many of this 'new' aristocracy bought land and adopted a lifestyle similar to that of the 'old' aristocracy.

changes. Thus, the industrial revolution transformed the socio-economic composition of the of the House of Commons during the nineteenth century, and the growing acceptance of collectivist ideas had a major impact on the composition of Liberal Party and was instrumental in the rise of the Labour Party.

The Changing Opportunity Structures

The Electoral System

Between the passing of the Septennial Act in 1715 and the Parliament Act of 1911 general elections had to take place at a maximum interval of seven years. This was reduced to the present five years in 1911 to allow a more frequent expression of opinion by the electorate, on the grounds that government legislation was no longer subject to the possibility of an absolute veto by the House of Lords. However, these were maxima and the dates of general elections have long been determined by the government of the day, since 1918 in fact, by the Prime Minister. Apart from the rare occasions when an election is brought about by an adverse vote in the House of Commons, as happened in 1924 and 1979, Prime Ministers choose the date they judge the most propitious. This inevitably affects the length of any particular Parliament, but on average general elections took place every to $4^1/_2$ years between 1832 and 1918 and every 3 to $3^1/_2$ years after 1918.

By-elections are a difference matter and vacancies occur for a variety of reasons, although the most frequent causes are the death

TABLE 4.1. *Frequency of general elections and by-elections, 1832–1997*

Period	General elections	By-elections
1832–68	1: 4.0 years	37.9 per year
1868–1918	1: 4.5 years	29.5 per year
1918–1945	1: 3.9 years	19.0 per year
1945–97	1: 3.5 years	8.3 per year

or the resignation of the sitting Member. By convention, the former
Member's party chooses the date of the by-election. The number of
by-elections per year has declined since the nineteenth century.
Two major factors account for this. Firstly, there was a marked
decline in the number of elections being overturned as a result of
election petitions, following the passage of the Corrupt and Illegal
Practices Act, 1883. The number of petitions declined from 979
between 1832 and 1885 to seventy-four between 1885 and 1910.
Similarly, the number of elections overturned declined from 272 to
thirty.[2] Secondly, until 1926, MPs appointed to ministerial posts
between rather than immediately after general elections were
required to seek re-election and this accounted for more than one
fifth of the by-elections between 1832 and 1926. There has,
however, been a further decline: between 1945 and 1970 the
number of by-elections per year was 11.2; between 1970 and 1997
it was 5.7. This resulted from a decline in the number of by-elections caused by governments appointing MPs to various positions
incompatible with continued membership of the Commons, since
governments increasingly found that they tended to lose the ensuing by-election. The opportunities for election at general elections
have therefore increased, but the opportunities via by-elections
have decreased.

The composition of the Commons is significantly affected by the
electoral system. The simple plurality or first-past-the-post system
distorts the relationship between votes and seats, especially in elections in which there is extensive third party intervention and
support. If that third party support is geographically concentrated
it will result in the party or parties concerned winning a disproportionately large number of seats *nationally*, as was the case with
the Irish Nationalists between 1874 and 1918, but the more thinly
third party support is spread, the fewer seats it or they will win
proportionate to their vote, as has been the fate of the Liberals and
their Liberal Democrat successors since 1918. On the other hand,
the party winning most votes usually has a disproportionately
higher number of seats to the point that it normally has absolute
majority in the Commons, even though it may not have an

---

[2] F. S. W. Craig, *British Electoral Facts, 1832–1987*, Parliamentary Research
Services, Dartmouth, 1989, Table 14.20.

absolute majority of the votes cast. Indeed, this has been the norm at almost every election in the twentieth century: one party has won an absolute majority of seats in every election except the two elections of 1910, and the elections of 1923, 1929, and February 1974, but only in 1900, 1931, and 1935 has the winning party secured more than 50 per cent of the votes cast. The number of uncontested seats distorts the situation in the nineteenth century. Even so, in all but the elections of 1832, 1835, 1837, and 1880 there was a significant distortion of the relationship between votes and seats. Crucially in the context of composition, this distortion produces a greater turnover of seats in the Commons than would be the case under a system of proportional representation.[3]

TABLE 4.2. *Turnover in seats in the House of Commons, 1832–1997*

Period	No. of elections	Mean	Median	Range
1832–68	9	37.9	40.1	25.7 (1859)–45.9 (1847 and 1865)
1874–1900	7	42.1	46.2	23.1 (1886)–60.6 (1885)
1906–18	4	44.1	49.5	14.9 (Dec 1910)–62.5 (1918)
1922–35	6	42.4	45.5	33.3 (1923)–58.7 (1922)
1945–97	15	27.1	24.8	7.2 (Feb 1974)–72.7 (1945)

Source: Calculated from lists of MPs in the first volume of Hansard for each Parliament.

The turnover of seats in the House of Commons inevitably varies according to party fortunes—large electoral swings produce large turnovers, but this tends to produce changes in composition that reflect socio-economic differences *between* the parties rather than *within* them. Thus, for most of the twentieth century an electoral swing to the Conservatives has produced a Commons with more

[3] For discussion of the electoral system see Robert Blackburn, *The Electoral System in Britain*, Macmillan, London, 1995; David Farrell, *Comparing Electoral Systems*, Macmillan, London, 1997; and Report of the Independent Commission on the Voting System (the Jenkins Commission), Cm. 4090, October 1998.

MPs with public school and Oxbridge backgrounds and more from business occupations; an electoral swing to Labour has produced more state-educated MPs and more manual workers. Changes *within* parties generally take effect more slowly, although major party splits involving the transfer of MPs from one party to another may result in a more dramatic change. This was certainly the case with the move of the Peelite Free Traders from the Conservatives to the Liberals after the repeal of the Corn Laws in the mid-nineteenth century, although this took place over a number of years. The more dramatic secession of the Liberal Unionists provides a further example, but more recent splits, such as the Labour split of 1980–81, leading to the formation of the SDP, had little effect on the socio-economic composition of the Parliamentary Labour Party.

Historically, there have been considerable variations in turnover. In the second half of the eighteenth and early part of the nineteenth centuries turnover averaged little more than a quarter, but the political upheavals over Catholic emancipation and, more especially, electoral reform resulted in a marked increase in turnover. Public interest in politics grew and the demands on MPs increased, both from their constituents and within Parliament. The proportion of uncontested constituencies fell from an average of 68.9 per cent in the eighteenth century to 47.5 per cent between 1832 and 1865. In 1832 itself only 31.2 per cent of constituencies were uncontested,[4] notwithstanding the fact that contested elections were an expensive business. The longer average period between elections before the Parliament Act of 1911 undoubtedly contributed to higher turnover in the nineteenth century, whereas the high average between 1922 and 1935 is attributable largely to changes in the party system, with the decline of the Liberals and the rise of Labour. In addition, the elections of 1918 and 1945 constitute special cases in that there was a longer than usual gap between elections because of the two world wars—eight years in the case of 1918 and ten in the case of 1945, quite apart from larger than usual electoral swings. Conversely, and not surprisingly, elections swiftly following one another usually

---

[4] Romney Sedgwick, *History of Parliament: The House of Commons 1715–54*, HMSO for the History of Parliament Trust, London, 1970, 116–24; Sir Lewis Namier and John Brooke, *History of Parliament: The House of Commons 1754–1790*, HMSO for the History of Parliament Trust, London, 1964, 513–21; and Craig, *British Electoral Facts*, Table 14.09.

produce below average turnovers, as happened in 1886, December 1910, and October 1974.

Turnover, however, also reflects changing career patterns among MPs, particularly since 1945. The lower average turnover between 1945 and 1997, in spite of the landslides in each of those elections, results partly from lower electoral swings, but they also stem from longer parliamentary service and the increasing number of full-time MPs, in short resulting from the professionalization of the Member of Parliament, which is discussed further in Chapter 5.

Legal Restraints

At no time in the history of the unreformed Parliament, certainly at no time subsequent to 1372, had constituencies an unrestricted choice in electing representatives to the House of Commons . . . First came the law of 1372, which excluded sheriffs of counties . . . Then came laws which restricted the choice of constituencies to men dwelling in their midst; next a series of enactments imposing religious tests; and concurrently with there were laws imposing oaths for the protection of the Crown, and subsequently of the settlement determined at the Revolution. Later still there was gradually enacted a code which made many office-holders ineligible; and about this time came the enactments which imposed property qualifications and were intended to restrict the choice of electors to men of means or of assured position.   (Edward Porritt, *The Unreformed House of Commons: Parliamentary Representation Before 1832*, Cambridge University Press, Cambridge, 1909, Vol. 1, 121).[5]

Edward Porritt traces in considerable detail the increasing restrictions on who could be elected to the House of Commons before 1832. The more significant of these restrictions were gradually removed: the residence qualification had fallen into to disuse by the seventeenth century; most religious restrictions were removed, although Catholics were barred until 1828 and orthodox Jews until 1858; and the property qualification was also finally abolished in 1858, although it had been widely evaded. Consequently, Porritt, writing in 1909, could say, 'the electors have had, so far as statute law is concerned, a much freer choice than at any time in the history of the representative system.'[6] In 1909, of course, women

---

[5] For more details see Porritt, *The Unreformed House*, chs. 7–10.
[6] Ibid., 121–2.

were still ineligible and remained so until 1918, but the restrictions that now remain are mostly ones that would be expected—minors, aliens, undischarged bankrupts, those certified as insane, convicted prisoners serving sentences of twelve or more months, and persons found guilty of corrupt or illegal electoral practices, but there are others, some of which could be seen as anachronistic, others retaining a contemporary logic.

The anachronistic exclusions are clergy of the Church of England and Church of Ireland, Roman Catholic priests, and ministers of the Church of Scotland, but not nonconformist ministers, although it is argued that the Church of England is represented by the two archbishops and twenty-four bishops in the House of Lords. The exclusions that retain a contemporary logic include members of the House of Lords, serving members of the armed services, judges, and civil servants. With the important exception of more senior civil servants, however, all those thus excluded may, in principle at least, stand for election to the Commons, but would be disqualified if elected and subsequently sought to take their seats. More senior civil servants, however, may not be parliamentary *candidates* unless they first resign, a restriction which, in its fullest form, dates back to 1884. This restriction on civil servants contrasts with practice in other European countries, where civil servants, and indeed judges, may be elected to the legislature and who invariably constitute a significant minority.[7]

The eligibility of women is undoubtedly the most important change of the twentieth century and it illustrates vividly that changing the *legal* opportunity structures seldom has an immediate and dramatic effect on the socio-economic composition of the House of Commons. There is a touch of irony in that fact that the first woman elected to Parliament, the Countess Markievicz, stood as a Sinn Fein candidate and, along with all other Sinn Fein candidates elected in 1918, refused to take her seat, leaving Lady Astor to become the first woman MP, following her election at a by-election

---

[7] See Heinrich Best and Maurizio Cotta (eds.), *Parliamentary Representatives in Europe 1848–2000: Legislative Recruitment and Careers in Eleven European Countries*, Oxford University Press, Oxford, 2000. The situation regarding civil servants in continental Europe is complicated by the fact that teachers and local government officials are classed as civil servants, which they are not in the UK.

TABLE 4.3. *The number and proportion of women MPs, 1922–1997*

(selected elections)

Election	No.	% of MPs	Election	No.	% of MPs
1922	2	0.3	1955	24	3.8
1923	8	1.3	1959	25	4.0
1929	14	2.3	1964	29	4.6
1931	15	2.4	1987	41	6.3
1945	24	3.8	1992	60	9.2
1951	17	2.7	1997	120	18.2

Source: David Butler and Gareth Butler, *Twentieth Century British Political Facts 1900–2000*, Macmillan, London, 2000, 261.

in 1919. Thereafter, the proportion of women MPs increased painfully slowly, so that it was not until 1987, almost seventy years after women became eligible, that the proportion exceeded 5 per cent, and, in spite of a doubling of the number of women MPs between 1992 and 1997, the proportion is still less than one in five.

The removal of legal barriers is therefore important, but its impact is not likely to be swift and extensive unless additional steps are taken to make it so. For instance, in the case of women, it would be so if there were a legal requirement that the parties must nominate women as 50 per cent of their candidates and even more so if this were combined in whole or part with a party list system of candidates.[8] Although such a system was not introduced for elections to the Scottish Parliament and National Assembly of Wales, the adoption of a proportional, added-member system, involving party lists, plus measures taken by the parties in their selection procedures, resulted in both legislatures having significantly larger proportions of women members than Westminster: nearly two-fifths in each case—38.8 per cent in Scotland and 41.7 per cent in

[8] See Michael Gallagher and Michael Marsh (eds.), *Candidate Selection in Comparative Perspective: The Secret Garden of Politics*, Sage, London, 1988; Pippa Norris and Joni Lovenduski, *Political Recruitment: Gender, Race and Class in the British Parliament*, Cambridge University Press, Cambridge, 1995; and Pippa Norris, 'Legislative Recruitment', in L. LeDuc, R. G. Niemi, and P. Norris (eds.), *Comparing Democracies: Elections and Voting in Global Perspective*, Sage, London, 1996.

Wales. The Labour Party in particular adopted a system which 'twinned' the two types of constituencies, resulting in half its members in the Scottish Parliament and sixteen out of twenty-eight of its members of the Welsh Assembly being women. Thus, short of legal compulsion, other factors account for the pace and extent of change in areas such as the recruitment of women MPs, and these relate to supply and demand. In the run-up to the general election of 1997, the Liberal Democratic and Labour Parties sought to influence the supply and demand equation, the former by engaging in affirmative discrimination, the latter in positive discrimination, and this largely accounts for the substantial increase in the number of women MPs in 1997. However, what began with a piece of irony in 1918, was marked by a further piece of irony in 1996, when an industrial tribunal ruled that the all-women short lists that Labour had adopted were illegal on the grounds of sexual discrimination. It is, in fact, supply and demand that does more to explain the composition of the Commons than legal restraints, important as they have been historically.

Financial constraints

... the House of Commons ... is only open to those who can pay the tariff. (G. J. Holyoake, *Working Class Representation*, Birmingham, 1868, 8–9, quoted by H. J. Hanham, *Elections and Party Management: Politics in the Age of Disraeli*, Harvester Press, Hemel Hampstead, 2nd ed. 1978, xxvi.)

Those words were written in 1868: they were true long before that date and for a considerable time after. It was not simply that MPs were not paid until 1912, which was of crucial importance to working-class MPs, but owed far more to the various financial demands made on candidates, successful and unsuccessful alike. The widespread corruption that characterized British elections before the passing of the Corrupt and Illegal Practices Act, 1883 meant that only the wealthy, or those with wealthy patrons, could afford to contest them. Before 1832 the choice of candidates—and therefore Members of Parliament—in a substantial proportion of borough constituencies was in the hands of wealthy landowners; these were 'nomination' or 'pocket' boroughs. In other boroughs the electors, often numbered in hundreds rather than thousands, were open to bribery, treating, and intimidation: these were 'rotten boroughs'. Matters were somewhat better in the county constituencies, but bribery and treating were widespread. Describing electoral practices in Exeter round about 1770, Robert Newton remarks that

... an electorate of a thousand or more was difficult and expensive to manage ... Candidates had to pay generously for the travelling expenses of voters who travelled to Exeter for the election, and for unstinted food and drink for their supporters, actual or potential, during the contest. Gangs of toughs had to be recruited to intimidate rival voters, if necessary by keeping them away from the hustings. (Robert Newton, *Eighteenth Century Exeter*, University of Exeter Press, Exeter, 1984, 55.)

The system was rather more decorous, but no less corrupt, just before the 1883 Act: James Lowther, later Speaker of the House, recounted his election for Rutland:

The election was the last held under the old system ... and in accordance with the electioneering practices which were then in vogue, my agent began operations by chartering every available conveyance for taking electors to the poll and by communicating with all out-voters and sending them return tickets to Oakham [in Rutland]. One gentleman eventually came all way from the south of France to vote—at my expense. (Viscount Ullswater, *A Speaker's Commentaries*, Edward Arnold, London, 1925, Vol. 1, 154.)

In addition to the cost of corrupt practices, candidates also had legitimate costs to meet. These involved the administrative costs of the election, which were shared among the candidates, the cost of printing election literature, the hiring of rooms, and, if elected, maintaining himself as a Member of Parliament and meeting any expenses arising out of his parliamentary duties.

In 1832 the local returning officer's expenses or administrative costs averaged £141 per constituency, but the costs in the 28.7 per cent of uncontested seats would have been less and those in contested seats higher. In January and December 1910, the last two elections in which candidates had to meet these expenses, the average returning officer's expenses were £340 and £280 respectively, with 11.2 and 24.3 per cent of the seats uncontested.[9] Systematic data on other legitimate costs is available from 1857, when candi-

---

[9] Craig, *British Electoral Facts*, Tables 3.03 and 14.09.

dates were first required to submit details of these expenses. In 1857 they averaged £493 per candidate and 1880 £1,472.[10] However, these costs fell significantly after the 1883 Act, which not only largely eliminated corruption but also placed strict and enforceable limits on candidates' legitimate election expenses. Thus, in 1885 the average fell to £610.[11]

The cost of fighting an election could also be considerably increased if the result was challenged by an election petition, as nearly a thousand were between 1832 and 1885. Since most petitions alleged corruption, bribery or some other form of improper influence, the number of petitions dropped dramatically after 1883,[12] undoubtedly to the financial detriment of lawyers specializing in the field: a barrister-MP, writing of his expenses in fighting a by-election and a general election in close succession in 1880, noted in his memoirs, 'My expenditure on the elections was soon made up. There was a large crop of election petitions, and I was retained in twelve.'[13]

In practice, election costs varied considerably and were a significant cause of the high number of uncontested seats. Before 1832 the overwhelming majority of seats were not contested and, although electoral competition increased markedly from 1832, a significant proportion of seats were uncontested at most ensuing elections up to and including that of 1900, but the trend was clearly downwards and the last two occasions when more than 50 per cent of seats were uncontested were 1857 (50.2 per cent) and 1858 (58.0 per cent). Only twice in the twentieth century did it exceed 10 per cent – 1918 (15.1 per cent) and 1931 (10.9 per cent) and since 1951 every seat has been contested at every general election.[14] Thus, while the elimination of corruption considerably reduced costs, the increase in the number of contested seats inevitably added to costs.

Just how expensive elections could be, can be illustrated anecdotally: contesting Liverpool in 1830 one candidate spent £65,000 and another £50,000;[15] and Lord George Hamilton claimed that his election for Middlesex in 1868, 1874, and 1880 'in aggregate

---

[10] Craig, *British Electoral Facts*, Table 3.01.
[11] Ibid., Table 3.02.   [12] Ibid., Table 14.20.
[13] Sir Edward Clarke, *The Story of My Life*, John Murray, London, 1918, 171.
[14] Craig, *British Electoral Facts*, Table 14.09
[15] Stanley Hyland, *Curiosities from Parliament*, Allan Wingate, London, 1955, 177.

amounted to £30,000.[16] Michael Pinto-Duchinsky has calculated that between 1867 and 1883 the average annual cost of standing for Parliament was £850 in county constituencies—with those with larger electorates always more expensive[17]—and £423 in borough constituencies. This included direct electoral or campaign costs,[18] the costs of maintaining the electoral register between elections, and subscriptions to the local party, local charities, and other bodies, but excluding living costs in London once elected and any expenses incurred in the course of carrying out parliamentary duties. Moreover, these figures—and the others cited—take no account of inflation and Pinto-Duchinsky estimated that at 1980 values these amounted to £20,000 and £10,000 a year respectively.[19]

Although the financial burden on candidates was much reduced after 1883, it remained a serious handicap for all but the wealthy and increasingly became a problem for the parties, who, on the one hand, had less wealthy candidates they wished to promote and, on the other, were faced with demands for support from such candidates. Pinto-Duchinksy points out that the 'demand for help from London grew fast during the 1880s. The £20,000–£30,000 that had normally been given as central subsidies to candidates in elections up to 1880 grew to £60,000–£80,000 by the 1890s.'[20] It was a problem for all parties, but especially the small socialist parties, such as the Social Democratic Federation and the Independent Labour Party (ILP). These relied on donations from wealthy supporters, but more electoral success was achieved by 'Lib-Lab' candidates. These were mainly working class men who ran with Liberal support, usually with some financial backing from individual trade unions. It

[16] Lord George Hamilton, *Parliamentary Reminiscences and Reflections, 1868–1885*, John Murray, London, 1916, 3.

[17] See R. Morris Coates and Thomas R. Dalton, 'A note on the cost of standing for the British Parliament, 1852–1880', *Legislative Studies Quarterly*, 17, 1992, 585–93.

[18] Before the introduction of the secret ballot in 1872 this included the cost of erecting the hustings, for which a 'top price was always charged . . . [and] . . . their abolition saw a considerable reduction in the expenditure which previously had to be incurred', Hamilton, *Parliamentary Reminiscences*, 8.

[19] Michael Pinto-Duchinsky, *British Political Finance 1830–1980*, American Enterprise Institute, Washington, DC, 1981, 17. See also William B. Gwyn, *Democracy and the Cost of Politics in Britain 1852–59*, Athlone Press, London, 1962; H. J. Hanham, *Elections and Party Management*; and Cornelius O'Leary, *The Elimination of Corrupt Practices in British Elections, 1868–1911*, Oxford University Press, 1962.

[20] Pinto-Duchinsky, *British Political Finance.*, 31.

was, however, the financing of working class representatives that was a major incentive in the formation of the Labour Representation Committee (LRC) in 1900, which adopted the name 'Labour Party' in 1906. The formation of the LRC not only concentrated resources, but, crucially, focused attention on sustaining working class MPs once they were elected. This had been a problem for both the Lib-Labs and early ILP MPs, such as Keir Hardie, but the LRC organized a modest salary for Members, as well as help with other expenses. While this did not solve the problem, it was an important step forward. However, much this support came from the trade unions affiliated to the LRC and the use of union funds for political purposes was successfully challenged by the Osborne Judgement in 1909. With the Liberals failing to win an overall majority in the two elections of 1910 and needing Labour and Irish Nationalist support, the court ruling became a major factor in the introduction of the payment of MPs from 1912 and in the reversing of the Osborne Judgement by the Trades Disputes Act, 1913.[21]

The payment of Members was intended to and did massively help early Labour MPs, almost all of whom had few means of their own, and it further reduced the financial burden on MPs generally. However, Members remained responsible for any costs incurred in relation to their parliamentary duties, although £100 of the original £400 salary was exempt from income tax as an expense allowance. The only free service MPs received was free telephone calls in the London area, an anomaly dating back to before 1896, when all telephone services were in private hands. Indeed, before 1896 MPs enjoyed free long-distance calls as well, but this ended when the Post Office took over all long-distance lines. Even when allowances to meet various expenses began to be introduced, most Conservative and Liberal, and not a few Labour MPs, found it necessary to supplement their income with outside earnings. Candidates were still expected to provide in whole or part their legitimate election expenses, to subscribe to their local parties and other bodies, so that personal wealth remained a considerable advantage. It was still possible, therefore, for Cuthbert Headlam (Conservative MP for Barnard Castle 1924–9 and 1931–5 and for Newcastle-upon-Tyne North 1940–51) to write in his diary in 1923:

---

[21] See Gwyn, *Democracy and the Cost of Politics.*, chs. 6–7.

... surely it is more difficult for a poor man, however much ability he might possess, to enter the House of Commons as a Conservative than for a rich man to enter the Kingdom of Heaven.   (Stuart Ball (ed.), *Parliament and Politics in the Age of Baldwin and MacDonald: the Headlam Diaries, 1923–1935*, The Historians' Press, London, 1992, 35.)

Headlam came from an old family in the north-east of England, but had no private source of wealth. His dilemma, however, was not confined to Conservatives, although for many Labour MPs the dilemma was that few had any means of supplementing a parliamentary salary that became increasingly inadequate.

The parties themselves slowly improved matters by eventually taking responsibility for electoral expenses and by placing strict limits on the contributions local parties could accept or demand from candidates and MPs. Labour took steps to deal with the matter in 1933, but the Conservatives did not introduce a limit until 1948. Two serious problems remained. The first, which mainly affected Conservatives, was that a significant number of MPs had earned more than the parliamentary salary before they were elected and had either to take a drop in income or, if they wished to maintain their standard of living, continue to earn or develop an outside income. It was this situation, for example, that led Oliver Lyttleton, a prominent Conservative, to give up his political career in 1954: '. . . I had a disturbing conversation with my accountant, who told me that in fairness to my wife and children I should not continue in politics for much longer.'[22] The same problem confronted Conservative backbenchers, to the point that some, like P. B. ('Laddie') Lucas (Conservative MP for Brentford and Chiswick 1950–9), refused ministerial office:

To support his family, in 1946 he had begun working for the Greyhound Racing Association, the company which operates White City and Belle Vue stadiums. In 1957 he had just become its managing director . . . and could not afford to give up these better-paid jobs to become a junior minister. In 1958 he decided not to stand again as an MP.   (the *Guardian*, Obituary for P. B. Lucas, 23 March 1998).[23]

[22] Oliver Lyttleton (Viscount Chandos), *The Memoirs of Lord Chandos*, The Bodley Head, London, 1962, 431.
[23] In 1957 the Prime Minister, Harold Macmillan, had offered Lucas the post of Parliamentary Under-Secretary for War.

Financial necessity aside, there was also a widespread view among
Conservative MPs that such work kept them in touch with the 'real
world' outside Westminster, but it too became a more serious problem as the demands on MPs increased.

The second problem was that, until 1972, no proper distinction
was drawn between the parliamentary salary and the expenses
incurred in carrying out parliamentary duties. Expenses could,
however, be claimed against tax and were by most MPs, so that in
1969–70, when the *gross* salary was £3,250, it was found that the
average *net* salary after expenses, but *before* tax was £1,920.[24] In
fact, some MPs were legitimately claiming the whole of their parliamentary salary as expenses against tax. The separation of salary and
expenses was accompanied by a considerable extension in
allowances, so that finance is no longer a serious barrier to
membership of the Commons. Even so, research carried out carried
out by members of the Study of Parliament Group found that,
among MPs first elected in 1992 and 1997, Conservatives were
more likely to have earned more than the prevailing parliamentary
salary or about the same, whereas Labour MPs were more likely to
have earned less or about the same, leading the former to be more
of the view that the salary remains inadequate.[25]

The 'Selectorate'—the Role of the Political Parties

The nineteenth century saw what might be termed the 'national-
ization' of political parties, with the development of national party
organization and the growing importance of national party leaders.
There was, however, an important exception to this nationalizing
process and that was political recruitment. In essence, local autonomy in the choice of candidates, which had been largely the norm
before 1832, remained largely the norm after 1832.

Political recruitment has never been a simple process, but before
the first Reform Act it was particularly complex because of the mix of
nomination, 'pocket', and 'rotten' boroughs, using a variety of
restricted franchises, and the English counties with larger electorates

[24] Review Body on Top Salaries, *First Report: Ministers of the Crown and Members of
Parliament*, Cmnd. 4836, December 1971, paras. 4–6.
[25] Unpublished research into the socialization of MPs, supported by an award
from the Nuffield Small Grants Scheme and ESRC Award No. RO000222470.

and a largely uniform franchise, with yet other variations in the Scottish, Welsh and Irish boroughs and counties, all subject to varying degrees of influence and corruption.[26] Using contemporary sources, Porritt reports that in 1827, 276 MPs were returned for nomination boroughs and that in 1830 there were nineteen or twenty such boroughs in Ireland, and concludes that 'from about 1760 to 1832 nearly one half of the members of the House of Commons owed their seats to patrons.'[27]

A small number of these boroughs—estimated at sixteen in England and Wales, but with others in Ireland[28]—were controlled by the Treasury, which in practice meant the government of the day. The numbers actually varied from election to election because some of the patrons who controlled seats were willing to negotiate a deal with the Treasury and yet other candidates were partly subsidized by the Treasury.[29] These were the only seats, however, subject to any form of national or central control, the rest—the overwhelming majority—were in the hands of individual patrons, often local or county-based landowners, or small electorates, locally and county-based and open to various forms of influence and corruption. MPs for most of the counties, especially the English counties, had local connections with their constituencies and were often drawn from landed families in the county. MPs returned for boroughs varied considerably and invariably had tenuous if any connection with the constituency they represented. It is anachronistic, but not inappropriate, to apply the term 'carpet-bagger' to many borough MPs in the unreformed Parliament but the *choice* of such candidates was essentially local in most cases. The centre of gravity of political recruitment was therefore at the constituency rather than the national level. Even where patrons and landowners controlled seats, they invariably had palpable links with the constituency.

The changes introduced in 1832, especially the registration of voters, stimulated the formation of local party organizations, not,

[26] See Chris Cook and John Stevenson, *British Historical Facts, 1760–1830*, Macmillan, London, 1980, 53–9; and Porritt, *The Unreformed House.*, Vol. 1, ch. 16.
[27] Ibid., 310 and 311. Systematic data on Ireland was not available.
[28] Cook and Stevenson, *British Historical Facts.*, 59; and Porritt, *The Unreformed House.*, Vol. 1, 341.
[29] See Porritt, *The Unreformed House.*, Vol. 1, 340–8.

of course, in every constituency, but sufficiently widespread and growing in number to underpin the local choice of candidates. This was reinforced by the provision that registers were to be maintained on an annual basis, not compiled once an election was called. In any case, such national party organization as existed was in no position to impose candidates on constituencies over which they had no control. The 1832 Reform Act also divided twenty-six of the forty English counties into two electoral divisions and similarly separated the three Yorkshire ridings, leaving thirteen less populous counties as single electoral divisions, further localizing political recruitment. It was inconceivable that party organizations developing at the local level, rather than being set up by a national party organization, would be willing to accept a passive role in the choice of candidates. This was especially so in constituencies held by one party with a substantial majority—the safe seats in which selection was tantamount to election. At the very least, local party organizations would demand a veto; in practice they established a proactive role and it was the national party organization that was to acquire the veto power.

Once formed, however, it became equally inconceivable that national party organizations would be willing to leave matters entirely in the hands of local parties. This was partly because local party organization was much stronger in some areas than others and the national party organization sometimes provided financial help for candidates in the constituencies concerned. This gave the national party organization some leverage over some selections, but only a minority. It became more important as party conflict grew and the number of uncontested seats fell, so that increasingly the parties were fighting seats they did not expect to win. In addition, there were always seats held by the party in which the local organization was financially weak, and this provided a small number in which the party leadership could place a candidate of its choice. Of much greater importance, however, was the desire of the party leadership to be able to veto candidates of whom it strongly disapproved. But the national veto is a negative weapon: it enables the party leadership to stop a candidate it dislikes; it is no guarantee of securing one that it does, let alone imposing a candidate of its own choice. Nevertheless, it is the case that the Conservative and Labour Party leaderships have been more *dirigiste* in recent years in the selection of candidates for by-elections. In the Conservative case this has tended to remain a negative power, amounting to keeping someone off the local short list of would-be candidates, but in the Labour case it has been strongly proactive to the point of occasionally imposing a candidate on a local party. That power has long been available to the leadership and was used during the interwar period to secure the return of leading members of party who had been defeated in a recent general election, but it fell into abeyance and was not used again until the 1980s and 1990s, under the leadership of Neil Kinnock, John Smith, and Tony Blair. This centralizing trend, especially in the Labour Party, is more apparent in the selection of candidates for the European Parliament and for the devolved legislatures in Scotland and Wales. This owes much to the adoption, in whole for the European elections and in part for the Scottish Parliament and the National Assembly for Wales, of party list systems as part of a proportional representation (PR) package. This would likely manifest itself in political recruitment at Westminster in the event of PR being adopted for national elections.

Local autonomy in political recruitment is thus the rule. The role of the national party organization and leadership in the overwhelming majority of candidate selections is threefold: providing a general framework of common rules by which local parties choose their candidates; maintaining an element of 'quality control' by requiring would-be candidates to secure a place on their lists of available candidates; and retaining a right to veto an unacceptable local choice.[30]

Martin Bell, who defeated Neil Hamilton (Conservative MP for Tatton 1983–1997) in 1997, was the first independent candidate to be elected to Parliament since 1945, when eight independents were elected. However, of these, six sat for the university seats abolished in 1950, so that only two prevailed against Conservative and Labour opponents in normal territorial constituencies. It is true that before and after 1945, candidates bearing labels such as 'Independent Conservative' and 'Independent Labour' have

[30] See Michael Rush, *The Selection of Parliamentary Candidates*, Nelson, London, 1969; and Pippa Norris and Joni Lovenduski, *Political Recruitment: Gender, Race and Class in the British Parliament*, Cambridge University Press, Cambridge, 1995.

defeated mainstream opponents, but they are only partial exceptions to the general rule of two-party domination, since they were mostly 'renegades' from their former parties. Thus, whom the parties select as their candidates crucially affects the membership of the House of Commons.

The Socio-Economic Composition of the House of Commons

The Impact of the Industrial Revolution

The data in Section A of Table 4.4 clearly shows the decline in landed interests in the House of Commons, from more than half the interests represented in 1832 to less than one in six by 1900, whereas industrial, commercial, and financial interests increased from rather more than a quarter to more than half. The increase in professional interests was much less dramatic, largely because the number of lawyers has always been relatively high. In 1832 9.3 per cent of MPs were lawyers, in 1900 20.4 per cent and, until 1992, lawyers were the largest single occupational group in the House of Commons.[31] The representation of working men, however, had hardly begun in 1900; that had to await the greater success of the Labour Party in 1906 and beyond. That, however, illustrates a crucial feature of the changes in the representation of economic interests and, by implication of social and ideological interests— the dominance of party meant that much depended on the fortunes of party.

Clear party differences emerge in Sections B and C of the table, with the Tory/Conservative Party more strongly representing landed interests and the Whig/Liberal Party industrial, commercial, and financial interests, but the difference is more dramatic in 1868 than either 1832 or 1900. In 1832 landed interests contributed nearly three-fifths of the economic interest among Tories and rather more than half among Whigs and Liberals, but by 1868 the difference between the parties was much more marked: landed

---

[31] See Michael Rush and Nicholas Baldwin, 'Lawyers in Parliament', in Dawn Oliver and Gavin Drewry (eds.), *The Law and Parliament*, Butterworths, London, 1998, 155–73.

TABLE 4.4. *The representation of economic interests in the House of Commons, 1832, 1868, and 1900 (%)*

A. *All MPs*

Economic interest	1832	1868	1900
Landed interests	52.4	34.0	15.5
Industrial, comm. & finan. interests	27.3	43.1	52.2
Professional interests	20.3	22.9	29.4
Workers' representatives	0.0	0.0	0.9
Miscellaneous	0.0	0.0	1.9
Total	100.0	100.0	99.9
N	934	1,224	1,319

B. *The Tory/Conservative Party*

Economic interest	1832	1868	1900
Landed interests	58.3	47.3	21.2
Industrial, comm. & finan. interests	22.3	30.9	50.4
Professional interests	19.4	21.7	28.4
Workers' representatives	0.0	0.0	0.0
Miscellaneous	0.0	0.0	0.0
Total	100.0	99.9	100.0
N	211	391	707

C. *The Whig/Liberal Party*

Economic interest	1832	1868	1900
Landed interests	52.8	26.7	9.0
Industrial, comm. & finan. interests	27.6	49.6	57.2
Professional interests	19.6	23.7	31.9
Workers' representatives	0.0	0.0	1.8
Miscellaneous	0.0	0.0	0.0
Total	100.0	100.0	99.9
N	608	738	332

Note: The totals exceed the membership of the House of Commons since many MPs represented more than one interest. The ratios of interests to MPs were 1:1.4 in 1832, 1:1.9 in 1868, and 1:2.0 in 1900.

Source: J. A. Thomas, *The House of Commons, 1832–1901: A Study of its Economic and Functional Character*, University of Wales Press, Cardiff, 1939, Section 1, Tables 1–5 and Section 2, Tables 1–6.

interests had declined by only 11 per cent among the Conservatives, but by half among the Whigs and the Liberals. Conversely, industrial, commercial, and financial interests increased by less than 10 per cent among the Conservatives between 1832 and 1868, but nearly doubled among Whigs and Liberals. By the end of the century, however, the contrast between the two parties was less marked: although the Conservatives were twice as prominent in representing landed interests, the party now represented substantial industrial, commercial, and financial interests, less than 7 per cent behind the comparable Liberal representation. With the subsequent decline of the Liberal Party, business interests were to become almost the exclusive prerogative of the Conservative Party, but in 1900 the contrast between the Conservative and Liberal Parties was less marked in terms of economic interests and what divided them more sharply was ideology.

The Socio-Economic Transformation of the House of Commons 1868–1997

The socio-economic composition of the House of Commons inevitably changes in the short-term in response to the electoral fortunes of the parties. There are significant differences between the candidates chosen by the parties for seats they hold and those they do not, with the important exception of those selected for marginal seats *not* held by the party. In socio-economic terms these candidates are more like their fellow-candidates chosen for seats held by the party, than with those selected to fight hopeless constituencies. This means that an electoral swing in one party's favour ushers in more MPs of a similar background.[32] Landslide victories offset this pattern, but landslides are relatively infrequent. It is therefore more illuminating to examine the parties separately, so that the patterns of change in each party are clear. There is also the question of what periods are most appropriate as a basis for analysis, given the very considerable continuity of membership that historically is a marked feature of the House of Commons. Certain dates clearly suggest themselves—1832 because of the

---

[32] See Rush, *The Selection of Parliamentary Candidates*, 98–100 and 220–2.

Reform Act, 1868 because the modern two-party system had clearly emerged, 1900 because it marks the advent of the Labour Party, 1918 because it signals the serious decline of the Liberal Party, and 1945 because it confirms Labour's status as one of the two major parties. Other dates could have been chosen—important changes took place in 1885, for instance, and, in the Labour case, 1922 provides a better break point than 1918, for reasons that will emerge.

The Conservative Party   Arguably, the Conservative Party under-went a greater socio-economic transformation between 1832 and 1900 than it has since. While not exclusively the party of the aristocracy, no fewer than 44.9 per cent of Conservative MPs had aristocratic connections[33] in 1868, a figure which was essentially no different at 43.4 per cent in 1880. However, the agricultural depression of the 1880s severely affected those whose wealth was in land and undermined the ability of those with landed interests to sustain a political career.[34] Moreover, their grip on many county constituencies was loosened by the electoral reorganization necessitated by the Reform Act of 1884. Consequently, aristocratic representation declined from 32 per cent in 1885 to 17 per cent in 1918. In 1974 it was still as much as 8 per cent, but by 1997 it had fallen to 2.4 per cent.

These changes are reflected in Section B of Table 4.4: landed interests declined, business and professional interests increased, but not to the extent that the Conservatives in 1900 could be described as the party of business and the professions; their Liberal rivals represented more extensive business interests and much the same proportion of professional interests. However, with the decline of the Liberal Party and the rise of Labour, the Conservatives inevitably became the party of business. The Labour Party has always had some from business among its supporters, some of whom became MPs, but that they were the exception to the rule is hardly surprising: until its wooing of business in the

---

[33] Aristocratic connections are defined as the son, grandson, or nephew of the holder of a hereditary peerage or baronetcy—i.e. hereditary knighthood—with a concomitant extension to women MPs from 1918.

[34] See David Cannadine, *The Decline and Fall of the British Aristocracy*, Macmillan, London, 1992, esp. chs. 3 and 5.

1990s, the Labour Party was ideologically antagonistic. Even so, although 1997 produced an increase in the number of Labour MPs with business experience, it was still fewer than the number elected in 1945.

TABLE 4.5. *The occupational backgrounds of Conservative MPs, 1868–1997 (%)*

Elected at general elections between

Occupation	1868–95	1900–10	1918–35	1945–97
Professions	44.5	48.6	47.9	33.7
Business	22.2	30.5	38.1	52.4
Workers	0.0	0.0	1.1	0.7
Miscellaneous	1.6	4.6	6.1	10.9
Private means	31.4	15.3	4.6	2.1
Not known	0.3	0.9	2.1	0.2
Total	100.0	99.9	99.9	100.0

Note: For definitions of each category see the Appendix to this book.

The Conservative Party may be widely seen as the party of business, but not to the extent that in occupational terms Conservative MPs are overwhelmingly drawn from business backgrounds. Nonetheless, as the figures in Table 4.5 show, the proportion of those with business occupations has increased markedly since 1868: in that year it was a mere 12.4 per cent; in 1997 it was 56.4 per cent, although it had been higher in the elections of February and October 1974 and 1979. Conversely, there has been a decline in the proportion of Conservatives from the professions. This is the result partly of a recent fall in the proportion of lawyers, whose numbers rose during the nineteenth century and earlier part of the twentieth, but more particularly to the greater decline in those with a service background, mostly military. Those with miscellaneous occupations, particularly various types of party officials and advisers, and, to a lesser extent, journalists, have increased. Least surprising of all is the considerable fall in those dependent on private means and the tiny proportion of genuine working-class Conservative MPs.

Traditionally, the Conservative may be regarded as the party of business, but it is even more the party of the middle class, whatever its aspirations have been and are to be the 'one-nation' party. This picture is strongly reinforced when the educational background of Conservative MPs is examined:

TABLE 4.6. *The educational background of Conservative MPs, 1868–1997 (%)*

Elected at general elections between

Education	1868–95	1900–10	1918–35	1945–97
All public schools	57.4	70.2	63.8	70.1
Clarendon schools	46.9	50.8	35.8	30.6
All graduates	58.1	64.1	58.5	72.6
Oxford	27.7	31.1	22.7	26.2
Cambridge	18.5	17.7	16.6	21.0
All Oxbridge	46.2	48.8	39.3	47.2
Other universities	11.9	15.3	19.2	25.4

Note: The 'Clarendon' schools—as defined by the Royal Commission on Public Schools, 1864, of which Lord Clarendon was chairman—are Eton, Harrow, Winchester, Charterhouse, Shrewsbury, Rugby, Westminster, St. Paul's, and Merchant Taylors'. For definitions of each category see the Appendix.

The public school system was created in the middle of the nineteenth century: the nine 'Clarendon' schools were all founded in the seventeenth century or earlier, but from the 1840s a growing number of fee-paying schools for the sons of wealthy landed and manufacturing interests were established, leading to the formation of the Headmasters' Conference in 1869. Many more schools were set up later in the nineteenth century and this expansion partly accounts for the increase in the proportion of public-school–educated Conservatives by 1900. However, it is much more a reflection of the social strata from which Conservative MPs are widely recruited, more a supply than a demand factor, to the point that the proportion has remained consistently high since 1900. As recently as October 1974 more than three-quarters of Conservative MPs had attended a public school and the proportion of 61.2 per cent in 1997 reflects a recent decline. The fall in the proportion who have attended 'Clarendon' schools has been more marked, but has been compensated for by non-Clarendon schools. To that extent the

Conservative Party could be said to have become less 'élitist', but it was not until 1959 that the 'Clarendon' school products were outnumbered by those from non-Clarendon schools; by 1997 the ratio was 1:2.

This educational élitism is repeated at the graduate level: given the expansion of higher education and, more particularly, the number of universities, a much higher proportion of Conservative MPs from non-Oxbridge institutions might have been expected, but here too the figures are remarkably consistent. What has expanded is the proportion of *graduates*, not the proportions from Oxford and Cambridge.

No matter how much Conservatives have owed their electoral success to working class support, as a parliamentary party they were and are overwhelmingly middle class. Conservative MPs, however, are less concentrated than they were in the upper echelons of the middle class, but a middle class party they remain.

The Liberal Party   In 1903 Herbert Gladstone, then the Liberal Chief Whip, negotiated an electoral pact with the Labour Representation Committee, by which Labour candidates in certain constituencies would not be opposed by Liberals and vice-versa. The pact undoubt-edly contributed to the size of the majority the Liberals won in 1906, but with hindsight it is clear that the Liberals would have won anyway and that the pact was a bonus, not a necessity. However, in 1886 the Liberal Party had split over Home Rule for Ireland. The defectors, who adopted the label Liberal Unionists, were a combina-tion of traditional Whigs and Radicals, but most Radicals remained in the Liberal Party and in the election of 1886 Whigs outnumbered Radicals by about two to one. A split between Whigs and Radicals was always a possibility, arguably a growing possibility as the nine-teenth century progressed, but the secession of a number of Radicals as well, led by as prominent a figure as Joseph Chamberlain, only damaged the Liberal Party more severely. The Liberal Unionists first supported and then allied themselves with the Conservatives. This produced the Conservative governments of 1886–92 and 1895–1905, with only a short interlude of weak Liberal government between 1892 and 1895. In the meantime, the Liberals' attempt to secure more firmly the working-class support it had enjoyed began to be threatened by the various parties that came together in the

LRC in 1900 and Liberal efforts to secure more genuine working-class MPs by running 'Lib-Lab' candidates had only limited success. The Liberal Party was therefore in danger of being squeezed electorally between the Conservatives and the nascent Labour Party. But this also meant that it was in danger of being similarly squeezed socio-economically.

Between 1832 and 1900 the Liberals had undergone a similar transformation to that of the Conservatives in terms of the interests they represented: landed interests had declined even more than among the Conservatives, and industrial, commercial, and financial, and professional interests had increased. Similarly, the aristocratic element in the Liberal party was 32.2 per cent in 1868, 22.8 per cent in 1880, 16.8 per cent in 1885, and a mere 8.6 per cent in 1918.

TABLE 4.7. *The occupational background of Liberal/Liberal Democrat MPs, 1868–1997 (%)*

	Elected at general elections between			
Occupation	1868–95	1900–10	1918–35	1945–97
Professions	39.7	42.6	43.0	39.3
Business	36.3	37.6	37.3	39.3
Workers	0.4	1.5	3.4	0.0
Miscellaneous	2.6	8.8	10.4	20.2
Private means	20.3	6.5	3.1	1.2
Not known	0.6	2.9	2.8	0.0
Total	99.9	99.9	100.0	100

However, between 1868 and 1997 the occupational profile of the Liberal/Liberal Democratic Party was remarkably consistent. Much more the party of business than the Conservatives in 1868 and attractive across the professions, the Liberals retained significant proportions in these occupations right through to 1997. Those reliant on private means declined more rapidly and sharply than among the Conservatives, but the greatest occupational contrast is the high proportion of Liberals falling within the miscellaneous category in the 1945–97 period. However, figures for this period need to be treated with some caution because of the small number of Liberal/Liberal Democrat MPs elected, but the figure of 20.2 per cent does reflect a trend for Liberal Democrats to be former political consultants or lobbyists, party organizers and advisers, or journalists. Like the Conservatives, the Liberals are essentially middle class and this too is reflected in their educational background.

TABLE 4.8. *The educational background of Liberal/Liberal Democrat MPs, 1868–1997 (%)*

	Elected at general elections between			
Education	1868–95	1900–10	1918–35	1945–97
All public schools	30.5	47.4	38.8	42.9
Clarendon schools	22.4	20.5	14.6	8.3
All graduates	50.1	57.6	51.1	75.0
Oxford	14.4	16.3	12.6	21.4
Cambridge	15.6	17.3	11.2	14.3
All Oxbridge	30.0	33.6	23.8	35.7
Other universities	20.1	24.0	27.3	39.3

Not surprisingly, a significant proportion of Liberal MPs attended public schools before 1900, but that proportion has remained high throughout the twentieth century. It has always been much lower than among the Conservatives and at no time has the number attending 'Clarendon' schools exceeded that of the non-Clarendon schools. Again, compared with the Conservatives, the proportion of graduates among Liberals tended to be lower until after 1945 and Oxford and Cambridge are less prominent. The picture that emerges is again one of an overwhelmingly middle class party, but drawn somewhat less from the upper echelons.

Given their strong Whig backgrounds, it is only to be expected that the Liberal Unionists should more closely resemble their Conservative allies educationally and in terms of aristocratic connections, but occupationally the leavening of Radicals tended to make the Liberal Unionists more like their erstwhile Liberal colleagues. However, by the time the Conservatives and Liberals formally merged to form the Conservative and Unionist Party in 1912, only a higher proportion of businessmen distinguished the Liberal Unionists from the Conservatives.

Conversely, the Lib-Labs were much closer socio-economically and educationally to early Labour MPs. More than four out of five Lib-Labs and Labour MPs had had an elementary education and were manual workers. Most had strong links with, and were often financially supported by, trade unions and, as the Labour Party grew in strength and the unions became increasingly sympathetic towards it, the Lib-Labs came under more and more pressure to leave the Liberals and join Labour, as many in fact did.

The Labour Party   The Labour Party was formed to secure working-class representation in the House of Commons. Two LRC candidates were successful in 1900, although one subsequently switched to Lib-Lab, but in 1906 the number of Labour MPs rose to twenty-nine, forty in January 1910, forty-two in December 1910, and fifty-seven in 1918. The latter, however, marked an important watershed, for Labour became the official opposition, since the Liberals were split between Coalition or Lloyd George Liberals, who with the Conservatives supported Lloyd George's coalition government, and the Asquith Liberals, who did not. From that point the Labour Party was either in government or was the official opposition, even when its number of MPs fell to fifty-two in the debacle of 1931.

The split in the Liberal Party was bitter because it was personal, but the impact of the electoral system on the divided party was devastating. In 1922 Labour and the divided Liberals won almost identical proportions of the vote—29.7 per cent and 28.8 per cent respectively, but for Labour this produced 142 seats, for the Liberals only 115. The two parties were almost equal in votes again in 1923 and the now reunited Liberals did better, with 158 seats, but it was Labour, with 191 seats, which formed a minority government with Liberal support. When that support was withdrawn, precipitating the 1924 election, the Liberal vote slumped to 17.8 per cent and the number of Liberal MPs fell to forty, pushing the party firmly into third place, a position from which it never recovered. Labour was now firmly entrenched as one of the two major parties.

A major consequence of this was that, as the electoral ground shifted under their feet, Liberal and would-be Liberal MPs had to face the dilemma of whether to stick with their party or change allegiance. A significant number chose to do the latter: some switched directly or were subsequently elected as Labour MPs; others started political life outside the Commons as Liberals and were subsequently elected for Labour; and yet others who, almost certainly would have been Liberals before the First World War, were Labour from the outset.[35] In contrast, Labour recruited few Conservatives – the most well-known being Oswald Mosley[36] and many more Liberals joined the Conservatives than Labour.

Nonetheless, this recruitment of Liberals was part of a wider *embourgeoisiement* of the Parliamentary Labour Party (PLP). It was a process that was helped by the adoption in 1918 of an explicitly socialist constitution, which undoubtedly attracted middle class intellectuals, who might earlier have favoured one of the various socialist groups that sprang up in the nineteenth century, or would otherwise have joined the British Communist Party when it was formed in 1920. *Embourgeoisiement*, however, was a continuing process and is clearly reflected in both occupational and educational backgrounds of Labour MPs between 1900 and the present.

TABLE 4.9. *The occupational background of Labour MPs, 1900–1997 (%)*

	Elected at general elections between		
Occupation	1900–18	1922–35	1945–97
Professions	2.3	18.6	33.9
Business	4.6	8.3	9.7
Workers	89.5	56.2	30.5
Miscellaneous	3.5	14.6	25.5
Private means	0.0	1.0	0.2
Not known	0.0	1.2	0.2
Total	99.9	99.9	100.0

[35] See Catherine Ann Cline, *Recruits to Labour: the British Labour Party 1914–1931*, Syracuse University Press, Syracuse, NY, 1963.

[36] Mosley was a Conservative MP 1918–22, an independent 1922–4, when he switched to Labour, but was defeated and then elected as Labour MP for Smethwick in 1926. He was a member of the Labour government elected in 1929, but resigned in May 1930, resigning from the Labour Party in December 1930 and forming the New Party in February 1931. He was defeated in the 1931 general election standing as the New Party candidate in the Stoke-on-Trent (Stoke). In 1932 the New Party was renamed the British Union of Fascists.

It is the Labour Party which provides the greatest contrast among the parties and which has undergone the most dramatic changes in the socio-economic composition of its MPs. Up to the election of 1922 Labour MPs came almost exclusively from the working class; after 1922 working-class representation steadily declined. Labour Members from manual occupations last constituted a majority of the PLP in 1935; in 1945 they comprised two-fifths, by 1966 a third, and by 1997 only one in eight.

TABLE 4.10. *The educational background of Labour MPs, 1900–1997 (%)*

	Elected at general elections between		
Education	1900–18	1922–35	1945–97
Elementary	88.4	55.7	16.2
All public schools	1.2	10.1	17.5
Clarendon schools	0.0	4.5	3.6
All graduates	1.2	22.2	50.3
Oxford	0.0	3.3	11.1
Cambridge	0.0	4.8	5.7
Oxbridge	0.0	8.1	16.8
Other universities	1.2	14.1	33.5

The stark contrast found in the occupational backgrounds of Labour MPs elected between 1900 and 1918 and those elected in 1922 and after is repeated educationally. Before 1922 the overwhelming majority of Labour MPs had had only an elementary education; after 1922 an increasing proportion were graduates and a minority had been to public school. On the one hand, these figures are further evidence of Labour's recruitment of a significant number of MPs from the middle class and, on the other, of a continuing and partly inevitable pattern of recruitment. The widening of educational opportunities meant that the levels of educational attainment of Labour recruits was bound to increase, but this applies much more to the period since 1945 than to the interwar period. The latter shows Labour's ability to attract middle-class recruits, for whom Labour was not the 'natural' party. Middle-class recruitment continued and grew after 1945, but in many cases those who became Labour MPs almost certainly had working class antecedents that many of their interwar predecessors lacked. After 1922 Labour was no longer a working-class party, narrowly seeking to represent the working class directly in Parliament; it had become the party claiming to represent the interests of the working class, of which direct representation was an important but incidental part.

In occupational terms this can be illustrated by the fact that, while both the Conservative and Labour Parties draw similar proportions of MPs from the professions, Conservatives are more commonly lawyers, especially barristers, whereas Labour professionals are more commonly teachers, especially in secondary and further education, or from other parts of the public sector. Similarly, Oxford and Cambridge graduates are heavily concentrated among Conservatives and public schools predominate, whereas non-Oxbridge graduates and those who attended state schools are more the norm for Labour MPs. In short, to a significant degree the Conservative and Labour Parties have increasingly come to recruit from different sectors of the middle class.

A Footnote on the Nationalists   In 1874 no fewer than sixty MPs were elected for Irish constituencies as 'Home Rulers'. This increased to sixty-three in 1880—less than one in ten MPs at Westminster, but comprising three-fifths of Irish Members. Under the leadership of Parnell the Irish Nationalists regularly won an eighth of the seats in the Commons, or four out of five Irish seats.[37] They therefore constituted a significant bloc in the Commons, all the more so because of their determined fight for Home Rule and, crucially, their tightly-knit organization at Westminster. After January 1910 the Nationalists and the smaller Labour Party held the balance of power and both were rewarded, the Nationalists by Home Rule and Labour by the payment of MPs and the reversing of the Osborne Judgement. In the event, the implementation of Home Rule was shelved on the outbreak of the First World War and in 1918 seventy-three of the 101 Irish constituencies were won by Sinn Fein, whose MPs refused to take their seats. Much more recently nationalist parties have secured the election of MPs in Scotland and Wales. Although neither the Scottish National Party

---

[37] T. P. O'Connor was elected as an Irish Nationalist for the Scotland Division of Liverpool from 1885 to 1929.

(SNP) nor the Plaid Cymru (PC) has managed to win more than a handful of seats at Westminster,[38] their impact has been much greater, especially during the periods of minority government between February and October 1974 and between 1976 and 1979. Electorally, they did more damage to the Conservatives in Scotland and Wales, but in the longer term they constitute a much greater threat to Labour's Scottish and Welsh hegemony, as Labour found when it failed to win a majority of seats in the first elections to the Scottish Parliament and the National Assembly for Wales in 1999.

In socio-economic terms the Irish Nationalists reinforced the growing middle-class composition of the House of Commons. Few were working class and occupationally they were drawn largely from the legal profession, teaching, journalism, and small businesses. Few were graduates and few had attended public schools. Their Scottish and Welsh counterparts bear more than a passing resemblance. They too are overwhelmingly middle class, with lawyers, teachers, and a significant business element predominant, but few journalists; and all are graduates.

Conclusion

The party composition of the House of Commons changes suddenly, but its socio-economic composition tends to change slowly. Changes of party composition are exaggerated by the electoral system: even a small swing can make a significant difference, ousting a government and usually bringing the main opposition party to power; a large swing will produce a landslide in seats, if not in votes. Such changes may make the Commons more conservative or more radical in its attitude towards the way it works and the role of its members and large turnovers of membership sometimes have a profound impact on the socio-economic composition of the House. In 1885, for instance, there was a marked fall in the proportion of MPs with

[38] The SNP's most successful election was October 1974, when it won eleven seats—15.5% of the seats in Scotland—and the PC's in 1992 and 1997, when it won four Welsh seats—10.5% of the thirty-eight Welsh seats in 1992 and 10.0 per cent of the forty Welsh seats in 1997. In the first elections to the Scottish Parliament and National Assembly of Wales in 1999 the SNP won 35 seats (27.1%) and the PC 17 (28.3%) respectively, benefiting in particular from the use of the proportional added-member electoral system used.

aristocratic connections and with landed interests; 1918 saw a further decline in those with aristocratic connections, but a massive influx of businessmen, especially among the Conservatives; 1945 resulted in many more graduates, a decline in working-class representation and an increase in the professions in the Labour Party and increased business representation among the Conservatives; and 1997 saw a doubling of the number and proportion of women MPs.

Change, however, has been accompanied by great continuity and the socio-economic composition of each party has tended to change gradually. The major exception was the onset of *embourgeoisiement* in the Labour Party in 1922, but this was a process that continued not only in that party, but also in the House of Commons generally. It has been said with almost monotonous regularity, but no less accurately, that MPs are white,[39] male, middle class, and middle-aged. The fact that the opportunity structures have widened enormously since the middle of the nineteenth century has greatly increased the supply of would-be MPs, but not to the extent that the House of Commons has become a microcosm of the adult population in socio-economic terms. It is a democratic body to the extent that it is a freely-elected body, but how far it represents those who elect it is a matter of judgement and that depends on how MPs carry out their various roles.

[39] Thirteen black and Asian MPs have been elected to the House of Commons, the first in 1892, the largest number in 1997, when 1.4% of MPs (9) (all Labour) were elected, compared with 5.1% of the population in the 1991 census. No black or Asian MPs were elected between 1929 and 1987.

5

The Professionalization of the Member of Parliament

The Professionalization of Politics

In 1918 Max Weber gave a lecture at the University of Munich that was to become one of his most famous pieces of work—'Politics as a Vocation',[1] in which he suggested:

There are two ways of making politics one's vocation: either one lives 'for' politics or one lives 'off' politics. By no means is this contrast an exclusive one . . . He who lives 'for' politics makes politics his life, in an internal sense. Either he enjoys the naked possession of the power he exerts, or he nourishes his inner balance and self-feeling by the consciousness that his life has *meaning* in the service of a 'cause' . . . He who strives to make politics a permanent *source of income* lives 'off' politics as a vocation . . . (Gerth and Mills, *From Max Weber*, 84, original italics.)

Weber goes on to define a professional politician as someone who is

. . . economically independent of the income politics can bring . . This means, quite simply, that the politician must be wealthy or must have a personal position in life which yields a sufficient income;   (Gerth and Mills, *From Max Weber*, 85.)

and cites lawyers as well-placed to become professional politicians. The legal profession has long been a source of politicians, not least because practising the law can often be combined practically and economically with practising politics. Yet Weber's concept of the professional politician appears to be almost the opposite of what

---

[1] H. H. Gerth and C. Wright Mills (eds.), *From Max Weber: Essays in Sociology*, Routledge and Kegan Paul, London, 1948, 77–128.

would nowadays be regarded as a professional, political or otherwise. However, Weber's principal concern was motivation, his interest was in those individuals who devoted most or much of their time to politics because they wanted to, not because they needed to do so. At the time he gave his lecture, most leading politicians were not economically dependent on politics, even though members of the German Reichstag and the United States Congress, for example, were paid salaries. On the other hand, Weber was very conscious that there were other individuals who, however strong their interest in politics, were economically dependent on it. The most prominent were the growing numbers of party officials, especially in countries like Germany.

Interestingly, Weber did not regard most members of legislatures, paid or not, as professional politicians, since they were 'politically active only during [legislative] sessions.'[2] Of course, most British MPs at the time and earlier certainly fitted Weber's condition that they were not economically dependent on being members of the House of Commons, but simply did not devote sufficient time to politics to be defined as professional politicians. More than sixty years later Anthony King, in part echoing Weber, published an important article entitled 'The Rise of the career politician in Britain—and its consequences'.[3] King objected strongly to the term 'professional politician' on the grounds that politics is not a profession in the sense that politicians do not have to undergo clearly-defined training in order to acquire specialized skills, do not have to belong to a professional organization which invariably sets the standards of the profession by controlling entry and playing a role in disciplining its members, and do not have a 'considerable degree of professional autonomy'.[4] King prefers the term 'career politician', who is

. . . a person committed to politics. He regards politics as his vocation, he seeks fulfilment in politics, he sees his future in politics, he would be deeply upset if circumstances forced him to retire from politics . . . What matters is not the individual's source of income but his degree of psychological commitment—his attitude towards what he regards as his *principal*

---

[2] Gerth and Mills, 83.
[3] *British Journal of Political Science*, 2, 1981, 249–85.
[4] Ibid., 256.

occupation . . . Moreover, this person, although deeply committed to politics, does not necessarily have *to work at politics full-time*. (King, 'The Rise of the Career Politician', 252, with added italics).

King's thesis is that in the '1980s career politicians are almost the only politicians left in the upper echelons of British politics and government'.[5] In support of it King points to the growth of the proportion of MPs who are full-time or nearly full-time, the tendency for an increasing proportion of MPs to be first elected in their 30s and 40s and to retire in their 60s, and then at the proportion of career politicians in selected Cabinets between 1945 and 1980.

TABLE 5.1. *The proportion of 'career politicians' among Cabinet ministers, 1945–1980 (%)*

Prime Minister	Period	Proportion of career politicians
Attlee	1945–51	54.3
Churchill & Eden	1951–57	56.3
Macmillan & Home	1957–64	69.4
Wilson	1964–70	70.3
Heath	1970–74	72.0
Wilson & Callaghan	1974–79	79.4
Thatcher	1979–(80)	77.3

Source: King, 'The rise of the career politician', Figures 1–7, 271–6.

The evidence is compelling, leading King to conclude that the 'serious politician cannot combine politics with a demanding job outside . . .'[6] and that 'with the rise of the career politician, there has also occurred a rise in the incidence of political ambition'.[7] In the latter case this is not ambition for political office, but ambition 'to express themselves politically—to influence the course of events, to have a say in the formulation of policy, to be in a position to challenge the executive'.[8]

The rise of the career politician, however, needs to be placed in

[5] Ibid., 259.   [6] Ibid., 277.
[7] Ibid., 279.   [8] Ibid., 279.

the context of the developments discussed in earlier chapters, which may be described as the professionalization of politics. Outside Parliament this involved the setting up of increasingly elaborate local and national party organizations to fight elections and sustain party activity between elections, a process which has resulted in more individuals who, in Weber's terms live both 'for' and 'off' politics. More extensive party organization developed in Parliament too, but it was also accompanied by procedural changes that increased the efficiency of the House of Commons in particular as a legislative machine, able to sustain a government in office and provide the legislative authority to implement the government's policies. That process could be said to have been completed by the early part of the twentieth century, but what, notwithstanding King's objections, may be described as the professionalization of the Member of Parliament lagged some way behind.

By the professionalization of the MP is meant the development of the full-time Member in both attitude and practice, the provision of a level of salary sufficient to sustain such a Member financially, accompanied by appropriate resources to support the performance of parliamentary duties, and, finally, the development of career patterns which reflect these developments.

From Part-Time to Full-Time

In 1971 the Top Salaries Review Body—(TSRB) later the Senior Salaries Review Body (SSRB)—concluded, 'By any reasonable standard . . . most Members must be considered as working on a full-time basis, and we consider that the level of remuneration should be assessed accordingly.'[9] This might have seemed an odd conclusion, given that a survey of MPs conducted on behalf of the Review Body had found that no fewer than 70 per cent of Members had outside occupations. However, this was considerably tempered by that fact that most devoted relatively few hours to such occupations and spent far more time on their various parliamentary activities. It was therefore evident that, for most,

---

[9] Top Salaries Review Body (TSRB), *First Report: Ministers of the Crown and Members of Parliament*, Cmnd. 4836, December 1971, para. 25.

being a Member of Parliament was their principal occupation or activity, certainly in terms of time, if not necessarily in terms of income. The life of the Member of Parliament is, in certain respects, a peculiar one and always has been. Bagehot described it as 'the worst of all lives—a life of distracting routine'.[10] There is no formal obligation on Members to attend either debates or committees, nor to participate if they do attend, nor even to vote. Attempts in medieval times to enforce attendance met with little success, even under the threat of withholding the wages and expenses then paid to Members, and such efforts had even less success later.[11] Of course, as the party system developed, the whips began to exert pressure on MPs, but the whips have a particular view of what constitutes participation. This view regards voting for the party in divisions as the most important form of participation, with other forms subject to various tactical considerations, but with support of the party leadership as a common purpose. Supportive parliamentary Questions, speeches, and motions are welcome, critical ones are not; attendance in numbers in support of the frontbench is similarly welcome, all the more so if it is vociferous, open dissent is not. The objectives of government and opposition whips may differ in that the government often wishes to limit debate and scrutiny, the opposition to extend them, but they are also mindful that their roles may be reversed after the next election. Constituents also have expectations and make demands, although the nature and extent of these has varied historically and could hardly be said to have been a burden on most MPs until well after 1945. As recently as 1958 Nigel Nicolson (Conservative MP for Bournemouth East and Christchurch 1952–9) could say,

A whole day can agreeably disappear answering half-a-dozen constituency letters in the morning while attending a standing committee with only a quarter-ear open to the debate, listening to Questions and ministerial statements from 2.30 to 4 p.m., looking in on one or two party committees in the evening, entertaining a couple of visiting Americans to drinks on the

[10] Walter Bagehot, *The English Constitution, Collected Works*, (ed.) Norman St. John Stevas, *The Economist*, London, 1974, Vol. 5, 275–6.

[11] See Charles Townsend, *History of the House of Commons*, Henry Colburn, London, 1843, Vol. 2, 362–72; and Edward Porritt, *The Unreformed House of Commons*, Cambridge University Press, Cambridge, 1909, Vol. 1, ch. 12.

terrace, and then gossiping in the Smoking Room till it is time for bed. (Nigel Nicolson, *People and Parliament*, Weidenfeld and Nicolson, London, 1958, 64–5.)

No wonder that John Morley, who served as a Liberal MP for twenty-four years and a member of every Liberal Cabinet between 1886 and 1914, could describe the life of a Member of Parliament as one of 'business without work and idleness without rest'.[12] This led Michael MacDonagh to observe in 1921 that

. . . the number of men in the House of Commons without social or political ambition is remarkably large; men, too, who are absolutely unknown outside their constituencies . . . During the day they are engaged in the direction of great industrial and commercial undertakings, and in the evening they go down to Westminster for that rest and recuperation which comes with a change of scene and occupation. (MacDonagh, *The Pageant of Parliament*, 92)

These were, of course, the very Members that Stanley Baldwin allegedly described as 'hard-faced men who looked as though they had done very well out of the war'.[13]

There are dangers in characterizing the House of Commons generally on the basis of a particular Parliament or particular period. Certainly, others have described the Parliament of 1918 as poorly-attended. Sir Arthur Griffith-Boscawen (Conservative 1892–1906, 1910–22) described it as 'a very listless Parliament, attendance in the House was slack and irregular'.[14] And Frank Grey (Liberal 1922–4) remarked, 'How some Members—and they are many—go there day after day content to sit in the House or in the smoke-room without either participating, or appearing to desire to participate personally, is a little difficult to understand.'[15] Parliaments, in fact, vary and each is to some extent unique. Writing of the 1888 parliamentary session, the former Speaker,

[12] Quoted in Michael MacDonagh, *The Pageant of Parliament*, T. Fisher Unwin, London, 1921, 85.
[13] Roy Douglas, *The History of the Liberal Party, 1895–1970*, Sidgwick and Jackson, London, 1971, 132, attributes this to Baldwin, but Sir Alexander Mackintosh, *Echoes of Big Ben: A Journalist's Parliamentary Diary (1881–1940)*, Jarrolds, London, 1946, attributes the phrase to 'an old Conservative' speaking to J. M. Keynes, who recorded it in *Economic Consequences of the Peace*.
[14] Sir Arthur Griffith-Boscawen, *Memories*, John Murray, London, 1925, 224.
[15] Frank Gray, *Confessions of a Candidate*, Martin Hopkinson, London, 1925, 157.

James Lowther (Viscount Ullswater), remarks: 'Although the sittings were not so prolonged or embittered as in 1887, constant attendance by the supporters of the government was essential and many "scenes" occurred.'[16] Similarly, Griffith-Boscawen says of 1893, 'we all had to attend the House regularly because of the frequent divisions'.[17]

More importantly, there are significant differences between Members, a point well put by Nigel Nicolson: 'There is no place where a man can occupy himself more intensively or usefully, and no place where he can hold down his job by doing so little.'[18] In 1930 Henry (later Lord) Snell (Labour 1922–31) asserted:

As a result of seven years' experience, I am convinced that the average Member of Parliament works at greater pressure and for longer hours than nine-tenths of those who elected him, and that if the factory worker, miner or engineer had the same strain put upon him, he would down tools within a month and demand better conditions of work. (Henry Snell, *Daily Life in Parliament*, 1930, cited by Strathearn Gordon, *Our Parliament*, Cassell for the Hansard Society, 6th rev. and enlarged ed., 1964, 56.)

Snell later described 'the daily life of a capable and conscientious Member of Parliament' as 'one of constant toil and much self-denial'.[19] A somewhat longer perspective can be gained by turning to other commentators. Sir Alexander Mackintosh, for instance, who covered Parliament as a lobby journalist from 1881 to 1940 was clearly of the view that

... the MP works harder now than in old times. In the early 'eighties he looked in at the House, went out to dine, returned in evening dress, and stayed late to cheer his leader and vote. There were, of course, more zealous Members, but that was the custom of many a man whose carriage waited in Palace Yard. Now there is much more for everyone to do and his constituency expects the MP to take an active and frequent part in the work. (Mackintosh, *Echoes of Big Ben*, 164.)

And Sir Edward Fellowes, Clerk of the House from 1954 to 1961 and a member of the Clerk s Department from 1919, took a similar view in surveying the period between 1918 and 1961:

[16] Viscount Ullswater, *A Speaker's Commentaries*, Edward Arnold, London, 1925, Vol. 1, 197.
[17] Griffith-Boscawen, *Memories*, 26.   [18] Nicolson, *People and Parliament*, 65.
[19] Lord Snell, *Men, Movements and Myself*, J. M. Dent, London, 1936, 209.

Members work much harder, since for many weeks in the year standing committees have to be attended. Constituents, too, make much greater demands on their Members, many of whom have to spend most weekends in their constituencies . . . and it is not surprising that there are more 'full-time' Members than there were fifty years ago.   (Sir Edward Fellowes, 'Changes in parliamentary life', 1918–1961, *Political Quarterly*, 36, 1965, 260.)

Similarly, Jo Grimond, the former Liberal Leader, writing in his memoirs, remarked: 'More and more MPs looked on it . . . as a full-time job.'[20]

More recent survey data, however, provides a clearer and more systematic picture, but one which is complicated by the fact that many MPs continue to have outside occupations.

TABLE 5.2. *Parliamentary work by backbench and unpaid frontbenchers during the parliamentary session, 1971—1982 (average hours/week and %)*

Year	At the House of Commons	Outside the House	Constituency work	Total
1971	42 (66.7)	10 (15.9)	11 (17.4)	63 (100.0)
1975	46 (65.7)	10 (14.3)	14 (20.0)	70 (100.0)
1978	41 (62.1)	11 (16.7)	14 (21.2)	66 (100.0)
1982	45 (67.2)	9 (13.4)	13 (19.4) ·	67 (100.0)

Sources: 1971: TSRB, *Report No. 1*, Cmnd., 4836, December 1971, Appendix A, Table 6; 1975: TSRB, *Report No. 8*, Cmnd. 6574, July 1976, Appendix A, Table 15; 1978: TSRB, *Report No. 12*, Cmnd. 7593, June 1979, Appendix C, Table 19; 1982: TSRB, *Report No. 20*, Cmnd. 8881-II, May 1983, Section I, Table 4.

The figures in Table 5.2 are remarkably consistent over the ten year period covered. Unfortunately, the surveys do not provide a party breakdown, but, given that they were conducted when different parties were in power and party representation varied, they suggest that party makes little difference. In 1971 the Review Body speculated that the figures might have been inflated because of the amount of time spent on the Conservative government's industrial relations legislation, but the later surveys would suggest that any

[20] Jo Grimond, *Memoirs*, Heinemann, London, 1979, 166.

such impact was limited or non-existent. All Parliaments and all sessions have their special features, but a further survey in 1996— see Table 5.3—does not deviate significantly from the earlier pattern. Similarly, if the figures reflect any exaggeration on the part of the Members surveyed, that exaggeration is also remarkable for its consistency. However, the data cover only time during the parliamentary session, when the Commons sits, and the average number of hours per week during recesses would be lower, as Table 5.3 confirms:

TABLE 5.3. *Parliamentary work by backbenchers and unpaid frontbenchers on during the parliamentary session and recesses, 1982 and 1996 (average hours/week)*

A. 1982

	Total		Constituency work	
	In session	In recesses	In session	In recesses
Backbenchers	67	40	13	23
Frontbenchers	76	50	16	29
All	69	42	14	25

Note: The figures for constituency work are included in the overall number of hours worked.*Source*: TSRB, Report No.20, Cmnd. 8881-II, May 1983, Section I, Table 4.

B. 1996

	Total		Constituency work	
	In session	In recesses	In session	In recesses
Backbenchers	70	50	} 27	} 31
Frontbenchers	70	53		
All	n.a.	n.a.	n.a.	n.a.

Note: The figures for constituency work are included in the overall number of hours worked.
Source: SSRB, Report No. 38, Cm. 3330-II July 1996, 30–1.

The earlier surveys distinguished between ministers and other paid office-holders, on the one hand, and non-office-holders, on the other, and therefore did not distinguish between backbenchers and unpaid frontbench spokespersons. This was rectified in the 1982 and 1996 surveys, which show a more marked difference between backbenchers and frontbenchers in 1982 than 1996. The figures also explain why, in 1971, the Review Body said that most MPs should be considered as full-time, even though the 1971 survey found that as many as 70 per cent of MPs had other paid occupations.[21] The surveys conducted in 1975, 1978, and 1982 all found similar proportions of Members with other paid occupations—67, 73, and 72 per cent respectively.[22] However, more detailed data gathered in the surveys found that the number of hours spent on these outside occupations were not, in most cases, very high: in 1971, for example, 52 per cent of MPs spent less than ten hours a week during the parliamentary session on such occupations, compared with 19 per cent who spent twenty or more hours a week; by 1978 these figures were 68 and 5 per cent respectively, changing slightly in 1982 to 64 and 7 per cent respectively. Not surprisingly, during recesses these MPs spent more time on outside occupations, with 31 per cent spending less than ten hours and 50 per cent twenty or more hours in 1971, but these figures had changed to 45 and 29 per cent in 1982.[23]

The 1996 survey did not gather data on this aspect of MPs' activities, so that there is nothing more recent than the 1982 figure of 69 per cent with outside occupations. However, it would be surprising if the number of hours spent on such occupations had not continued to decline, and this is supported by data gathered by members of the Study of Parliament Group (SPG). This shows that of 129 MPs surveyed in the 1992 Parliament and 196 in the 1997 Parliament—no less than 87.6 and 88.8 per cent respectively—thought that the job of being a Member of Parliament *should* be full-time, many expressing the view that the demands of the job

---

[21] TSRB, *Report No. 1*, Cmnd. 4836, December 1971, Appendix A, Table 15.

[22] 1976: TSRB, *Report No. 8*, Cmnd. 6574, July 1976, Appendix A, Table 18; 1978: TSRB, *Report No. 12*, Cmnd. 7593, June 1979, Appendix C, Table 22; and 1982: TSRB, *Report No. 20*, Cmnd. 8881-II, May 1983, Section I, Table 6.

[23] TSRB, *Report No. 1*, Cmnd. 4836, December 1971, Appendix A, Table 16; and TSRB, *Report No. 20*, Cmnd. 8881-II, May 1983, Section I, Table 7.

were such that it could be nothing other than full-time. There were, however, significant differences between Conservatives and MPs of other parties: 28.3 per cent of Conservatives in the 1992 Parliament and 40.0 per cent in the 1997 Parliament thought that the job should be part-time, although many acknowledged that the *demands* made on MPs rendered the job full-time in terms of the number of hours per week needed to meet those demands. This reflected a widely and often strongly-held Conservative view that the full-time, professional MP is likely to be cut off from 'the real world' of work and that it was desirable, even essential, that MPs should be allowed to have outside occupations to keep them in touch with that 'real world'. It almost certainly reflects another factor, however, found in the SPG surveys. This is that newly-elected Conservatives in both 1992 and 1997 were more likely to have earned about the same as or more than the prevailing parliamentary salary, whereas Labour and other MPs were more likely to have earned about the same or less than the parliamentary salary. The need felt by Conservatives to supplement their parliamentary salary is therefore likely to be greater.[24]

In spite of the high proportion with outside occupations, what the available data suggest is that for the overwhelming majority of MPs, being a Member of Parliament is their main occupation or activity. And, for those with other, paid occupations, it is these occupations that are part-time and their parliamentary role essentially full-time. It was this that led the TSRB to recommend a salary that, for the first time, treated being a Member of Parliament as a full-time occupation and that practice has been followed in successive reports, eventually linking the salary to civil service pay.[25] Until 1971, however, the question of Member's pay was always

[24] Unpublished research conducted by members of the Study of Parliament Group, supported in 1992–7 by a grant from the Nuffield Foundation and since 1997 by an ESRC award (R0000222470). Henceforth cited as unpublished SPG research.

[25] For a detailed account of pay, services, and facilities see Michael Rush and Malcolm Shaw (eds.), *The House of Commons: Services and Facilities*, Allen and Unwin, London, 1974 and Michael Rush (ed.), *The House of Commons: Services and Facilities, 1972–82*, Policy Studies Institute, London, 1983. For an international comparison see Michael Rush, 'The Pay, Allowances, Services and Facilities of Legislators in Eighteen Countries and the European Parliament: A Comparative Survey', and Tom Stark, 'International Comparisons of the Remuneration of Members of Parliament' in SSRB, *Report No. 38*, Cm. 3330-II, July 1996, 38—59 and 60–8 respectively.

complicated by the related question of the expenses incurred by MPs in carrying out their parliamentary duties.

The Payment of Members of Parliament

As noted earlier, MPs were paid in medieval times, but the practice had largely died out by the end of the fifteenth century, although Porritt cites three instances in the seventeenth century. These were Devizes in 1641, King's Lynn in 1643 and, the most well-known, Andrew Marvell at Hull up to his death in 1678.[26] Moreover, such payments came from constituents, not the state. The state funding of MPs was not introduced until 1912, although the issue of the payment of Members received periodic attention from the late eighteenth century onwards. In 1780, for instance, a parliamentary committee reported in favour of payment and the proposal was subsequently taken up by the Society for Constitutional Information, one of the pressure groups urging parliamentary reform. Fifty-four years later Lord Blandford introduced a Reform Bill that included a provision for the payment of MPs. It was also one of the demands of the Chartists in 1838 and proposals for payment were considered by the House of Commons on no fewer than five occasions between 1870 and 1895. The Liberals were the first major party formally to propose the payment of Members, including it in the Newcastle Programme of 1891, but it was not a very strong commitment[27] and not vigorously pursued by the Liberal government of 1892–5. Resolutions in favour of payment were passed by the Commons in 1893 and 1895, but the proposals were rejected by the House of Lords. Not surprisingly, individuals such as Keir Hardie advocated payment, as did radical pressure groups, such as the National Democratic League and the Metropolitan Radical Federation.

Inevitably, opinion among Members was divided. In 1870 Gladstone, then Prime Minister, opposed a motion in favour of payment, arguing that it was not an appropriate charge upon the public purse, but also arguing that, if it were introduced, it should be borne by local ratepayers—a reversion, in effect to the medieval

---

[26] Porritt, *The Unreformed House*, Vol. 1, 153.
[27] See Sir Robert Ensor, *England, 1870–1914*, Clarendon Press, Oxford, 1936, 207.

practice.[28] By the time of the Newcastle Programme, however, Gladstone had changed his mind: 'Mr Gladstone's view was that if any MP could procure a certificate from the Board of Inland Revenue to the effect that his income was under £400 he should receive a salary, and that a return should be made to Parliament of MPs receiving payment.'[29] Richard Cobden was also in favour of MPs receiving 'a modest salary for their services'.[30] On the other hand, John Stuart Mill was strongly against paying MPs. He did not accept that the payment of Members would provide 'a means of rendering Parliament accessible to persons of all ranks and circumstances' and, while conceding that

[i]f, as in some of our colonies, there are scarcely any fit persons who can afford to attend to an unpaid occupation, the payment should be an indemnity for loss of time and money, not a salary. The greater latitude of choice which a salary would give is an illusory advantage. No remuneration which anyone would think of attaching to the post would attract it to those who were seriously engaged in other lucrative professions with the prospect of succeeding in them. The business of a Member of Parliament would therefore become an occupation in itself; carried on like other professions, with a view to its pecuniary return . . . It would become an object of desire to adventurers of a low class. (John Stuart Mill, *Representative Government* [1861], J. M. Dent, London, 1910, 311.)

Sir Alfred Pease (Liberal 1885 92 and 1897 1902) was proud of the fact 'that I was the last Liberal MP, and a solitary one, who voted against payment of Members', deploring what he described as MPs having 'become little more than the *paid* delegates of party organisations'.[31] And the Conservative, Sir Arthur Griffith-Boscawen, stressed the importance of public service and of being 'a member of the greatest political institution in the world, to the service of which you have given a great part of your life without the hope of any material or pecuniary reward'. Griffith-Boscawen was writing retrospectively and added, 'MPs get £400 a year nowadays

---

[28] Alpheus Todd, *On Parliamentary Government in England*, Longman, London, 2nd ed. 1889,Vol. 1, 70.

[29] Horace G. Hutchinson (ed.), *The Private Diaries of Sir Algernon West*, John Murray, London, 1922, 28.

[30] James E. Thorold Rogers, *Cobden and Modern Public Opinion*, Macmillan, London, 1873, 273.

[31] Sir Alfred Pease, *Elections and Recollections*, John Murray, London, 1932, 6, original italics.

and a free railway ticket to their constituencies, and more is the pity, but even so, we have not yet produced a race of "professional politicians", partly because the payment is so small, but chiefly because the idea is so abhorrent to our people'.[32]

It took not just the advent of the Labour Party but the conjunction of the final Osborne Judgement of December 1910 with the Liberal government's loss of its overall majority in the two elections of 1910 to move the payment of Members close to the top of the political agenda. The Osborne Judgement by the House of Lords, as the final court of appeal, upheld the case of a trade union member who objected to his union's funds being used to support Labour MPs. This was a serious threat to the financial viability of many Labour MPs, but the pressure on the Liberal government was increased by the loss of its majority in January 1910. The government's survival was not under threat, since it could normally rely on the support of the Labour Party and the Irish Nationalists, but it was one of the factors that encouraged the Liberals to include the payment of MPs in its manifesto for the election of December 1910. The Osborne Judgement was effectively reversed by the passing of the Trades Union Act, 1913, which allowed unions to establish political funds.

The House of Commons' resolution providing for the payment of Members was introduced by the Chancellor of the Exchequer, David Lloyd-George, whose speech echoed the sentiments of John Stuart Mill and Gladstone. The £400 payment was

... an allowance to a man to enable him to maintain himself comfortably and honourably, but not luxuriously, during the time he is rendering service to the state ... it is not a recognition of the magnitude of the service, it is not a remuneration, it is not a recompense, it is not even a salary. It is just an allowance, and I think the minimum allowance, to enable men to come here, men who would render incalculable service to the state, and whom it is an individual loss to the state not to be here because their means do not allow it.   (HC Debs., 29, 10 August 1911, cc. 1382 and 1383).[33]

Once introduced, Members' pay continued to be a problem, partly because raising its level has always been politically sensitive

---

[32] Griffith-Boscawen, *Memories*, 256.
[33] In fact, the resolution used the term 'salary'.

TABLE 5.4. *Members' salaries, 1912–2000 (selected years) (£s)*

Year	Salary	Year	Salary
1912	400[a]	1957	1,750[d]
1931	360[b]	1964	3,250[e]
1934	380	1972	4,500
1935	400	1982	14,510
1937	600	1992	30,854
1946	1,000	2000	48,371
1954	1,250[c]		

Notes: [a] From 1912 £100 was exempt from income tax, being regarded as an average allowance for necessary parliamentary expenses.
[b] In 1931 the salary was reduced by 10 per cent as an economy measure, half of which was restored in 1934, half in 1935.
[c] In 1954 the £100 tax-free allowance was abolished and a sessional allowance averaging £250 was substituted and included in the salary.
[d] The sessional allowance was abolished in 1957 and replaced by an additional sum of £750 to cover parliamentary expenses. This was included in the salary.
[e] £1,250 of the salary was regarded as an expense allowance.

and partly because it increasingly became entangled with the expenses associated with the job. In the sixty years since its inception the problem of dealing with changing economic circumstances—notably increases in the cost of living—was dealt with in *ad hoc* fashion, sometimes by a select committee of the House, sometimes by government initiative, and then, in 1963, by the appointment of committee outside Parliament—the Lawrence Committee.[34] The problem of expenses, apart from the introduction of free travel between London and the Member's constituency in 1924, was addressed by making a proportion of the salary a tax-free expense allowance, as indicated in Table 5.4. In addition, MPs could claim further expenses for tax purposes against the total parliamentary salary, resulting, as the Lawrence Committee discovered, that most MPs were legitimately claiming significantly more than the £750 expense allowances dating from 1957. Indeed, in its

[34] *Committee on the Remuneration of Ministers and of Members of Parliament* (the Lawrence Committee), Cmnd. 2516, November 1964.

first report the TSRB found that, in 1969–70, the average net pay of a Member, after meeting necessary expenses, but before tax was £1,920.[35] Although a secretarial allowance had been introduced in 1969, the Review Body regarded the arrangements for meeting parliamentary expenses as unsatisfactory and this led to its second and crucial conclusion: 'a clear separation should be observed between salary, on the one hand, and provision for expenses on the other . . . It should not be the responsibility of the individual Member to finance the facilities he needs to do his job.'[36]

The Provision of Services and Facilities

In an autobiographical note written towards the end of his long life, Gladstone recalled the sheer lack of facilities in the old Palace of Westminster, when he first entered the House in 1833: 'What I may term corporeal conveniences were . . . marvellously small. I do not think that in any part of the building it afforded the means of so much as washing the hands.'[37] The destruction of the old Palace by fire in 1834 created the opportunity to build what one former Clerk of the House called a 'mid-Victorian masterpiece'.[38] The neo-gothic splendour of the Palace of Westminster, the edifice by Sir Charles Barry and the sumptuous interior by Augustus Welby Pugin, has many admirers, but it was designed primarily as a worthy meeting place for the two houses of a historic legislature. Certainly, the facilities it afforded Members were vastly superior to those of its ancient predecessor—two legislative chambers, various committee rooms, a suite for the library, a smoking room, dining rooms and bars, and a splendid terrace overlooking the Thames, but these were all *public* facilities. They were the sort of facilities usually associated with a London club and it became a common-place to describe the Palace of Westminster as 'the best club in London'.[39] Private facilities for ministers, let alone Members, did

[35] TSRB, *Report No. 1*, Cmnd. 4836, Part I, paras. 4–6.
[36] Ibid., para. 33.
[37] John Morley, *Life of Gladstone*, Macmillan, London, 1903, Vol. 1, 101.
[38] Sir Barnett Cocks, *Mid-Victorian Masterpiece: The Story of an Institution Unable to Put Its Own House in Order*, Hutchinson, London, 1977.
[39] According to T. H. S. Escott, *Club Makers and Club Members*, T. Fisher Unwin, London, 1914, 58, the term first became current about 1840, but this predates the opening of the new Palace—the House of Lords first used its new chamber in 1847

not enter into the equation. Lord George Hamilton pointed out in his memoirs, recalling the Parliament of 1868–74: 'There were no private rooms for ministers, except one for the Prime Minister and a kind of small den . . . for the Leader of the Opposition.'[40] In 1871 'a room was provided in the gallery of St Stephen's Cloister to enable Members to receive persons who might wish to see them on business', but the idea of anything more extensive was firmly resisted.[41]

Complaints about the inadequacy of facilities were to continue long after 1871. Writing of the Commons in 1936, Lord Snell, remarked:

As a workshop, it is badly equipped, it is overcrowded, and it is unhealthy. Its recreative amenities are restricted to one smoking-room which would not hold more than fifty of its 615 members. The research side of its library is shamefully inadequate, the facilities provided for its members for the storage of their papers are limited to a locker about the size of a hat-box. (Snell, *Men, Movements and Myself*, 208–9.)

And this was echoed by the former Speaker, George Thomas (Lord Tonypandy), remembering what it was like when he was first elected in 1945:

Sometimes I received thirty or forty letters in one day, and had to write all my replies in longhand as I could not afford a secretary . . . We had no special room to work in, and if the Library was full, Members had to sit in the corridors. (George Thomas, *Mr Speaker*, Century Publications, London, 1985, 54.)

However, perhaps the most well-known comment was that quoted by the pseudonymous Anthony Hill and Anthony Whichelow in *What's Wrong with Parliament?* published in 1964:

When I came here in 1950, I was given a key to a locker, which was no bigger than that which I had at school. That was the only accommodation, the only amenity, I had in the building.

---

and the House of Commons in 1852. Michael MacDonagh, *The Pageant of Parliament*, Vol. 1, 80, attributes it to E. M. Whitty, a sketch-writer in the Reporters' Gallery in the mid-Victorian period.

[40] Lord George Hamilton, *Parliamentary Reminiscences and Reflections, 1868 to 1885*, John Murray, London, 1916, 47.

[41] HC Debs., CCVI, 25 May 1871, c.1255.

But things did improve:

I now have (in addition to my locker) a little desk . . . with another seven Members in a room the size of the average dining room in the average council house . . . We have to have artificial light . . . The room is ideal for a suicide.   (Anthony Hill and Anthony Whichelow, *What's Wrong with Parliament?*, Penguin, London, 1964, 84–5.)

Soon after this things really did begin to improve, though fairly slowly and incrementally. Hill and Whichelow was one of a series of books questioning the effectiveness of British institutions. In the case of Parliament this coincided with the publication of Bernard Crick's *The Reform of Parliament*, which had developed out of a Fabian Tract published in 1959.[42] Nothing would have happened, however, without pressure from Members themselves. Sir Edward Fellowes, looking back over the period 1918–61, noted the decline on the Conservative benches of what he termed 'the country gentlemen' type of Member, more commonly called the 'knights of the shire' and, on the Labour benches, of the traditional, working-class, trade union MP.[43] Another study found evidence of dissatisfaction and reformist attitudes among MPs first elected in 1959, 1964, and 1966, not, as was widely thought at the time, just among younger Labour MPs, but among younger Conservatives as well.[44] It was also during the 1960s that backbench dissent began to become more common.[45] These were Members who were not content, as the 'knights of the shire' and the trade union MPs largely were, to play an essentially passive role, faithfully supporting their leaders in the House and the division lobbies. They wanted to be involved; they wanted an active role in Parliament. Added to this, were growing demands from constituents: letters to MPs increased in volume and almost all MPs held 'surgeries' to deal with constituents' problems.

The desire for a more active role and the growth in constituency

[42] Bernard Crick, *Reform of the Commons*, Fabian Tract 319, Fabian Society, London, 1959 and Bernard Crick, *The Reform of Parliament: The Crisis of British Government*, Weidenfeld and Nicolson, London, 1st ed. 1964, 2nd rev. ed. 1968.

[43] Fellowes, 'Changes in parliamentary life', 260.

[44] Anthony Barker and Michael Rush, *The Member of Parliament and His Information*. Allen and Unwin, London, 1970, 378–86.

[45] See Philip Norton, *Dissension in the House of Commons, 1945–74*, Macmillan, London, 1975

work inevitably led to the demand for better services and facilities. Bernard Crick could still write in 1967,

Clearly a Member should be able to draw on public funds, or be reimbursed from them, for those essentials he needs to do his job properly: secretary, office, postage, telephone and travel. (Crick, *The Reform of Parliament*, 66–7.)

Of these, only desks spaces—not individual offices—for about half the backbenchers, travel between London and their constituencies, postal correspondence with government departments and various other public authorities, and telephone calls in the London area were then available, but soon after there were significant developments in all the areas listed by Crick.

The dates when the services and facilities shown in Table 5.5 were introduced are instructive, but they have also been accompanied by

TABLE 5.5. *The provision of services and facilities for MPs*

Allowance or facility	Date introduced	Provision in 2000
Staff and office costs	1969	£51,572 (linked to RPI)
Telephone and postage	1969	Free on parliamentary business within the UK
Travel	1924	Free to and from constituency and between home and Westminster, plus some provision for family. Free travel to EU institutions, subject to approval.
Subsistence	1972	Allowance when the House is sitting: £1,473 London supplement (inner-London MPs) or maximum of £13,322.
Pension	1964	Payable at 65 (60 with reduced benefit), according to length of service; minimum of 4 years' service.
Resettlement grant	1974	Lump sum equivalent to 50–100% of salary, depending on age and length of service.

Source: House of Commons Factsheet No. 17.

other important developments, notably the provision of office accommodation for Members and their staff and in the provision of information services. As early as 1969 the House of Commons (Services) Committee made it clear that in providing office accomodation the objective should be a 'room for every Member'[46] and in 1973 the House of Commons approved a proposal for new parliamentary accommodation to be built close to the Palace of Westminster. In the meantime, additional accommodation was provided by the reallocation and refurbishment of space within the Palace and by the redevelopment of nearby buildings for parliamentary use. However, following the energy crisis that began later in 1973, plans for the new parliamentary building were abandoned. Nonetheless, further *ad hoc* development took place and by 1982 desk spaces were available to all backbench MPs who required them, about three-quarters in single or double rooms. In addition, desk spaces were available for the staff of about 350 MPs.[47] Since then, yet more nearby buildings have been redeveloped to accommodate MPs, their staff, and House of Commons' staff and the objective of a 'room for every Member' was realized in 2000 when, with an undoubted sense of *déjà vu*, a new parliamentary building was opened on the same site planned for the building abandoned in 1975. The reluctance to spend public funds on office accommodation for MPs parallels the similar reluctance over salaries, but in both cases, once the principle of adequate provision was conceded, practice eventually matched principle.

In the provision of other services and facilities there has tended to be less difficulty, partly because in areas such as the provision of procedural and similar advice and of information services, the benefits are seen as less personal.

There has, in fact, been a considerable expansion in the services and facilities provided to Members by the staff of the House of Commons (see Table 5.6). In general this expansion has been one of scale rather than the introduction of new services or facilities, with the important exception of the House of Commons Library. The Library was established in 1818 and the second Librarian,

[46] House of Commons (Services Committee), *Third Report: Accommodation in the New Parliamentary Building*, HC 295, 1968–9, para. 3.
[47] Robert Rogers, 'Accommodation, Car-parking and Security', in Michael Rush (ed.), *The House of Commons: Services and Facilities, 1972–1982*, 70–90.

TABLE 5.6. *The growth of House Commons' staff, 1972–2000*

Department	1972	1982	1992	2000	% increase 1972–2000
Clerk	95	145	166.5	272	186.3
Sergeant at Arms	152	183	206.5	307.5	102.3
Speaker	9	10	11.5	9.5	5.6
Library	55	126	199	200.5	264.5
Administration/Finance & Admin.[a]	20	72	103	131	555.0
Official Report (Hansard)	53	74	91	110	107.5
Total[b]	384	610	777.5	1,030.5	168.4

[a] The considerable increase in the Administration/Finance and Administration Department is the result of the range and variety of allowances available to MPs and the massive extension of MPs' staff, whose salaries are administered by the Department.
[b] This figure excludes the Refreshment Department, for which no figures are available for 1972. In 1982 it had 234 staff; in 1992, 305.5; and in 2000, 313.5.

Thomas Vardon, saw his task as one of providing Members with 'instant information'.[48] Its main source of relevant information was its 'comprehensive collection of parliamentary papers and official documents', with which it had been restocked after the fire of 1834, but, rather in keeping with the club-like facilities if the Palace, 'a great deal of general literature, more suited to a country gentleman's private library, was also acquired during the nineteenth and early twentieth centuries'.[49] In fact, in terms of seeking to provide an information service the modern House of Commons Library dates from 1946, when, following a select committee report, a research division was set up. The Library, said the committee, '. . . should be far more than a repository of books and parliamentary papers. It should aim at providing Members rapidly with precise and detailed information on subjects connected with their

[48] Standing Committee appointed to assist Mr Speaker on the Direction of the Library, HC 104, 1835, evidence, 11.
[49] Rush and Shaw, *Services and Facilities*, 135.

duties.'[50] This is exactly what the then Librarian and his successors set about doing. It was, however, for the first twenty years a slow and gradual process. In 1946 the Library had seven staff, by 1965 it had risen to thirty-five, and by 1968 to fifty-three. Similarly, the Library gradually developed a comprehensive information service for MPs, but the greater part of that expansion dates from the 1960s and later. In the early fifties the Library dealt with about 200 research enquiries a year; by the early sixties it had risen to about 300, and 450 in 1964, but there then followed an exponential expansion—in 1967 there were 1,800 enquiries; in 1973, 3,291; and in 1982 7,561.[51] In 1990–2000 the number of enquiries was 34,759, with a further 31,009 made at the branch library in Parliament Street, mostly by Members' staff.[52]

In 1967, Barker and Rush found that 43.1 per cent of the backbenchers and opposition frontbenchers they surveyed were satisfied with the services offered by the Library's Research Division, with a further 4.6 per cent also satisfied, but fearing that without further expansion the Research Division would not be able to cope. As many as 45.9 per cent were dissatisfied, leaving a small residue of 'don't knows'.[53] This, however, was a comment not on the quality of the service, but on the pressures it was under. Responses to the two SPG surveys of the 1992 and 1997 Parliaments undoubtedly reflect both the quality and the massive expansion that the Library's information services have undergone, with the overwhelmingly majority regarding them very highly.[54]

The House of Commons Library provides the most directly relevant example of the extent to which the professionalization of the MP has been accompanied by the extension of services and facilities. What has happened with the Library has, to varying degrees, been repeated with the other departments of the House, particularly in the Department of the Clerk, but also in more mundane departments, such as that of the Serjeant at Arms, as the figures in

---

[50] Select Committee on the Library (House of Commons), *Second Report*, HC 99-I, 1945–6, para. 8.

[51] Barker and Rush, *The Member of Parliament and His Information*, 295, 305; and Rush and Shaw, Services and Facilities, 151; and Rush, *The House of Commons: Services and Facilities*, 60.

[52] House of Commons Commission, *Annual Report, 1999–2000*, HC 808, Annex A.

[53] Barker and Rush, *The Member of Parliament and His Information*, Appendix 3, Table 32.   [54] Unpublished SPG research.

Table 5.6 show. In short, the professionalization of the Member of Parliament has been more than matched by the professionalization of the House of Commons.

Changing Career Patterns

The professionalization of the Member of Parliament has, in turn, been reflected in changing career patterns. In the nineteenth century, particularly before 1868, parliamentary careers were more fragmented and shorter on average. This was partly because electoral defeat became more common than it had been in the eighteenth century as more constituencies were contested, but of at least equal importance was a tendency to retire after one or two Parliaments. Serving as a Member of Parliament was widely seen as a form of public service, but it was an expensive business and many of those who were elected had other important matters to attend to—their estates, their business, or professional livelihoods.

In the first half of the eighteenth century the average length of service was fifteen years, and a little longer in the second half of the century. After 1832, however, it fell to ten years, rising slowly after 1868, but did not begin to match eighteenth century levels until after 1945. Since 1945 it has risen further, until the average length of service is now eighteen years. As the figures in Table 5.7 show, the proportions of Conservative MPs with less than ten years' service and of Labour MPs with less than five years' service have fallen, whereas those with twenty or more years have risen. The Liberals present a less clear pattern, but this is a reflection of the severe decline of the Liberal Party after the First World War.

Length of service is, of course, reflected in the age patterns of parliamentary careers. The proportion of MPs elected under the age of thirty has fallen markedly, especially among Conservatives, and it never was high in the Labour Party—the number of young Labour MPs elected in 1997 being the exception to the general rule. Increasingly, it became the norm that would-be MPs had to make their way in the world before getting elected to Parliament and most MPs are now aged between thirty-five and forty-five when first elected. The nineteenth century, especially after 1868, saw the election of a number of Members with household names, several of

TABLE 5.7. Length of parliamentary service, 1868–1997 (%)

A. *Conservative*

No. of years	1868–99	1900–17	1918–44	1945–97
Less than 5	8.0	6.5	22.0	6.6
5–9	27.5	19.0	19.5	19.9
10–14	24.2	29.0	23.6	18.3
15–19	14.9	15.0	11.5	18.8
20–24	10.4	12.4	11.5	15.4
25 or more	15.0	18.1	11.9	21.0

B. *Liberal*

No. of years	1868–99	1900–17	1918–44	1945–97
Less than 5	14.9	20.0	38.8	10.2
5–9	28.2	15.1	15.2	25.6
10–14	18.8	26.1	15.7	23.1
15–19	14.3	16.7	14.6	12.8
20–24	10.3	11.3	7.6	12.8
25 or more	13.5	10.7	8.1	15.4

C. *Labour*

No. of years	1868–99	1900–17	1918–44	1945–97
Less than 5	—	13.0	29.2	7.3
5–9	—	19.6	17.8	23.9
10–14	—	17.4	14.2	16.4
15–19	—	26.1	16.4	18.7
20–24	—	8.7	9.4	13.6
25 or more	—	15.2	13.0	20.0

whom were at least fifty when first elected—W. H. Wills (50), H. M. Stanley (51), Sir Edward Harland—of Harland and Wolff (54), William McEwan—one of many brewers (59), Sir Frederick Mappin—former Master Cutler (59), Spencer Charrington— another brewer (67), and Sir Philip Mansfield—shoe manufacturer)

TABLE 5.8. *Age at which MPs entered and left Parliament, 1868–1997 (%)*

A. *Age at which first elected*

Conservative	1868–99	1900–17	1918–44	1945–97
Under 30	20.6	16.1	12.3	7.5
30–49	55.7	60.7	56.5	80.7
50 or over	23.7	23.2	31.2	11.8

Liberal	1868–99	1900–17	1918–44	1945–97
Under 30	15.8	9.6	8.5	7.1
30–49	54.2	64.6	60.7	73.8
50 or over	29.9	25.8	30.8	19.0

Labour	1868–99	1900–17	1918–44	1945–97
Under 30	—	—	2.7	3.2
30–49	—	69.6	60.4	74.1
50 or over	—	30.4	36.9	22.7

B. *Age on leaving Parliament*

Conservative	1868–99	1900–17	1918–44	1945–97
Under 30	1.2	0.4	0.2	0.1
30–49	26.3	22.4	24.2	20.4
50 or over	72.5	77.2	75.6	79.5

Liberal	1868–99	1900–17	1918–44	1945–97
Under 30	1.2	0.6	1.1	—
30–49	22.7	23.5	27.1	41.0
50 or over	76.1	75.9	71.8	59.0

Labour	1868–99	1900–17	1918–44	1945–97
Under 30	—	—	—	0.2
30–49	—	13.0	21.0	18.4
50 or over	—	87.0	79.0	81.3

(72).[55] Whether all or any of these were among MacDonagh's MPs who repaired 'to Westminster for the rest and recuperation which comes with a change of scene and occupation' is less clear, but they are examples of individuals who almost certainly saw election to Parliament as a fitting fulfilment to their contributions to society in general and public life in particular.

The age at which MPs left Parliament presents a more complex picture, since a significant proportion of parliamentary careers are ended involuntarily by electoral defeat or death. The proportion of MPs whose political careers—at least as members of the Commons—have been terminated by electoral defeat depends inevitably on party fortunes. During periods of electoral instability and party realignment defeat becomes more common, as was the case between 1918 and 1945, when electoral defeat was the largest single cause of leaving the Commons. However, before 1918 and since 1945 voluntary retirement was the most common cause, accounting for more than a third before 1918 and more than two-fifths since 1945. Indeed, between 1974 and 1992 the proportion of MPs ending their Commons' careers by retirement was 49.2 per cent[56] and, in spite of the massive Conservative defeat in 1997, no fewer than 47 per cent who left Parliament in April 1997 retired. Death, which brought to an end the parliamentary careers of a fifth of Members before 1900, now accounts for fewer than one in eight, an important factor in which has been the introduction of a parliamentary pension scheme from 1964. Retirement at or near normal retirement age has become increasingly common and Members such as Michael Foot—nearly 84 when he retired in 1997—and Sir Edward Heath—81 when he was re-elected in 1997—are exceptions to the general rule. In short, provided electoral defeat does not bring a parliamentary career to a premature end, the age at which MPs start and finish their political lives has more and more come to resemble a normal occupation, with the proviso that they have normally established themselves occupationally outside Parliament before first being elected.

[55] Other well-known individuals elected at an earlier age were W. H. Smith, Sir Frederick Fison, George Palmer (biscuit manufacturer), Jerimiah Colman (mustard manufacturer), H. S. Samuel (jeweller), Henry Stephens (ink manufacturer), and George Newnes (publisher).

[56] Michael Rush, 'Career patterns in British politics: First choose your party . . .', *Parliamentary Affairs*, 47, 577.

What, then, marks a political career from a normal occupation? For what is probably an increasing number, it is ambition for ministerial office. The idea that *all* MPs hope, let alone expect, to achieve ministerial office, does not bear close examination. Of course, neither hope nor expectation may accord with reality and an important part of that reality is the frequency and extent to which different parties hold office. Thus, no Liberal MP has held ministerial office since the election of the first majority Labour government in 1945[57] and, in terms of fulfilling ministerial ambitions, it is not without cause that the twentieth century has been described as 'the Conservative century'. Although there is plenty of anecdotal evidence to show that there has been no shortage of highly ambitious individuals in British politics, there is no reason to doubt MacDonagh's 1921 assessment that 'the number of men in the House of Commons without social or *political* ambition is remarkably large'.[58] In the eighteenth century a significant group of MPs hoped to benefit from appointment to official posts, particularly sinecures, or to receive government pensions. Others, especially in the nineteenth and early twentieth centuries, hoped for and, in some numbers, received peerages, knighthoods, or other honours. Furthermore, as the state expanded its activities, other opportunities arose for appointments to positions of power and influence on various public bodies, some executive, others advisory, now commonly called non-governmental organizations (NGOs) or quangos. However, in the absence of clear systematic evidence, there is no way of knowing to what extent appointments and honours represented rewards or consolation prizes. Data from the SPG survey would suggest that more MPs are ambitious for ministerial office than in 1921. Newly-elected MPs in 1992 and 1997 were asked whether they had ministerial ambitions. The contrast between the two main parties was marked: no newly-elected Conservative denied ministerial ambitions—some modestly recorded 'don't know' or 'too early to say'—but nearly a fifth of new Labour MPs did, compared with more than two-fifths in 1992 and nearly half in 1997 who did admit such ambitions.[59]

---

[57] Some Liberal-Democrat MPs have more recently held office in the Labour-Liberal-Democrat coalition government in Scotland, following the setting up of the Scottish Parliament and executive in 1999, and several Liberal-Democrat MPs are member of a consultative Cabinet committee on constitutional developments.

[58] Italics added.   [59] Unpublished SPG research

TABLE 5.9. *Number of ministerial posts*[a] *and MPs holding ministerial office, 1900–1997*

Year	Total no. of ministerial posts	No. of MPs holding office	% of MPs holding office
1830 (Whig)	47	23	48.9
1840 (Whig)[b]	60	31	51.7
1850 (Lib.)	57	35	61.4
1860 (Lib.)	56	31	55.4
1870 (Lib.)	58	29	50.0
1880 (Cons.)[c]	55	30	54.5
1890 (Lib.)	60	34	56.7
1900 (Cons.)	60	33	55.0
1910 (Lib.)	62	43	69.3
1917 (Coalition)	85	60	70.6
1920 (Coalition)	81	58	71.6
1930 (Lab.)	58	50	86.2
1940 (Coalition)	74	58	78.4
1950 (Lab.)	81	68	83.9
1960 (Cons.)	82	65	79.3
1970 (Lab.)	102	85	83.3
1980 (Cons.)	107	86	80.4
1990 (Cons.)	103	80	77.7
1997 (Lab.)	112	88	78.6

[a] Except for 1997, the figures relate to the 1 January each year. Unpaid Parliamentary Private Secretaries are excluded.
[b] The figures for Peel's Conservative government are 60, 34, and 56.7. respectively.
[c] The figures for Gladstone's Liberal government are 57, 32, and 56.1. respectively.
Sources: Chris Cook and Brendan Keith, *British Historical Facts 1830–1900*, Macmillan, London, 1975, 2–47; and David Butler and Gareth Butler, *Twentieth British Political Facts, 1900–2000*, Macmillan, London, 2000, 48–50 and 71.

What is clear from the data in Table 5.9 is that the *opportunity* to achieve ministerial office has increased significantly since the middle of the nineteenth century. The total number of government posts varied between fifty and sixty for much of the nineteenth century, but members of the House of Lords held a significant minority of ministerial posts. Even in 1900 peers held twenty-seven out of sixty posts and the proportion has remained as high as one in five or six since 1945. However, it is MPs who have been the principal beneficiaries of the expansion of government, with the number of posts rising from sixty in 1900 to over a hundred in most governments since 1964. With the decline in the number of peers holding ministerial posts, the number of MPs in office has risen from thirty-three in 1900 to eighty-eight in 1997, an increase of 166.7 per cent, and the proportion of MPs has risen from rather more than half to four-fifths. There have been fluctuations and the increase in the number of MPs holding office has tended to occur under Liberal and Labour governments, but subsequent Conservative administrations have either made only small reductions or consolidated increases; the overall trend has been clearly upwards.

TABLE 5.10. *Proportion of MPs achieving ministerial or parliamentary office, 1868–1997 (%)*[a]

Party	1868–1900	1900–18	1918–45	1945–97
Conservative	14.3	17.9	19.1	39.0
Liberal	14.6	23.2	23.6	9.6
Labour	—	32.6	28.2	31.3

[a] Parliamentary offices consist of Speaker or Deputy Speaker of the House of Commons.

Table 5.10 shows just how dramatic the increase in achieving ministerial and parliamentary office has been, especially for Conservative MPs, contrasting with the sharpness of the Liberal decline. The figures for Labour MPs are a reflection of the smaller numbers of Labour Members before 1945 and the Conservative and Labour proportions since 1945 suggest another dimension to the career patterns of MPs—that between a third and two-fifths can expect to hold office.

Political careers have thus become more like other careers, starting at a similar age—if pre-election experience is taken into account—and continuing until normal retirement age—unless electoral defeat intervenes. A significant proportion hope to achieve ministerial office and a significant minority succeed. Ambitions realized or not, MPs now fulfil their roles in a manner

akin to that of many other occupations: being a Member of
Parliament is their only or overwhelmingly principal occupation
and in terms of salary they are treated as full-time; in the provision
of services and facilities they are treated as professionals. What
distinguishes being a Member of Parliament from most other occupations is that, for the overwhelming majority of MPs, politics is a
vocation. Anthony King's career politician has become the norm;
the professional politician has arrived.

6

Parliamentary Participation: Continuity and Change 1

An Anecdotal Picture of Participation

There is no shortage of anecdotal material on parliamentary participation, though most of it focuses on low levels of participation, either generally or in respect of individual MPs. Townsend, for instance, relates at some length efforts from the time of Edward III onwards to enforce attendance.[1] Jeremy Bentham, in 'An Essay on Political Tactics' actually proposed that each Member should deposit an annual sum that would be forfeited at a per diem rate for non-attendance.[2] The comments of John Hatsell, Clerk of the House of Commons from 1768 to 1820, therefore come as no surprise:

Notwithstanding the great anxiety, trouble, and expense which many persons put themselves to, to obtain a seat in the House of Commons, it is inconceivable how many of these very persons neglect their duty, by not attending and taking a part in the business that is depending, and with what difficulty they are prevailed upon to give up their amusements, and other less important avocations, from this, which, whilst they continue members ought to be their first and principal object . . . It is, therefore, the duty of the House . . . to compel the attendance of members by frequent calls, and not to permit the indolence of some, the inattention of others, or the love of amusement in many to leave the most important and interesting questions to be discussed and decided upon in

[1] Charles Townsend, *History of the House of Commons: From the Convention Parliament of 1688 to the Passing of the Reform Bill in 1832*, Henry Colburn, London, 1843, Vol. 2, 361–75.

[2] Jeremy Bentham, 'An Essay on Political Tactics', in Michael James, Cyprian Blamires, and Catherine Pease-Watkin (eds.). *The Collected Works of Jeremy Bentham: Political Tactics*, Clarendon Press, Oxford, 1999, 58–60, originally published in 1791.

a House not consisting of half the number of members, who ought to be present on such occasions.   (John Hatsell, *Precedents of Proceedings in the House of Commons* (originally published in 1776), London, 1781, 62 3.)

Hatsell pointed out that that one of the consequences of poor attendance was that the 'control which the independent members ought to have over the conduct of ministers is entirely lost; and the direction and detail of the measures of government are left without attention or examination to those in whose official department they happen to be'.[3] Some later and more recent Parliaments have been characterized by allegations of poor or low attendance. Sir Courtney Ilbert, in his supplementary chapter to Redlich, for example, says 'The Parliament of 1900 was not a very hard-working body. Attendance was slack, especially towards the beginning and the end of the week'.[4] Arthur Griffith-Boscawen's description of the 1918 Parliament as 'very listless . . .' and attendance as 'slack and irregular' and Frank Gray's comment on the 'many' inactive Members in the 1920s were noted in Chapter 5.[5]

Similarly, there is no shortage of examples of MPs who have rarely, if ever, spoken in the House. One, William Gerard Hamilton, acquired the sobriquet of 'Single-speech Hamilton' because, after his maiden speech, he never spoke again in all his forty-two years (1754–96) years in the Commons.[6] However, Colonel H. C. Lowther, who sat for fifty-five years (1812–67) without making his maiden speech, surpassed even Hamilton.[7] There is also the case of Lowther's near-contemporary, Sir Graham Montgomery, who represented Peeblesshire for twenty-eight years (1852–80) without ever speaking in the House.[8] Rather more recently, Sir John Leigh (Conservative MP for Wandsworth (Clapham) 1922–45) became

---

[3] Hatsell, *Precedents of Proceedings*, 63.

[4] Sir Courtney Ilbert, Supplementary Chapter in Josef Redlich, *The Procedure of the House of Commons*, Constable, London, 1908, Vol. 3, 203.

[5] Sir Arthur Griffith-Boscawen, *Memories*, John Murray, London, 1925, 224; and Frank Gray, *Confessions of a Candidate*, Martin Hopkinson, London, 1925, 157.

[6] See Townsend, *History of the House of Commons*, Vol. 2, 391; and Romney Sedgwick, *History of Parliament: The House of Commons 1715–54*, HMSO for the History of Parliament Trust, London, 1970, Vol. 2, 103.

[7] See Viscount Ullswater, *A Speaker's Commentaries*, Edward Arnold, London, 1925, Vol. 2, 292.

[8] See Mark Bonham Carter, 'Introduction', to his edited edition of *The Autobiography of Margot Asquith*, Weidenfeld and Nicolson, London, 1995 (originally published in two volumes, 1920 and 1922), xx.

known as 'the silent MP', never speaking once in the chamber, although he did table Questions for written answer in the earlier part of his parliamentary career—eight in 1922, as many as forty in 1923, none in 1924, and fourteen in 1924–5. Thereafter, there is no record of any activity on his part.

Such cases might be thought to be very much in the past, but MPs who rarely speak in the chamber can still be found, although they are far less numerous. In the 1994–5 session, for example, only ten Conservative MPs, three of whom were ministers, and one Labour MP did not take any part in debates. Moreover, apart from obvious explanations, such as serious illness, non-participation in debates does not preclude activity in other areas, such as committees, asking Questions, tabling or signing motions, or taking action on behalf of constituents. Nor, for that matter, does relative silence in the chamber necessarily mean absence from the chamber, as the example of John Morrison (later Lord Margadale), Conservative MP for Salisbury from 1924 to 1964 illustrates: 'his voice was rarely heard in the chamber (though he was diligent in his attendance)'.[9] Another Conservative, Arthur Jones (Northants, South Daventry 1962–79), is an example of a different case: '. . . his attendance record was not what it might have been – in 1968 he missed 200 votes . . . [but] . . . Jones was a diligent member of both party and Commons committees'.[10] Similar examples can be found among Labour MPs: Freda Corbet (Member for Camberwell, North-West-Peckham, 1945–74)—'though the rareness of her speeches caused some comment, she worked efficiently behind the scenes for her constituents';[11] and Edwin Wainwright (Dearne Valley, 1959–83)—'Although he spoke rarely in the Commons, he was diligent in pursuing . . . [constituents'] . . . interests in parliamentary Questions, and in party and Commons committees'.[12]

It is also the case that participation by individual Members can vary considerably over time. Lord Ullswater, who, as James Lowther, was Speaker from 1905 to 1921, could hardly be called an inactive Member, but he recounts how, as a young MP, he was rebuked by Lord Randolph Churchill for his irregular attendance at

---

[9] Obituary, the *Daily Telegraph*, 29 May 1996.
[10] Obituary, the *Daily Telegraph*, 23 December 1991.
[11] Obituary, the *Daily Telegraph*, 6 November 1993.
[12] Obituary, the *Daily Telegraph*, 2 February 1998.

debates.[13] This was at the beginning of his parliamentary career: low participation towards the end of a career is, understandably, more common. Joseph Chamberlain, for instance, was unable to attend the House after suffering a stroke in July 1906, although he was twice re-elected and remained an MP until his death in 1914.[14] More recently, Sir Winston Churchill rarely spoke after leaving office as Prime Minister in 1955, although he remained a well-known spectator on the government benches below the gangway in the chamber.[15]

The problem, however, with anecdotal evidence is that it provides a partial picture; it is not clear whether particular examples, whether of Parliaments or individuals, are typical and, while comparisons over time may well be valid, they remain impressionistic. This is well-illustrated by an observation made by Sir Robert Inglis (1824–54) during the debates on the Reform Bill of 1832: 'Formerly, very few Members were wont to address the House; now the speaking Members are probably not less than four hundred'.[16] Later in the century, however, Alpheus Todd actually calculated the number of MPs speaking at different times: before 1832 he estimated the number speaking each year to be 'about 150' (23 per cent); by 1841 this had risen to 231 (35 per cent), by 1861 to 300 (46 per cent); and by 1876 to 385 (59 per cent),[17] still below Sir Robert Inglis' estimate. Thus, useful as anecdotal material is, more systematic data are necessary to provide the basis for judging the extent and nature of parliamentary participation and how far it has changed since the middle of the nineteenth century.

[13] Ullswater, *A Speaker's Commentaries*, Vol. 1, 162.

[14] The seriousness of Chamberlain's illness was kept secret for some time after his stroke. He made extensive contributions to debates until May 1906, but there is no further mention of his name in the *Hansard* index until his death.

[15] Churchill spoke twice in 1956–7 and once more in November 1959, when he accepted good wishes on his 85th birthday. In 1961 he tabled a Question for written answer and the final references to him while he was still a Member consisted of tributes paid to him shortly before he retired from Parliament in 1964.

[16] Cited by Townsend, *History of the House of Commons*, Vol., 390.

[17] Alpheus Todd, *On Parliamentary Government in England: Its Origins, Development and Operation*, Longman, London. 2nd ed., 1889, Vol. 2, 401.

Measuring Participation

Measuring parliamentary participation is no easy task. Parliament has long kept a record of its proceedings, but only in the sense of formal minutes of each day's business: the *Journal of the House of Lords* dates back to 1510 and that of the Commons to 1547. The *Journals* are based on daily votes and proceedings (each House's agenda) and include a record of all divisions. However, this consists of the number of Members voting 'Aye' or 'No' and does not list their names. Such lists are found in *Hansard*—the record of actual debates, which dates from 1803 if the reports of debates in William Cobbett's *Political Register*, published by Thomas Hansard, are included, which they should.[18] The record of what was actually said in Parliament has a much more haphazard history and the *official* verbatim record dates only from 1909. Before that reports of parliamentary debates were unofficial and the quality was dependent on the vagaries of reporters and publishers. During the nineteenth century parliamentary reporting came under the control of the Hansard family, but an official Hansard reporter was not appointed until 1878. In fact, from 1803 until 1878 parliamentary reportage consisted of summaries of debates culled from newspapers. From 1878 the Hansard reporter supplemented these. Before 1909, therefore, published debates need to be treated with a degree of caution, especially those before 1878.[19]

In addition to being a verbatim record of debates, *The Official Report of Debates*—commonly known as *Hansard*—also contains the answers to all parliamentary Questions, including those tabled for written answer, first introduced in 1902. There is, however, no record of attendance in the chamber of the House of Commons, other than actual participation in debates or Question Time and, although *Hansard* includes full division lists, voting in a division

[18] Before 1803 journalists, of whom the most famous was Dr Samuel Johnson, published their own accounts of debates. These were based on memory, hearsay, or surreptitious notes, since the reporting of debates was regarded as a breach of parliamentary privilege. They were subsequently published as *Parliamentary History*. Cobbett's *Political Register* was bought by Hansard in 1812.

[19] For a brief account of the development of *Hansard* see Malcolm Shaw, 'Hansard' in Michael Rush and Malcolm Shaw (eds.), *The House of Commons: Services and Facilities*, Allen and Unwin, London, 1974, 112–33. For a more extensive account see William Law, *Our Hansard*, Pitman, London, 1950.

does not mean that a Member has attended the debate preceding the division. Nonetheless, division lists provide a basic indication of attendance, or at least presence. More detailed analyses of division lists, however, have formed the basis of much useful research on nineteenth century parliamentary parties and behaviour, especially in measuring party cohesion, and, more recently, in measuring backbench dissension. However, these two aspects of participation are discussed in more detail in Chapter 7.

Committees also maintain records of their proceedings. For select committees these consist of formal minutes, including a record of attendance and any divisions that took place, and a verbatim record of all oral evidence, and much of the written evidence submitted. However, there is no verbatim record, only formal minutes, of select committee deliberations on draft committee reports and any other matters, such as discussions of a committee's programme of inquiries. For standing committees the records consist of formal minutes and a verbatim in the form of the *Standing Committee Hansard*. Committee attendance records, however, do no more than record that a Member was present at some point during the proceedings, so that a Member may have attended the whole of a meeting or no more than a few minutes. Committee attendance records therefore also need to be treated with a degree of caution as a measure of participation. Of course, the verbatim record provides a clearer indication of actual participation, but, in the case of standing committees dealing with legislation, it is commonly said that the job of government supporter is 'to turn up and shut up' in order to secure the smooth passage of government bills and that of the opposition supporter 'to turn up and speak up' to slow down their passage.

Apart from the various records of its proceedings, the House of Commons has for many years published other data about its activities, some periodically, some systematically. The Select Committee on Procedure, for example, has from time to time published information about the incidence or impact of various procedures and practices.[20] More systematically, the House has long published annual returns on committee activity, although none were published for standing committees between 1931–2 and 1946–7

---

[20]   e.g. Select Committee on Procedure, *Third Report*, HC 189, 1945–6.

and none for select committees between 1931–2 and 1967–8. And, since 1977–8 there has been a *Weekly Information Bulletin* and from 1983–4 an annual *Sessional Digest*. Information about the number of Questions asked, the number of bills introduced and what happened to them, the use of closure, the number of motions tabled by backbenchers, and so on, as well as data on committee activity, is now made available. From these and from the formal and verbatim records of activity in the chamber and committees, it is possible to build up a picture of the nature and extent of Members' participation over time.

This has been done by selecting nine parliamentary sessions between 1871 and 1995 at roughly fifteen-year intervals and, using *Hansard* indexes, committee and other records, creating a series of snapshots to assess levels of activity by individual MPs.[21] Division lists have been used to provide a basic indicator of participation, though not by individual Members. Other records have been analysed to examine the activity of each Member in three key areas—participation in debates, the asking of Questions, and committee attendance. In the latter case a distinction was drawn between committees dealing with legislation, both primary and secondary, and those conducting various forms of policy investigation or scrutiny.[22] The caveats mentioned earlier need to be borne in mind, especially for the pre-1909 period of *Hansard*. Moreover, no attempt was made to adopt a more qualitative approach, even in a quantitative way, by measuring the extent of individual activ-

[21] The sessions selected were 1871, 1887, 1901, 1913, 1928, 1947–8, 1961–2, 1976–7, and 1994–5. In general, sessions in mid-Parliament were chosen, but it was necessary to avoid particular sessions because they were election years or known to be untypical, the most obvious example being 1916 in the middle of the First World War.

[22] Legislative committees include all standing committees dealing with the committee stage of public bills, all committees (select or standing) dealing with delegated legislation (including European legislation), and second reading committees. It was decided to treat the Scottish and Welsh Grand Committees as legislative rather than investigatory committees. Investigatory committees include the Public Accounts Committee, the former Estimates, Expenditure and Nationalized Industries Committees, the former Select Committee on the Parliamentary Commissioner for Administration, departmental select committees, and all *ad hoc* select committees established to investigate particular matters in each of the sessions covered. 'Domestic' committees dealing with various aspects of the operation of the House of Commons, including the Privileges and Procedure Committees, have been excluded, so that the data is based on committees dealing with the passage or scrutiny of public business.

ity by counting column inches in debates or the number of questions asked in the taking of oral evidence in select committees. One speech or intervention in a debate was enough, asking one parliamentary Question, attending one committee meeting was sufficient for participation to be recorded. However, the actual number of speeches or interventions, Questions, and committee attendances were recorded, so that data on the extent of participation was generated. In addition, a record was made of whether Members raised matters about their constituencies in Questions or debates, with 'one strike' again being enough to register such activity.

The purpose was to create a broad, overall picture of participation by Members of Parliament, which, it was judged, a more selective, in-depth approach was less likely to produce. In particular, the purpose was to explore the nature and extent of parliamentary participation since the mid-nineteenth century, whether there were significantly different patterns of participation between government and opposition, between frontbenchers and backbenchers, and between parties. In short, in what ways has the undoubted growth of government affected MPs and their roles? This chapter focuses on the picture of parliamentary participation that the data gathered presents; the penultimate chapter seeks to relate that picture to the three roles performed by MPs—as partisans, as scrutineers, and as constituency representatives.

Patterns of Participation

Table 6.1 clearly shows that participation in divisions has increased markedly since 1871, especially in divisions in which 300 or more Members voted. These rose from a quarter of all divisions in 1871 to three-quarters in 1961–2 and 1994–5. The 1976–7 session, however, defies the trend, with only 55.3 per cent such divisions. This was a period of minority government and therefore one in which party management was at a premium, but the party arithmetic in the Commons was such that the government was only ultimately vulnerable if *all* the opposition parties and the single Independent Irish Republican voted against it. Furthermore, between March 1977 and July 1978 a 'Lib-Lab Pact' operated, by which Liberal MPs gave support to the Labour government in

TABLE 6.1. *Participation in divisions, 1871–1995 (% of MPs voting)*

Session	Less than 100	100–199	200–299	30–399	400–499	500–599	600+	300+
1871	17.8	26.5	29.2	17.8	6.8	1.9	0.0	26.5
1887	2.9	23.8	29.8	33.1	8.3	0.8	1.4	43.6
1901	0.0	9.1	36.9	42.1	11.2	0.6	0.0	53.9
1913	0.4	5.3	33.1	37.3	19.0	4.2	0.8	61.2
1928	0.0	5.5	26.0	60.7	7.8	0.0	0.0	68.5
1947–8	0.4	6.7	22.9	50.6	13.8	5.5	0.0	70.0
1961–2	0.4	9.0	14.6	31.5	37.8	5.9	0.8	76.0
1976–7	11.4	14.9	18.4	14.0	21.1	19.7	0.4	55.3
1994–5	2.7	9.4	12.5	9.8	13.4	46.4	5.8	75.4

Source: *Journal of the House of Commons* for each session.

return for policy concessions, so that a serious 'war of attrition' did not develop until the 1978–9 session. In the meantime, the Conservative opposition adopted a selective approach, attacking the government and forcing votes where it thought it most vulnerable and trying to avoid devaluing confidence motions by not using them too frequently. This contrasts with the 1992–7 Parliament, which rapidly developed into a war of attrition, especially as the Conservative majority was whittled away by by-election losses and defections, leading to much more intense party warfare in the division lobbies.

Of course, what the figures in Table 6.1 most strongly reflect is the growth of party cohesion, although this is implicit rather than explicit. However, it is not just a case of MPs increasingly voting with their parties, nor, indeed, of two-party conflict and dominance, but also of the growth of party management. The handling of parliamentary business increasingly came to be decided between government and opposition, with, of course, the initiative mostly in the hands of the government. Pairing normally ensured the attendance of sufficient MPs to preserve the government's majority in most divisions, but MPs increasingly expected to support their parties in the division lobbies: their parties expected no less. What other parliamentary activities they engaged in were a different matter, over which they had more control.

TABLE 6.2. *Participation in debates, committees, and the asking of parliamentary Questions, and overall participation rate, 1871–1995 (% of MPs)*

Year	Debates	Committees	PQs	Overall
1871	63.0	41.5	55.4	78.2
1887	74.9	38.2	76.2	89.1
1901	64.1	43.0	81.3	85.8
1913	64.1	50.4	84.8	89.1
1928	78.3	57.5	81.0	92.3
1947–8	91.5	67.3	90.4	98.0
1961–2	92.0	66.5	89.8	97.9
1976–7	95.7	79.7	98.1	99.2
1994–5	98.5	85.1	97.5	99.5

Notes: The figures for Questions exclude ministers and relate to opposition frontbenchers and all backbench MPs. The overall participation rate is based on participation in one of more of the activities.

Source: *Hansard* indexes and committee votes and proceedings/returns for each session.

What is striking about the figures in Table 6.2 is the high level of participation in the later nineteenth century, with four-fifths of MPs in 1871 and nearly nine out of ten in 1887. However, this observation needs to be strongly tempered by bearing in mind that a single action—one speech or intervention in a debate, attending one committee meeting, asking a single Question—is sufficient to be recorded as participation. Moreover, it also needs to be borne in mind that committee attendance is in part a function of the number of committees established and how often they met, that the practice of asking Questions was far less developed in 1871, and, by no means least, that parliamentary sessions vary in length and intensity. These factors are indeed reflected in Table 6.2, particularly in the data on committee activity, which now involves the great majority of MPs, and on Questions, the asking of which is now almost universal among opposition frontbenchers and backbench MPs. What is now required is a more detailed analysis of the data to explore the intensity of participation and whether it differs between different groups in the House, notably frontbenchers and backbenchers, and the parties.

Frontbenchers[23] *and Backbenchers*

The overall participation rates shown in Table 6.3 do not show major differences between frontbenchers and backbenchers. It would appear that, apart from 1871, backbenchers did not lag far behind their frontbench colleagues before the Second World War and since then they have been the same. On the other hand, it is clear from Table 6.3 that between 1871 and 1928 opposition front-benchers and backbenchers were more active than ministers and government frontbenchers and backbenchers, with the exception of opposition backbenchers in 1871. However, if account is taken of the levels or intensity of activity a somewhat different picture emerges, as shown in Table 6.4.

Frontbench activity, as measured by participation in two out of the three forms of activity—debates, committee attendance, and Questions, remained considerably greater than that of back-benchers until as recently as the 1970s, by which time the two groups were on a par. The high levels of frontbench participation are hardly surprising, since ministers must lead on government business, both in the chamber and in most legislative committees, and reply to Questions, though the latter are not measured here. Similarly, the opposition frontbench wishes to confront and criti-cize the government and establish itself as a credible alternative.

[23] The 'Shadow Cabinet'—the core of frontbench spokespersons for the official opposition—is now an established part of British politics. The Shadow Cabinet, in the case of the Conservatives, is appointed by the Leader of the Party, but mostly elected by the Parliamentary Labour Party in the case of Labour. It is now that prac-tice for the opposition to have something more akin to a 'shadow government', an extensive, if not full complement of frontbenchers speaking on its behalf, with, of course, others in the House of Lords. In 1961–2, for instance, the Labour opposition had forty frontbenchers in the Commons; in 1976–7 the Conservatives had fifty-four, and in 1994–5 Labour had ninety-four. The numbers have grown, but this has essentially been the case for the Conservatives since the early part of the twentieth century, when Arthur Balfour was Leader, and since 1923 in the case of the Labour Party. Before this, a more amorphous 'Shadow Cabinet' existed, usually consisting of ex-Cabinet members of the party in opposition, although this presented problems the longer the party remained in opposition and both Conservative and Liberal Party leaders reserved the right to consult whomever they wished. For a detailed discussion see R. M. Punnett, *Frontbench Opposition*, Heinemann, London, 1973, particularly ch. 2. For the purposes of this study, where a clearly-designated list of the 'Shadow Cabinet' and other frontbenchers exists—as is the case for most of the twentieth century—that list was used. For the 1871, 1887, and 1901 sessions members of the immediately-preceding government of the party concerned were used.

TABLE 6.3. *Participation rates of frontbenchers and backbenchers, 1871–1995 (% of MPs)*

Year	Ministers	Opp. FBs	Govt. BBs	Opp. BBs
1871	84.8	96.2	78.4	74.9
1887	89.7	95.8	82.7	95.8
1901	96.4	95.0	79.9	90.2
1913	86.8	100.0	83.3	91.5
1928	91.8	100.0	90.8	96.5
1947–8	100.0	93.8	96.6	99.5
1961–2	94.2	100.0	98.2	98.6
1976–7	98.9	96.3	99.5	99.6
1994–5	97.7	100.0	99.6	100.0

Source: Hansard indexes and committee votes and proceedings/returns for each session.

TABLE 6.4. *Participation by frontbenchers and backbenchers in two out of three activities, 1871–1995 (%)*

Session	Frontbenchers	Backbenchers
1871	81.1	25.5
1887	69.8	27.3
1901	68.8	29.0
1913	70.2	37.1
1928	68.8	46.7
1947–8	82.0	59.0
1961–2	84.1	59.6
1976–7	79.9	79.9
1994–5	83.9	89.6

Source: Hansard indexes and committee votes and proceedings/returns for each session.

This illustrates an important aspect of participation—the opportunities for frontbenchers are inevitably greater than those for backbenchers. Of the measures used, only in the tabling of Questions for written answer is the initiative solely in the hands of the backbenchers. Attendance at committees rests with the individual backbencher, but membership does not; taking part in debates requires catching the eye of the chair; and participation in Question Time is a combination of chance and similarly securing the attention of the Speaker. Hence, opportunity alone cannot explain the differences between frontbench and backbench activity. At least three factors account for the growth in backbench participation. First, the massive expansion of parliamentary Questions, particularly for written answer, means that Questions now constitute by far the largest numerical activity by Members. Second, and much more recently, there has been an expansion in the use of committees for both legislative and investigatory purposes. And third, but not so easily quantifiable, backbenchers increasingly wish to be actively involved in the work of the House of Commons. All this can be seen more clearly if frontbenchers and backbenchers are examined separately.

Ministers and Opposition Frontbenchers

The figures in Table 6.5 show consistently high percentages of ministers and opposition frontbenchers participating in debates, but with much greater variation in the actual levels, whether measured by the mean number of speeches or the proportion of frontbenchers with twenty or more listed in the *Hansard* indexes. These variations almost certainly reflect what was happening in each session—current issues and the impact of events, the extent of the government's legislative programme, the state of morale in the governing and opposition parties, and so on. For example, the extraordinarily high mean for ministers in 1887 reflects the intensity of the session, especially as a result of Irish Nationalist obstruction. The very low mean for 1901 may in part result from the fact that less than twelve months before the Liberals had lost heavily in a general election and were facing a further period in opposition. In any case, as already noted, contemporaries described the 1900 Parliament as being poorly attended. The lower means for the two most recent sessions probably reflect the marked increase in the number of MPs holding ministerial office and the concomitant expansion of the opposition frontbench. However, these variations are less important than the overall picture of considerable activity in the chamber by frontbenchers going back well into the nineteenth century.

TABLE 6.5. *Participation by ministers and opposition frontbenchers in debates, 1871–1995*

Session	Ministers			Opposition frontbenchers		
	% partic.	Mean no.	% 20 +	% partic.	Mean no.	% 20+
1871	84.8	38.6	45.4	88.5	22.9	42.3
1887	82.1	99.0	58.9	87.5	41.3	54.1
1901	89.3	30.7	35.1	90.0	17.7	30.0
1913	86.8	44.7	52.6	100.0	36.5	57.9
1928	83.7	25.2	38.8	100.0	28.5	53.4
1947–8	90.4	51.1	58.9	93.8	90.2	81.2
1961–2	94.2	35.6	53.6	100.0	79.6	77.5
1976–7	95.8	28.0	54.7	92.6	29.7	63.0
1994–5	96.5	20.6	39.6	100.0	22.4	46.9

Notes: % partic. = the percentage of frontbenchers participating in debates; Mean no.= the mean number of speeches in debate; % 20 + = the proportion of front-benchers with 20 or more speeches listed in the *Hansard* indexes.

Source: *Hansard* indexes for each session.

TABLE 6.6. *Committee attendance by ministers and opposition frontbenchers, 1871–1995*

Session	Ministers			Opposition frontbenchers		
	% partic.	Mean no.	% 20+	% partic.	Mean no.	% 20+
1871	60.6	8.6	18.2	73.1	10.7	26.9
1887	48.7	5.7	5.1	58.3	6.5	12.5
1901	57.1	4.5	0.0	50.0	2.5	0.0
1913	42.1	2.6	0.0	36.8	3.2	5.3
1928	30.6	3.9	6.1	53.3	5.1	0.0
1947–8	71.2	6.8	15.1	50.0	6.6	12.5
1961–2	61.6	9.1	21.0	55.0	11.8	22.5
1976–7	71.5	6.4	4.2	61.1	6.3	5.6
1994–5	68.6	9.9	19.8	75.5	9.0	21.3

Source: Committee votes and proceedings/returns for each session.

The data for committee attendance shown in Table 6.6 relates almost entirely to legislative committees, mostly standing committees taking the committee stage of legislation, although frontbenchers—including ministers—occasionally served on investigatory select committees until the earlier part of the twentieth century. That the figures show a lower level of activity than for debates is not surprising, since ministers and opposition frontbenchers serve on standing committees to lead for the government and the opposition on the committee stage of government bills, but only for bills sponsored by their department or within their 'shadow' responsibility respectively. However, the figures also reflect changes in the use of committees, with an increase in legislative committees and a decline and subsequent revival of investigatory committees. The 1976–7 session also illustrates the influence of particular factors: in this case it was the relative reluctance of the then Labour government to use standing committees, rather than the floor of the House, since the latter was easier to manage in a minority situation.

Procedurally the asking of Questions has been the major growth area in parliamentary activity and, not surprisingly, opposition frontbenchers have made increasing use of them since 1871. Their number inevitably varies, but the strong upward trend is clear, a trend which, of course, directly affects ministers, since it is they who must answer Questions.

TABLE 6.7. *The use of parliamentary Questions by opposition frontbenchers, 1871–1995*

Session	% partic.	Mean no.	% 20+
1871	92.3	5.4	3.8
1887	83.3	15.2	37.5
1901	85.0	15.4	30.0
1913	100.0	35.9	42.1
1928	93.3	42.9	26.6
1947–8	87.5	37.8	37.5
1961–2	95.0	41.3	65.0
1976–7	94.4	48.3	75.9
1994–5	98.9	147.2	85.1

Source: *Hansard* indexes for each session.

The overall picture that emerges is one of high levels of participation by both ministers and opposition frontbenchers. The figures for debates suggest that, from some time between 1913 and 1928, the opposition became more organized and systematic, given the higher means and proportion with twenty or more speeches among opposition frontbenchers. This is not found with committee attendance, but that is not to be expected, since attendance equals votes, whereas speeches do not. This is reinforced by the data on Questions, which, though not an exclusively opposition procedure, are an important weapon in the opposition's armoury. More detailed analysis presents a more complex picture, supporting the clear trend towards greater activity, accompanied by a convergence in the two most recent sessions. That there should be tendency for more frequent activity, though not consistently so, either temporally or in relation to particular forms of activity, is to be expected. Ministers' participation is driven largely by the government's programme and opposition's reactions to it. Opposition frontbench participation, however, while inevitably driven to a large extent by the government's programme, is also much affected by the extent of its attempts to keep a check on the government and scrutinize its polices. However, the opposition has a significant degree of latitude, raising levels of activity generally or specifically, operating on a broad front or focusing on particular matters. Whether the same patterns are found among backbenchers is now the question.

Backbench Participation

Two trends are clearly discernible in Table 6.8: first, there is a strong upward trend in participation in debates among backbenchers generally; but, second, as measured by the mean and the proportion making twenty or more speeches, opposition backbenchers are always more active, until, interestingly enough, the two most recent sessions.

Committee attendance (see Table 6.9) presents a less clear pattern, largely because of the growth in the use of legislative committees, most of which are subject to heavy whipping. This tends to increase the attendance of government backbenchers—as indeed was the case in the four post-1945 sessions—in order to ensure the smooth passage of government bills. Nonetheless, the broader pattern of growing backbench participation is clearly sustained.

TABLE 6.8. *Participation in debates by government and opposition backbenchers, 1871–1995*

Session	Government backbenchers			Oppositon backbenchers		
	% partic.	Mean no.	% 20 +	% partic.	Mean no.	% 20+
1871	65.5	6.0	7.6	54.2	8.3	12.0
1887	65.3	7.3	10.6	85.1	22.9	13.1
1901	54.4	2.5	1.9	74.8	6.9	8.6
1913	68.0	7.5	10.1	65.0	10.3	13.8
1928	72.3	6.2	7.8	86.7	22.5	34.3
1947–8	88.8	18.0	29.4	96.0	37.8	53.5
1961–2	91.7	16.0	27.8	89.9	26.7	40.6
1976–7	97.7	23.8	51.7	97.3	27.0	46.9
1994–5	97.1	21.0	42.8	99.4	23.4	42.6

Source: *Hansard* indexes for each session.

TABLE 6.9. *Committee attendance by government and opposition backbenchers, 1871–1995*

Session	Government backbenchers			Opposition backbenchers		
	% partic.	Mean no.	% 20 +	% partic.	Mean no.	% 20+
1871	38.8	4.8	5.9	39.4	4.1	7.2
1887	36.4	4.2	5.1	41.1	4.5	7.7
1901	40.5	3.0	0.0	49.7	3.7	1.2
1913	61.0	6.7	10.1	43.8	4.1	4.6
1928	61.9	6.1	7.2	60.8	5.8	5.6
1947–8	66.1	9.2	17.0	69.5	8.1	13.5
1962–2	71.0	11.1	22.8	64.1	10.1	18.4
1976–7	84.4	12.5	19.8	80.1	14.1	21.2
1994–5	94.7	25.1	59.2	85.8	20.8	65.3

Source: Committee votes and proceedings/returns for each session.

The data on the backbench use of Questions (see Table 6.10) not only illustrates the enormous growth in Questions and therefore in backbench participation, but strongly reinforces and extends the image presented by the data on participation in debates, with

TABLE 6.10. *The use of parliamentary Questions by government and opposition backbenchers, 1871–1995*

Session	Government backbenchers			Oppositon backbenchers		
	% partic.	Mean no.	% 20 +	% partic.	Mean no.	% 20+
1871	53.4	2.1	0.9	53.8	2.5	2.0
1887	67.0	5.0	4.8	82.7	12.4	18.5
1901	73.2	4.8	5.9	91.4	16.8	22.0
1913	82.0	14.3	20.6	82.3	23.6	30.0
1928	76.8	11.2	13.7	88.8	48.6	50.4
1947–8	87.0	29.0	35.2	96.5	56.7	62.0
1961–2	88.4	13.8	22.8	90.8	30.6	43.3
1976–7	97.7	60.3	51.7	99.1	60.8	72.6
1994–5	96.3	37.0	56.7	97.2	111.2	75.0

Source: Hansard indexes for each session.

opposition backbenchers considerably more active than government backbenchers. Government backbenchers can and do use Questions to probe government policy and to extract information, but they also use them to defend the government they support, not least with the device of the 'planted Question'. However, the incentive for opposition backbenchers to ask Questions is much greater: they offer an effective means of extracting information with which to criticize the government and, especially with Questions for oral answer, of seeking to put the government on the spot at relatively little cost to the individual Member.

Backbench activity grew more slowly than frontbench activity, which was already at a relatively high level in the late nineteenth century. Moreover, there is clear evidence that opposition backbenchers are more active than government supporters, although the two latest sessions show a near balance in debates, whereas it remains strongly in favour of opposition backbenchers in the use of Questions. From a partisan view this is to be expected: the job of the opposition is to expose the government's shortcomings; the job of government supporters is to facilitate the passage of government business, as the data on committee attendance suggests. The convergence shown in the two most recent sessions probably

reflects in part the fine party balance in both cases, with a minority Labour government in 1976–7 and a Conservative government
with a dwindling majority in 1994–5. But, more importantly, these
figures can be seen as prime facie evidence of the extent to which
MPs have become largely full-time and increasingly professional-
ized.

The Impact of Party

Organizationally and procedurally the House of Commons
depends on party, but it is normally the two largest parties, one
forming the government, the other the official opposition, that are
crucial. Indeed, the analysis of the data so far suggests that the
government–opposition divide is of more significance than which
party is in government and which in opposition. Further analysis,
however, shows that there is some evidence that party does make a
difference. In particular, it suggests that ministers in left-of-centre
governments and their backbench supporters are more active than
those of right-of-centre governments. Thus, with the exception of
the 1887 session, Conservative ministers have lower mean levels of
participation in debates than their counterparts in the preceding
Liberal or Labour governments over the nine sessions covered.
Similarly, Conservative backbenchers have lower mean levels of
participation in both debates and Questions than the backbench
supporters of the preceding Liberal or Labour governments, with
the exception of Questions in 1887. This is despite a general
upward trend of participation. However, the same does not hold for
committee attendance or for Conservative frontbenchers or backbenchers when in opposition. This would therefore appear to be a
function of more active left-of-centre governments: a function of
ideology.

Third Party Participation

Further analysis also suggests that third parties *qua* third parties
have some distinctive patterns of participation. Although the
House of Commons has long been dominated by two major parties,
third parties have never been absent in modern times and have
sometimes formed a significant proportion of its membership,

notably between 1874 and 1935—though not involving the same parties—and since February 1974. The analysis of third party participation in the nine sessions suggests two interesting patterns, the first concerning the extent of their participation, the second nascent early professionalization.

Third parties have very little time at their disposal, certainly much less than the official opposition.[24] Furthermore, as the main opponent of and threat to the government, the latter is normally able to bargain much more effectively with the government's business managers on the allocation of time. Governing parties need little reminding that, sooner or later, they are likely to find themselves in opposition and allowing the opposition to have its say, or at least a reasonable say, is good parliamentary politics. Of course, third parties, like all minorities in the House, benefit from the duty imposed on the Speaker to see that they get a fair chance to put their points of view, but this does not fully compensate for their distinctly minority position. On the other hand, there are times when the government is dependent for its survival on one or more third parties, as was the case following both elections of 1910 and again for much of the period 1974–9, but the impact is usually greater on policy than participation.

Data based on the nine sessions (see Table 6.11) suggests that third parties work harder than the official opposition, probably out of necessity, to get their message across. This is most easily achieved in using Questions and particular debates, less easily through committee activity. This is because the official opposition is guaranteed proportionate representation on committees, whereas third party representation on committees depends on their overall number in the House and, in the case of the nationalist parties in Scotland, Wales, and Ireland, the more limited focus of their interests. Table 6.11 shows that in most of the nine sessions members of third parties asked more Questions and participated in more debates that either government or opposition backbenchers. The Irish Nationalists were particularly active in 1887—a session in which they engaged in a good deal of obstruction as the government sought to tighten its procedural grip. Of course, the figures on

---

[24] The Liberal Democrats are currently allocated three of the twenty opposition days, but these are shared with the other third parties.

TABLE 6.11. *Participation by third party MPs in debates and asking parliamentary Questions, 1887–1995 (mean no. per MP)*

A. Debates

Session	Irish Nat.	Labour	Liberal/LD	Plaid Cymru	Scot. Nat.	Ulster Union.	SDLP	Govt. BBs	Opp. BBs
1887	63.5	—	—	—	—	—	—	7.3	22.9
1901	11.4	23.5	—	—	—	—	—	2.5	6.9
1913	3.5	6.5	—	—	—	—	—	7.5	10.3
1928	2.0	—	19.5	—	—	—	—	6.2	22.5
1947–8	—	—	30.6	—	—	—	—	18.0	37.8
1961–2	—	—	39.9	—	—	—	—	16.0	26.7
1976–7	—	—	55.5	52.3	42.7	38.8	20.0	23.8	27.0
1994–5	—	—	36.2	33.1	34.6	33.1	10.3	21.0	23.4

B. Parliamentary Questions

Session	Irish Nat.	Labour	Liberal/LD	Plaid Cymru	Scot. Nat.	Ulster Union.	SDLP	Govt. BBs	Opp. BBs
1887	28.2	—	—	—	—	—	—	5.0	12.4
1901	41.1	45.0	—	—	—	—	—	4.8	16.8
1913	21.4	31.3	—	—	—	—	—	14.3	23.6
1928	0.0	—	35.8	—	—	—	—	11.2	48.6
1947–8	—	—	24.2	—	—	—	—	29.0	56.7

Table 6.11. (cont.)

B. Parliamentary Questions

Session	Irish Nat.	Labour	Liberal/ LD	Plaid Cymru	Scot. Nat.	Ulster Union.	SDLP	Govt. BBs	Opp.
1961–2	—	—	20.7	—	—	—	—	13.8	30.6
1976–7	—	—	89.9	205.7	86.7	71.5	51.0	60.3	60.8
1994–5	—	—	141.8	268.8	92.5	55.5	54.8	37.0	111.2

Notes: the number of MPs in each party was as follows, including by-election changes:
(a) *Irish Nationalist:* 1887: 85; 1901: 82; 1913: 84; 1928: 1 (T. P. O'Connor-Liverpool (Scotland)).
(b) *Labour:* 1901: 2; 1913: 40.
(c) *Liberal/Liberal Democrat:* 1928: 43; 1947–8: 10; 1961–2: 7; 1976–7: 13; 1994–5: 24.
(d) *Plaid Cymru:* 1976–7: 3; 1994–5: 4.
(e) *Scottish National Party:* 1976–7: 11; 1994–5: 4.
(f) *Ulster Unionist (including the Democratic Ulster Unionist Party and other Unionist parties):* 1976–7: 10; 1994–5: 13. Before the imposition of direct rule in Northern Ireland in 1972, the Ulster Unionists took the Conservative whip and are therefore counted as Conservative MPs in earlier sessions.
(g) *Social Democratic and Labour Party:* 1976–7: 1; 1994–5: 4.

Source: Hansard indexes and committee votes and proceedings/returns for each session.

debates for the third parties—the Liberals since 1945 and the various nationalist parties—in part reflect the 'frontbench' opportunities they secure, since all or most of their MPs have some frontbench responsibilities in their respective parties. Nonetheless, third party activity in debates and Questions shows a clear tendency to be higher than that of government backbenchers and often of opposition backbenchers as well. It is also the case that the SNP is more active than other parties in standing committees dealing with Scottish legislation. With this exception, however, third parties tend to be less active in committee work, particularly investigatory committees, though more by lack of opportunity than willingness to participate.

The second pattern produced by the analysis of third party participation was that of nascent or early professionalization among Irish Nationalist and Labour MPs and among the 'Lib-Labs', who took the Liberal whip.

Although overall backbench participation was high in 1887, 1901, and 1913, these three groups of MPs had the highest levels of overall participation, as Table 6.12 shows, but it is in mean levels of activity that the contrast is sharpest.

TABLE 6.12. *Overall participation rates among Irish Nationalist, Labour and Lib-Lab MPs, 1887–1913 (% of MPs)*

Session	Irish Nat.	Labour	Lib-Lab	Cons. BBs	Lib. BBs
1887	100.0	—	100.0	82.7	95.6
1901	97.6	100.0	100.0	79.9	89.7
1913	92.9	95.0	100.0	91.5	82.7

Notes: For the number of Irish Nationalist and Labour MPs in each session see the notes to Table 6.11. The number of Lib-Lab MPs was 8 in 1887 and 1913 and 7 in 1901.

Source: *Hansard* indexes and committee votes and proceedings/returns for each session.

In both 1887 and 1901 Irish Nationalist and Lib-Lab MPs and Labour Members in 1901 asked many more questions than either Conservative of Liberal backbenchers. A similar situation prevailed in debates. However, in 1913 Conservative backbenchers asked on

TABLE 6.13. *Participation by Irish Nationalist, Labour, and Lib-Lab MPs in debates and asking parliamentary Questions, 1887–1913 (mean no. per MP)*

A. Debates

Session	Irish Nat.	Labour	Lib-Lab	Cons. BBs	Lib. BBs
1887	63.5	—	44.8	7.3	21.8
1901	11.4	23.5	10.7	2.5	6.7
1913	3.5	6.5	13.8	10.3	7.5

B. Questions

Session	Irish Nat.	Labour	Lib-Lab	Cons. BBs	Lib. BBs
1887	28.2	—	15.1	5.0	12.3
1901	41.1	45.0	8.4	4.8	17.1
1913	21.4	31.3	28.9	23.6	13.8

Notes: See the notes to Table 6.12.

Source: *Hansard* indexes and committee votes and proceedings/returns for each session.

average more questions than Irish Nationalists, though fewer than Labour or Lib-Lab Members, and in debates both Conservatives and Liberals had higher means than either Irish Nationalists or Labour MPs, but were less active than Lib-Labs.

In the case of the Irish Nationalists the explanation probably lies in the fact that the main Home Rule battle had been won in the previous session, with the passing by the Commons of a Government of Ireland Bill. The Lords had rejected this, but the Parliament Act of 1911 would ensure its passage in 1914. The Nationalists now had less reason to participate in debates; their main concern was the survival of Asquith's minority Liberal government, a matter which required support at appropriate times in the division lobbies, not participation in debates of the asking of Questions.

Labour also had a vested interest in Asquith's survival. The 1909 Osborne Judgement had seriously affected the financial support the party received from the trade unions, especially the sponsorship of individual MPs. The introduction of the payment of MPs from 1912 helped considerably, but the Osborne Judgement was not reversed until 1913, with the passage of the Trades Union Act that year. More generally, Labour supported the welfare policies of the Liberal government and in many respects Labour MPs behaved more like government backbenchers.

Nevertheless, Nationalist, Lib-Lab, and Labour MPs were generally considerably more active than backbench MPs in the two major parties. Unlike their Conservative and Liberal counterparts, few were able to support themselves financially. The majority of Irish Nationalist Members were supported by funds raised through the Irish National League, which was controlled by Parnell and his successors. Lib-Lab and Labour MPs were mostly supported by trade union funds. This is not to say that they were financially well-off or even comfortably-off; on the contrary, many led a financially precarious existence, but it also meant that few were engaged in any other remunerative activity—essentially they were full-time politicians—the first *players*.

Robert Kee, one of Parnell's biographers, has argued that the Irish Nationalist Party was 'the first disciplined democratic party of modern times'.[25] There is no doubt that the Nationalists were highly-organized and operated a system of strict party discipline. In 1896 John Redmond, later leader of the Nationalists, described how the Irish Members organized themselves for the debates on the Irish Coercion Bill in 1881:

Half of Mr Parnell's followers were out of the chamber snatching a few moments' sleep in chairs in the Library or Smoke-room. Those who remained had each a specified period of time allotted to him to speak, and they were wearily waiting their turn.   (John Redmond, 'Fifteen Years in the House of Commons', lecture given in New York, 29 November 1896, quoted in Christopher Sylvester (ed.), *The Literary Companion to Parliament*, Sinclair-Stevenson, London, 1996, 30.)

Herbert Gladstone, William Ewart's son, then at the beginning of his parliamentary career, had a similar recollection of the 1880–5 Parliament:

[25] Robert Kee, *The Laurel and the Ivy: the Story of Charles Stewart Parnell and the Irish Nationalists*, Penguin, London, 1994, 443.

The Parnellites made use of not only Irish questions but of every question. Every man spoke on any subject as long as his physical endurance permitted. The party was organised in relays. They brought in Conservatives by raising Conservative issues, and many Conservatives gladly joined in the fun. By moving amendments to raise questions they got fresh rights to speak. They came to the House loaded with blue-books from which they made interminable quotations.

The Speaker had no power to stop them. All the government could was to keep a quorum and tire them out by protracted sittings . . .

Members in these days had to read their Questions to the House though they were printed on the Order Paper. The Irishmen wrote immensely long Questions and read them slowly to the House. If a Member was not satisfied with the answer he could make a speech and end with a motion.   (Herbert (Viscount) Gladstone, *After Thirty Years*, Macmillan, London, 1928, 184).[26]

Any thought that such organization and activity was peculiar to the 1880–85 Parliament is mistaken—far from it; it continued throughout Parnell's leadership and beyond, subsequently tempered by the procedural changes described in Chapter 3 and lessening somewhat when the legislative objective of Home Rule had almost been achieved in 1913. In a study of party behaviour between 1886 and 1918, John D. Fair points out that the Irish Nationalists had the highest level of cohesion of all the parties represented in the Commons, although the Conservatives were not far behind.[27] William B. Gwyn has remarked that the 'history of the Home Rule party is one of ever-increasing control of the majority over the individual'.[28]

Although the Labour Party had much broader and longer-term objectives than the Irish Nationalists and in that sense was much less single-minded, it too exhibited similar characteristics. Like the Nationalists, pledges of party loyalty were demanded and strong party discipline was enforced. Indeed, there is evidence that Labour leaders like Keir Hardie were fully conscious of the Irish example. Gwyn cites Hardie as arguing in 1886 that the 'the democracy of Ireland has taught us a lesson we will not be slow to learn'.[29]

[26] For a detailed account see T. P. O'Connor, *Gladstone's House of Commons*, Ward and Downey, London, 1885.

[27] John D. Fair, 'Party voting behaviour in the British House of Commons 1886–1918', *Parliamentary History*, 5, 1986, 67.

[28] William B. Gwyn, *Democracy and the Cost of Politics in Britain*, Athlone Press, London, 1962, 143.   [29] Quoted in ibid., 145.

It may be going too far to claim that the Irish Nationalists were Britain's first professional parliamentary party and that Labour was to become the second. The Conservatives and Liberals already had organizations outside Parliament—it was these that gave Ostrogorski such concern, but neither had to any significant degree developed more than a few dozen full-time MPs and most of these were to be found on the frontbenches. Irish Nationalist and Labour Members, and the Lib-Labs, were for all intents and purposes full-time MPs, not fully-professionalized in terms of services and facilities, but in effect setting what would eventually become the norm.

Conclusion

Parties may be the engines of Parliament, driving government and opposition, but it is largely these roles of government and opposition which determine levels of participation, with third parties having to exert themselves much more to make their presence felt. Thus, while there is some evidence that parties to the left of centre are more active than those to the right, this too operates within the government–opposition dichotomy, with a number of Conservative governments, and therefore their backbench supporters, being less active than Liberal or Labour governments and their backbench supporters. Even this difference seems to have disappeared in more recent Parliaments.

The government–opposition dichotomy is hardly surprising: governments wish to expedite business, oppositions to prolong it. Government backbenchers, whether individually hopeful of office or not, wish to assist *their* government in achieving its policy objectives and the prolonging of debates, whether in the chamber or standing committees, is not seen as conducive to this. Opposition backbenchers, again whether individually hopeful of office or not, wish to assist *their* shadow government in exposing the flaws in government policy and laying the foundations for success at the next election, and the prolonging of debates is seen as a means to this end. This is the essence of the partisan role, but Members are widely expected to perform two other roles, whether supporters of the government or the opposition or neither, that of calling the government to account—the scrutiny role—and that of advancing and defending their constituents' interests—the constituency role. And it is these three roles with which the penultimate chapter is concerned.

7

The Role of the Member of Parliament: Continuity and Change 2

The Role of the Member of Parliament

The role of the Member of Parliament can be divided into three inter-linked roles—that of the partisan, the scrutinizer of the executive, and the constituency representative. Each would have been recognized by a nineteenth as much as by a twenty-first century MP. What has changed is the balance and relationship between them. Analytically, they can be separated, but in practice they are far from separate; they both complement and conflict with one another.

An analysis on the basis of these three roles does not preclude, nor is it intended to preclude, other approaches, as was argued in Chapter 1 in respect of Donald Searing's positional and preferential roles. Rather, it is to argue that whatever positional and preferential roles MPs may fulfil, all MPs fulfil the partisan, scrutiny, and constituency roles. Though analytically separate, they are not mutually exclusive and in carrying out one role a Member may be implicitly or explicitly fulfilling another. Moreover, each role can and should be seen as collective, as well as individual, especially in the context of the conflict between government and opposition. Collectively, MPs normally support their parties in the division lobbies, but they are also involved in the collective scrutiny of the executive through committee activity, especially investigatory committees. They also act together in tabling and signing motions, especially Early Day Motions (EDMs), as means of expressing back-bench opinion—sometimes in partisan fashion, sometimes as a genuine expression of cross-party opinion, and any serious promotion of a Private Member's bill requires collective action. It has long been the case that, party aside, like-minded Members have hunted in packs, some large, some remarkably small. The Fourth Party in the early 1880s literally had four 'members', though that was not, of course, the derivation of its name, and in the 1999–2000 session a small group of Conservative ex-ministers conducted a sustained 'guerrilla war' against Labour's huge majority. On other occasions much larger groups of MPs have worked together, often against their own party—the initial breakaways of the Peelite Free Traders and of the Liberal Unionists being cases in point. Much more recently left-wing groups in the Labour Party—the 'Keep Left Group' in the late 1940s, the Tribune Group from the early 1950s, and the Campaign Group from the early 1980s—and right-wing groups in the Conservative Party—the Monday Club, formed in 1961, and the Eurosceptics of the 1990s—have played a significant part in intra-party politics inside and outside Parliament. Centre groups, at least influential ones, have been less common, but the Campaign for Social Democracy in the Labour Party in the early 1960s and the Bow group, dating from the late 1950s, were important. From time to time MPs also co-operate over constituency matters, within a city or region, sometimes more widely, in relation to matters of common constituency interest, and such co-operation is often across party lines.

Of course, much of what MPs do is done individually, most obviously as constituency representatives, but also in the asking of Questions and the tabling and signing of motions. However, the whips can and do play a part in some of these activities, with the government whips 'assisting' their backbenchers in the tabling of friendly, even sycophantic, Questions and motions; and the opposition whips likewise 'assisting' in the generation of hostile and highly critical Questions and motions, in both cases often providing 'the script'. Nonetheless, party activity of this sort, especially by opposition backbenchers, is also part of the scrutiny process and even sycophancy can inadvertently expose government inadequacies. Individual and collective activities thus intermingle, but so do the three roles: partisan activity involves scrutiny, scrutiny may be highly partisan, and the constituency role can provide grist for the partisan and scrutiny roles.

Members also play different roles at different times. A minority, but a significant and growing proportion, serve as frontbenchers as well as backbenchers. Not only has the number of MPs who become ministers increased, but so also has those who serve on the opposition frontbench without achieving ministerial office, usually because, by the time their party regains office, their places on the frontbench have been taken by other, younger, more recently-elected colleagues. A few Members spend all or most of their parliamentary careers in the Commons on the frontbench, but most serve an 'apprenticeship' as backbenchers and not a few have a post-frontbench career as backbenchers. Frontbench roles, as Searing points out, set fairly clear parameters for MPs, especially for those holding ministerial office. As MPs, for both ministers and opposition frontbenchers the partisan role dominates, but for opposition frontbenchers there is also a major scrutiny role, even though it is conducted in a largely partisan fashion. Ministers, however, by definition, have no scrutiny role in Parliament, but both they and opposition frontbenchers continue to have a constituency role, though this is carried out mainly behind the scenes, rather than through overt parliamentary activity, especially, of course, in the case of ministers.

Backbench MPs, again as Searing notes, can choose how to perform their roles, focusing on one more than another and choosing different means of fulfilling them. Thus Searing is able to show in considerable detail that his four backbench types have different patterns of parliamentary behaviour and activity.[1] Policy advocates make considerable use of parliamentary Questions, adjournment debates, and Private Members' bills and are committee members; ministerial aspirants speak regularly in the chamber and involve themselves in particular aspects of committee work; constituency Members make especial use of Questions for written answer and adjournment debates, but are also very active in formal and informal contacts with ministers and departments; and, among 'Parliament men', some are 'spectators', but others are much involved in the House's domestic committees and many are 'good constituency' Members. There are also significant variations *within* Searing's four types: for example, 'generalist' policy advocates make particular use of Private Members' bills, and 'specialist' policy advocates of

---

[1] See Donald Searing, *Westminster's World: Understanding Political Roles*, Harvard University Press, Cambridge, MA, 1994, ch. 2–5.

committees. The data gathered for this study does not lend itself to analysis by Searing's categories, but offers an alternative and additional way of looking at the role of the MP. It suggests that Members perform three basic, but interlinking roles on a continuing and, in many respects, simultaneous basis, so that, for instance, however partisan MPs may see themselves, all to one degree or another, fulfil the three roles of partisan, scrutinizer, and constituency representative.

The Partisan Role

Damn your principles!
Stick to your party!
(Remark to Edward Bulwer Lytton, attributed to Disraeli)

I always voted at party's call,
And never thought of thinking for myself at all.
(W. S. Gilbert, *HMS Pinafore*)

The idea that party cohesion was something of a novelty in the middle of the nineteenth century is at best misleading. That it was considerably lower between 1846 and 1867 is not in dispute, but Gilbert *would not* have written what he did in *Pinafore* without knowing what his audience's reaction would be.[2] Furthermore, political memoirs throughout most of the nineteenth century are replete with references to the activities of the whips, nor did they escape the attention of Dickens.[3] In July 1858 Sir John Mowbray, then Conservative MP for Derby City and a member of the government as Judge-Advocate General, was presented with a silver spoon

---

[2] In 1877 Sir Wilfred Lawson, the Conservative MP for Carlisle, described the whipping system to his constituents, referring not only to one, two and three-line whips, but also to *four*-line whips (G. H. Jennings, *An Anecdotal History of the British Parliament*, Appleton & Co., New York, 1881, pp. 446–7). See also T A. Jenkins, 'The whips in the early Victorian House of Commons', *Parliamentary History*, 19, 2000, pp. 259–86.

[3] In one of his 'Sketches by Boz', published between 1833 and 1835, Dickens facetiously refers to a 'whipper-in for the government [who] brought four men out of their beds to vote in the majority, three of whom died on their way home again.' (Charles Dickens, *Collected Works*, Gresham, London, 1911, Vol. 1, 115).

for attending the largest number of divisions, and Sir John Pakington, the Conservative MP for Droitwich, also a member of the government as First Lord of Admiralty, was presented with a wooden spoon for attending the fewest. Mowbray remarks that Sir John 'appeared incapable of tolerating a harmless joke'.[4] Sir Herbert Williams-Wynn, briefly Conservative MP for Denbigh, recounts how, following his by-election victory in May 1885, '. . . I arrived in the House while a division was in progress. I did not know what it was about. I was pushed into the lobby'.[5]

Lawrence Lowell's study of party cohesion in the nineteenth century—see Table 2.3—shows clearly that, by the end of the century, party voting had become the norm, but it also shows that it was not a smooth progression from low to high levels of cohesion. In fact, there was a sharp decline in the middle of the century, largely caused by party splits and a party realignment that was not complete until after the breakaway of the Liberal Unionists in 1886. Hugh Berrington reanalysed Lowell's figures and, in order to clarify the post-1880 period, gathered data for three further sessions— 1883, 1890, and 1903.[6] Thus, in 1836 'true two-party votes', when both major parties voted on opposite sides, accounted for 34 per cent of whipped divisions, but in 1850 for only 18 per cent and in 1860 for a mere 5 per cent. In 1871, however, 'two-party votes' had risen to 38 per cent and in 1881 to 49 per cent, only to fall again in 1883 to 35 per cent. Thereafter, apart from a fall in 1899, the trend was firmly upward: 1890—65 per cent, 1894—84 per cent, 1899—75 per cent, and 1903—86 per cent. It is likely that an even more detailed, session by session analysis, would show variations and fluctuations, but equally unlikely that it would contradict the basic conclusion that by 1900 party cohesion was virtually compete. Berrington concludes:

The last two decades of the nineteenth century and the early years of the twentieth were marked by a rapid growth of party conformity in

---

[4] Sir John Mowbray, *Seventy Years at Westminster* (ed. Edith Mowbray), Blackwood, London, 1900, 158.

[5] Cited by Sir Henry Morris-Jones, *Doctor in the Whips' Room*, Robert Hales, London, 1955, cited in Christopher Sylvester (ed.), *The Literary Companion to Parliament*, Sinclair-Stevenson, London, 1996, 41.

[6] Hugh Berrington, 'Partisanship and dissidence in the nineteenth century House of Commons', *Parliamentary Affairs*, 21, 1967–8, 338–74.

Parliament. On the Conservative side there is a remarkable contrast between the quarrelling and ill-led party of the early eighties, and the almost monolithic party of 1890. By that year (and perhaps earlier) all forms of dissidence . . . had virtually disappeared; and though in later Parliaments the party's unity was a little less rigid than in 1890, the picture remains one of a faithful following.

Amongst the Liberals, the growth of party unity was slower, and less regular. Yet even here we can see, in the sessions of 1894 and 1903, a unity which approached, if it did not equal, that of a modern parliamentary party . . .

By 1903 the gap between the radicals and the official leadership of the party, had largely closed. In that year there were only four divisions in which Liberals cast extremist non-party votes.   (Berrington, 'Partisanship and dissidence', 348 and 359.)

This picture of strong party cohesion is confirmed by John Fair's study of voting behaviour in the House of Commons between 1886 and 1918. Fair used a unanimity test—more a stringent test than Lowell, and therefore Berrington—which defined party votes as those in which 90 per cent or more of the MPs of one party voted in the same division lobby. Excluding divisions in which less than 10 per cent of a party's MPs voted, unanimity meant those divisions in which all those taking a party whip voted with their parties, regardless of the overall numbers voting. On this basis, Fair found that the cumulative average of party voting between 1886 and 1918 was 95.35 per cent. The highest level was recorded by the Irish Nationalists, with 96.88, closely followed by the Conservatives, with 96.86. Labour, the Liberal Unionists and the Liberals were marginally less cohesive, recording figures of 94.55, 94.43, and 93.41 respectively.[7] A further study of party cohesion found that between 1924 and 1928 the percentage of party votes was 95 per cent.[8]

Strong party cohesion was not only the norm but came to be taken for granted by practitioners and scholars alike, to the point that, in his study, *Modern British Politics*, published in 1965, Samuel

[7] John D. Fair, 'Party voting behaviour in the British House of Commons 1886–1918', *Parliamentary History*, 5, 1986, 67.

[8] Russell Jones, *Party Voting in the English House of Commons*, unpublished MA thesis, University of Chicago, 1933, 24, cited by Robert J. Jackson, *Rebels and Whips: Discipline and Cohesion in British Political Parties since 1945*, Macmillan, London, 1968, 4–5.

Beer remarked that party cohesion 'was so close to 100 per cent that there was no longer any point in measuring it.'[9] This view was echoed by Geoffrey Hosking and Anthony King even for the period 1906–14: 'given the high level of party cohesion, the rewards of our labour [in analysing every division] would almost certainly have been meagre.'[10] And Christopher Hollis, Conservative MP for Devizes 1945–55, famously suggested that 'it really would be simpler and more economical to keep a flock of tame sheep and from time to time drive them through the division lobbies in appropriate numbers.'[11] These were not unreasonable comments, but even before Beer's comment, in the 1959–64 Parliament, there had been a sharp rise in dissidence, falling back in 1964–6, but rising again in 1966–70. These levels rose further after 1970 and have remained at about a fifth of divisions in most Parliaments since then.[12]

The figures in Table 7.1. show that, on the one hand, party cohesion has continued to be the norm, but that, on the other, there has been a significant growth in dissidence. However, they also show that, even before 1970 dissenting votes 'have been more prevalent than has been generally realised'.[13] What distinguishes the period before 1970 from that since, however, is the willingness of government backbenchers to inflict defeats on their own government, as the figures in Table 7.2 clearly show.

Of course, the ability of government backbenchers to defeat the government on the floor of the House is much greater when the government only has a small majority, as was the case in 1950–1,

[9] Samuel H. Beer, *Modern British Politics: A Study of Parties and Pressure Groups*, Faber, London, 1965, 350.
[10] Geoffrey Hosking and Anthony King, 'Radicals and Whigs in the British Liberal Party, 1906–1914', in William O. Ayedelotte (ed.), *The History of Parliamentary Behaviour*, Princeton University Press, Princeton, NJ, 1977, 146.
[11] Christopher Hollis, *Can Parliament Survive?*, Hollis and Carter, London, 1949, 36.
[12] There was, in fact, a decline in dissidence in the Parliament elected in 1997— about 9% overall, lower in the first two sessions but rising in the third. See Philip Cowley and Mark Stuart, 'Parliament: a few headaches and a dose of modernisation', *Parliamentary Affairs*, 54, 2001, 238–56.
[13] Norton, *Dissidence in the House of Commons, 1945–74*, 609. Norton also points out that between 1905 and 1972 there were 'at least' thirty-four government defeats on the floor of the House, but this compares with 301 between 1847 and 1905. See Philip Norton, 'Government defeats in the House of Commons: myth and reality', *Public Law*, 1978, 361.

TABLE 7.1. *Proportion of divisions in the House of Commons with dissenting votes, 1945–97*

Parliament	% with dissenting votes	% with unanimous votes
1945–50	7.0	93.0
1950–1	2.5	97.5
1951–5	3.0	97.0
1955–9	2.0	98.0
1959–64	13.5	86.5
1964–6	0.5	99.5
1966–70	9.5	90.5
1970–4	20.0	80.0
1974	23.0	77.0
1974–9	28.0	72.0
1979–83	19.0	81.0
1983–7	22.0	78.0
1987–92	19.0	81.0
1992–7	21.0	79.0

Sources: Philip Norton, *Dissension in the House of Commons, 1945–74*, Macmillan, London, 1975 and *Dissidence in the House of Commons, 1974–79*; and Philip Cowley and Philip Norton, 'Rebellions in the British House of Commons', Paper presented to the Third Workshop of Parliamentary Scholars and Parliamentarians, Wroxton College, Banbury, Oxon., August 1998.

1964—6, and October 1974 to April 1976, or, even more so, when it has no overall majority at all, as was the case in March–October 1974 and April 1976 to the end of the 1974–9 Parliament. Although governments between 1945 and 1970 suffered eleven defeats, none of these was the result of deliberate dissent by government back-benchers, but, as Philip Norton points out, 'resulted from poor organisation by the whips or deliberate opposition ploys . . . and were concentrated in two Parliaments of small government majorities (1950–51 and 1964–66).'[14] In contrast, 'six defeats experienced in the 1970–74 Parliament . . . were inflicted as a result of dissension by government backbenchers'.[15] The Labour government of

[14] Norton, *Dissension in the House of Commons*, xviii.
[15] Ibid.

TABLE 7.2. *Number of government defeats in the House of Commons, 1945–97*

Period	No. of defeats
1945–70	11
1970–4	6
March–October 1974	17
1974–9	42
1979–83	1
1983–7	2
1987–92	1
1992–7	9

Sources: David Butler and Gareth Butler, *Twentieth Century British Political Facts 1900–2000*, Macmillan, London, 2000, 201.

1974–9 was particularly vulnerable and suffered seventeen defeats in the short-lived 1974 Parliament and no less than forty-two in the 1974–9 Parliament, of which as many as twenty-three were directly inflicted by its own backbenchers.[16] Governments in succeeding Parliament all had overall majorities, in two cases very large majorities.[17] Nonetheless, all suffered defeats on the floor, none more spectacular than the defeat of the second reading of the Shops Bill in 1986, when seventy-two Conservatives rebelled, obliterating a normal government majority of 140.[18] The 1992–7 Conservative government began with a majority of twenty-one, but this was gradually whittled away as a result of by-election losses and defections to the Liberal Democrats and Labour. The Major government was especially vulnerable to rebellions over Europe by Eurosceptic Conservatives, but always survived votes of confidence. The number of defeats may have declined, but levels of dissidence

[16] Philip Norton, 'Behavioural Changes' in Philip Norton (ed.), *Parliament in the 1980s*, Blackwell, 1985,. 26.
[17] Between November 1995 and April 1996 Conservative government was technically in a minority, when the whip was withdrawn from eight Conservatives and another resigned the whip.
[18] See Francis Bown, 'The Defeat of the Shops Bill, 1986', in Michael Rush (ed.), *Parliament and Pressure Politics*, Clarendon Press, Oxford, 1990, 213–33.

have not, other than from the high point of 28 per cent of divisions in the 1974–9 Parliament. Furthermore, in spite of—perhaps partly because of—Labour's huge majority, dissidence at the rate of about one division in ten continues to occur in the Parliament elected in 1997

To what can this growth of backbench dissidence be attributed? This continues to be a matter of dispute. One thing is clear, however, there is neither a simple nor a single explanation. Various explanations have been suggested—poor party leadership, the impact of cohorts or 'generations' of MPs, and a realization among government backbenchers that defeating the government did not necessarily result in its resignation or a dissolution of Parliament. One further explanation can be confidently dismissed—that the dissidence of the 1970s was an aberration and that party cohesion would return to 'normal', since it patently did not happen.[19]

The poor leadership hypothesis was advanced by Norton in relation to Conservative dissidence in the early 1970s, to the point that he argued, 'No other explanation for the upsurge in Conservative *division-lobby* dissent in the 1970–74 Parliament is as plausible as that of Mr Heath's style of prime ministerial leadership.' He went on to suggest that there were 'indications that Mrs Thatcher, emboldened by a large majority, may be changing her leadership style. If that is the case, it is likely to result in backbench dissent being expressed more often . . .'.[20] Robert Jackson also suggests that poor leadership may be a factor, quoting a chief whip as saying that 'ministers are responsible for revolts, not whips.'[21] Yet it is doubtful whether poor leadership explains all or even most dissidence, not least because the continuation of dissidence into the 1980s and 1990s and beyond implies a continuation of poor leadership which all but the most cynical would not accept.

The 'generational' hypothesis appears to offer a longer-term explanation, whether in the form that newly-elected MPs, initially at least, are more likely to rebel, or, more importantly, that a 'new breed' of Member, unwilling simply to be lobby fodder, has entered

---

[19] See Philip Norton, 'Are MPs Revolting? Dissension in the British House of Commons, 1979–92', Paper presented to the Second Workshop of Parliamentary Scholars and Parliamentarians, Wroxton College, Banbury, August 1996.

[20] See Norton, 'Behavioural Changes', 37–9, original italics.

[21] Jackson, *Rebels and Whips*, 299.

the Commons. To take the second generational argument first, there is no doubt that, in socio-economic terms, a 'new breed' of Member has been elected and that they are more likely to be full-time rather than part-time, with greater expectations in terms of pay, services, and facilities. Moreover, the fact that they are more active than their predecessors would support the view that they are not content to be lobby fodder. But, unless it can be shown that these MPs are more likely to rebel than their 'old breed' colleagues are, the explanation remains a hypothesis. Similarly, while it may be thought that newly-elected MPs might be more inclined to rebel until such time as they have been socialized into the norm of supporting their parties, the proof would lie in their behaviour. A statistical analysis of rebels in the 1970–4 Parliament found limited evidence between socio-economic background and dissidence, but only for Conservatives and 'not younger or more recently elected' Conservatives. For Labour MPs no socio-economic connections emerged, although Labour rebels were more likely to be union-sponsored and elected in 1970 or later.[22]

What may be called the 'absence of dire consequences' hypothesis, more specifically the realization that defeating the government would not bring about its fall, either by 'forcing' it to resign or through a 'forced' dissolution and loss of the consequent general election, was specifically advanced by John Schwarz.[23] He argues that the growth in dissidence is explained mainly by what he calls a change in the interpretation of 'the parliamentary rule', that is 'the understanding that, following a defeat of the government on the floor on an important issue, the government may well resign.'[24] This is, of course, the ultimate operation of collective responsibility, but practice has long been more complex than the constitutional theory. The fact that this is a constitutional convention, unenforceable by law and open to interpretation, means that, while there are particular circumstances in which a government would resign on losing a vote, there are many more when it might

[22] Mark Franklin, Alison Baxter, and Margaret Jordan, 'Who are the rebels? Dissent in the House of Commons, 1970–74', *Legislative Studies Quarterly*, 11, 1986, 151.
[23] John E. Schwarz, 'Exploring a new role in policy-making: the British House of Commons in the 1970s', *American Political Science Review*, 74, 1980, 23–37. Schwarz also provides evidence refuting the 'new breed' hypothesis.
[24] Ibid., 33.

and it might not and, in most instances, it would not resign. The obvious case is that of a confidence motion or a vote that the government has said it would regard as a matter of confidence. Of course, the government may *choose* to resign after a defeat which is not a matter of confidence, as Lord Rosebery's did in 1895, but it is under no obligation, constitutional or otherwise, to do so. Similarly, even a defeat on the second reading of a government bill does not mean the government will resign or that the Prime Minister will recommend a dissolution of Parliament, although it is possible to hypothesize that a defeat on a major aspect of the Budget or the government's expenditure proposals would result in resignation or a dissolution. The fact that a former Prime Minister's private secretary claimed that a three-line whip was 'a formality which warns supporters of an administration that the government will resign if the vote in question goes against them',[25] does not mean that it is true. Governments have lost votes on three-line whips before and since 1971—many more times since than before—and remained in office. It is neither the rule that has changed, nor its application; it is the behaviour of backbenchers as partisans that has changed.

Of course, as long as and whenever MPs *believe* that a defeat will result in resignation or a dissolution, they will presumably act accordingly, as they will if they believe the government will take neither course. Thus, the realization that governments invariably survive parliamentary defeats, however embarrassing they may be, has probably contributed to the growth and maintenance of dissidence, but it is a factor more likely to influence government than opposition backbenchers. The latter may, of course, forbear rebellion when dissidence among government backbenchers threatens the government, but opposition backbench dissent mostly follows a course of its own.

However, there are, allegedly, other 'dire consequences' that could ensue for dissident Members, whether government or opposition backbenchers, such as withdrawal of the whip, deselection by their local parties, refusal of endorsement as a candidate at the

---

[25] Sir Philip Zuleta in a letter to *The Times*, 13 July 1971, quoted by Norton 'Government defeats in the House of Commons', 360. Norton goes on to spell out the relative frequency of government defeats and the rarity of consequent resignations.

next general election by the national party leadership, lack of preferment for ministerial office, and exclusion from membership of parliamentary committees or delegations, quite apart from the 'black arts' in which the whips are said to engage.[26] Examples of all these can be found and, although it was deliberately disingenuous of a whip to claim, 'We have no real sanctions, but we don't tell that to rebels',[27] they form only one side of the coin of party cohesion.

The other side of that coin is that for much of the time backbenchers agree with their parties and, in any case, much prefer their own party's view to that of the their opponent's. Robert Dowse and Trevor Smith argued this in the early sixties.[28] They suggested that MPs toed the party line because their concerns, especially on legislation, had either been dealt with by pre-legislative consultation with pressure groups or by the network of subject committees found in the two major parliamentary parties. Their assumptions about pre-legislative consultation were almost certainly too sanguine[29] and their trust in backbench party committees misplaced, at least as far as the Labour Party was concerned.[30] Nonetheless, their underlying argument remains valid. MPs are elected almost exclusively under party labels: their parties choose them, of course, but they first choose their parties; they are first and foremost partisans and, as Dowse and Smith conclude, 'the fact of persistent support need not be interpreted as stemming simply from pressure.'[31]

There was clear evidence of a growth in backbench dissidence in the 1959–64 Parliament, but more among Conservative than Labour MPs, with Conservatives rebelling in 120 divisions and

[26] For a lively account of the role of the whips see Gyles Brandreth, *Breaking the Code: Westminster Diaries*, Phœnix, London, 2000, 365–503 *passim* and 519–22. See also Jackson, *Rebels and Whips, passim*; and Austin Mitchell, *Westminster Man: A Tribal Anthropology of the Commons People*, Thames Methuen, London, 1982 *passim*.

[27] Jackson, *Rebels and Whips*, 307.

[28] Robert E. Dowse and Trevor Smith, 'Party discipline in the House of Commons—a comment', *Parliamentary Affairs*, 16, 1962–3, 159–64.

[29] See The Hansard Society, *Making the Law: report of the Hansard Society Commission on the Legislative Process*, London, 1992, ch. 3.

[30] See Anthony Barker and Michael Rush, *The Member of Parliament and His Information*, Allen and Unwin, London, 1970, 284, n1; and John P. Mackintosh, *People and Parliament*, Saxon House, Farnborough, 1978, 82, 104, and 128.

[31] Dowse and Smith, 'Party discipline', 164.

Labour Members in only twenty-six. In the 1966–70 Parliament, however, the roles were reversed, with Conservative rebellions numbering forty-one and Labour 109. More crucially, Labour dissent tended to increase session on session: in 1966–7 the number of divisions in which one or more Labour MPs rebelled was nine, in 1967–8 it rose to twenty-two, and to fifty-six in 1968–9, falling in the short session of 1969–70 to twelve.[32] Some of these rebellions were substantial, numbering thirty, forty, fifty or more Members, although most involved fewer and the government was normally secure from defeat, given its considerable overall majority. Even so, it was backbench opposition among its own supporters that played a major part in forcing the government to withdraw its bill to reform the House of Lords, ostensibly to make way for its proposals to legislate on industrial relations, but opposition by government backbenchers forced the government to withdraw that too.

One of the factors that probably encouraged dissent, apart from the government's large majority, was a lighter rein on party discipline during the period that Richard Crossman and John Silkin were Leader of the House and Government Chief Whip respectively, with the implicit message that the party leadership could tolerate rebellion provided it was contained and did not threaten the government's legislative programme, a message that hindsight was to steep in irony. The adoption of harsher discipline under a new chief whip appears to have limited the number of dissidents, but not dissidence itself. Indeed, it was under the 'new regime' that the 'disasters' of the House of Lords and industrial relations occurred. Moreover, Labour dissidence continued when the party went into opposition after the 1970 general election, although a show of party unity was maintained over opposition to Britain's entry to the European Economic Community (EEC). After an initial rebellion over the principle of entry, in which sixty-nine Labour Members defied a three-line whip by voting in favour and a further twenty abstained, Labour solidly opposed the European Communities Bill.

On the Conservative side of the House there was extensive dissent over entry to the EEC and, although this may have been exacerbated by Edward Heath's relations with his backbenchers, for

---

[32] See Norton, *Dissension in the House of Commons*, 1945–74, 258–377.

most of the rebels it was a matter of principle or serious disagreement. Like its Labour predecessor, the government survived, but
dissidence in the 1970–4 Parliament was the prelude to much
greater dissidence in succeeding Parliaments on a wide range of
issues. Furthermore, dissidence affected both government and
opposition, but it is a feature of most Parliaments from 1945 that
dissidence has been greater amongst government than opposition
backbenchers. The exceptions were the Parliaments of 1951–5 and
1979–83, when Labour was seriously split between left and right,
and the two knife-edge Parliaments of 1964–6 and 1974, when
cohesion in the government party was at a premium. Government
backbenchers, of course, are in a position to influence government
policy directly, whereas opposition backbenchers are so placed only
when they are able to combine with sufficient government backbenchers to threaten the government's majority. Governments
therefore take threatened rebellions among their own supporters
seriously, but usually welcome opposition dissidence as sign of
disunity in the opposition. Government backbenchers thus have a
greater incentive to threaten rebellion, in the hope of changing
government policy. Of course, actual, as opposed to threatened
backbench dissidence, may be interpreted as an admission of a failure to persuade the party leadership to make concessions that
would have headed off rebellion and there is no doubt that the
threat of rebellion sometimes secures concessions. Neither government nor opposition welcomes dissent, since it draws attention to
party disunity. In some cases dissent is clearly related to a particular issue on which the party leadership has misread backbench
opinion and, possibly, public opinion, rather than being related to
an on-going issue, such as Europe, or one of a number of issues that
form an ideological cluster. Richard Rose has argued that the
Conservative Party is a party of 'tendencies', in which divisions
relate to issues that cut across rather than conform to ideological
lines, whereas Labour is a party of 'factions', in which divisions are
ideological.[33] Norton found some evidence to support this view,

---

[33] Richard Rose, 'Parties, factions and tendencies in Britain', *Political Studies*, 12,
1964, 34–46. See also Samuel E. Finer, Hugh B. Berrington, and D. Bartholomew,
Backbench Opinion in the House of Commons, 1955–59, Pergamon Press, London,
1961; and Hugh B. Berrington, *Backbench Opinion in the House of Commons, 1945–55*,
Pergamon Press, London, 1973.

but has pointed out that the appearance of 'new right' ideas among Conservatives have introduced a more ideological or factional element to the party.[34]

This suggests that, although dissent inevitably focuses on particular issues, it often sends a broader message, not only that the party leadership should listen to its parliamentary supporters, but that there are directions, ideological or otherwise, in which significant numbers of backbenchers wish the party to move—or, in some cases, to abandon. Dissent among government backbenchers—or the threat of it—is often clearly directed at specific polices, but it may also be a sign that some backbenchers feel that the government is moving in the 'wrong' direction, even the sign of a disintegrating government, as in the periods before the 1979 and 1997 general elections. Dissent among opposition backbenchers may also be directed at specific policies, but on other occasions they are part of a concerted effort to shift the party's ideological centre of gravity, sometimes successfully, sometimes not. This was certainly the case with the Labour Party after losing office in 1951, 1970, and 1979.[35]

Dissidence therefore has a variety of objectives and is almost certainly the product of a variety of causes, some specific, others longer-term. Factors such as poor leadership, MPs generally rather than generationally being willing to defy the whips, and an absence of 'dire consequences' have probably all played their part, but so also have issues, including some, notably Europe, which cut across traditional party lines. In addition, there has been a loosening of the party system in a wider sense, with the growth of electoral support for nationalist parties in Scotland and Wales, the breakaway of the Unionists in Northern Ireland from the Conservative Party, and the short but electorally-significant life of the SDP, all of which contributed to the loosening of party ties and a process of electoral dealignment.[36] Party membership declined,

[34] Norton, *Dissidence in the House of Commons 1974–79*, 432–6; and *Conservative Dissidents*, Temple Smith, London, 1978, 248.

[35] The other, and usually more successful, means by which such ideological shifts are achieved, of course, is by a change of leadership, as occurred, for example, with the election as leader of the Conservative Party of Margaret Thatcher in 1975 and, arguably, of William Hague in 1997 and of Neil Kinnock in 1983 and Tony Blair in 1994 as Labour leaders.

[36] See Anthony Heath, Roger Jowell, and John Curtice, *How Britain Votes*, Oxford

voter identification with parties weakened, but political participation took other forms, with a growth in pressure group activity and greater involvement in direct action.[37] MPs must have been affected by these wider developments in British politics; indeed, they were part of it.

The partisan role of the MP is much affected by whether a party is in government or opposition, or whether it is a third party, as was clear from the data presented in Chapter 6, but it has also changed. That change, however, has been one of modification, not transformation. MPs remain largely faithful to their parties and party cohesion remains the norm. Nonetheless, backbench dissidence might appear at first sight to be a limited reversion to mid-nineteenth century parliamentary politics, the period 1846–67, sometimes called 'the golden age of Parliament'. But was it? Was the mid-nineteenth century a period when MPs were willing to thrust aside party allegiance and subject the government to genuine parliamentary scrutiny? Was this not only the golden age of Parliament, but also the golden age of parliamentary *scrutiny*?

The Scrutiny Role

The Myth of 'the Golden Age of Parliament'

The short period of thirty or forty years, lasting until the results of the next extension of the franchise, in 1867, became apparent, deserves its title of the 'Golden Age of Parliament'. It was an age of reason in politics, of individualism and *laisser-faire* [sic]. Power was reasonably balanced between the executive and the legislature; the problems of the period were chiefly political—of a nature within the competence of the average member of the

University Press, Oxford, 1985; Mark N. Franklin, *The Decline of Class Voting in Britain: Changes in the Basis of Electoral Choice, 1964–83*, Oxford University Press, Oxford, 1985; Richard Rose and Ian McAllister, *Voters Begin to Choose: From Closed Class to Open Elections in Britain*, Sage, London, 1986; Anthony Heath, John Curtice, Roger Jowell, Geoff Evans, Julia Field, and Sharon Witherspoon, *Understanding Political Change: the British Voter, 1964–87*, Pergamon, London, 1991; and Anthony King and Ivor Crewe, SDP: *The Birth, Life and Death of the Social Democrat Party*, Oxford University Press, Oxford, 1995.

[37] See Geraint Parry, George Moyser, and Neil Day, *Political Participation and Democracy in Britain*, Cambridge University Press, Cambridge, 1992; and William L. Miller, Annis May Timpson, and Michael Lessnoff, *Political Culture in Contemporary Britain: People and Politicians, Principles and Practice*, Clarendon Press, Oxford, 1996.

House of Commons.   (Gilbert Campion, 'Parliamentary Democracy', in Lord Campion (ed.), *Parliament: A Survey*, Allen and Unwin, London, 1952, 14.)

Your business is not to govern the country, but it is, if you think fit, to call to account those who do govern it.   (W. E. Gladstone, speech on a motion to set up a select committee to investigate the conduct of the Crimean War (Roebuck's motion), HC Debs., 3rd series, 136, 29 June 1855, c.1202.)

In his introduction to a new edition of Bagehot's *The English Constitution*[38] Richard Crossman, a Labour MP from 1945 to 1974 and a prominent member of the Cabinet from 1964 to 1970, described the period 1846 to 1867 as 'the classic age of parliamentary government' in which 'the Commons was the place where the most of vital decisions were made.'[39] He went on to suggest:

What [Bagehot] liked most about Parliament was the existence of a solid centre, composed of the majority of solid, sensible independent MPs, collectively able to make and unmake ministries, to defy when necessary their own whips and above all to frustrate the growth of 'constituency government' outside.   (Crossman, 'Introduction', 40.)

However, Crossman's picture of the golden age does not stand up to close examination. In his reanalysis and extension of Lowell s work on party cohesion, Berrington draws a distinction between three types of dissidence: crossbench dissidence—deviation towards the centre—extremist dissidence—deviation from the centre—and bi-partisan dissidence—an alliance of backbenchers against their party leaders. Of these three the least common was the last: 'revolts by backbench alliances against the leaders of the two main parties were uncommon—especially after 1883.'[40] In the earlier part of period covered, that is in 1836, 1850, and 1860, the proportions of crossbench and extremist votes were essentially the same and in 1871 there were more crossbench than extremist votes. However, in '1881 and 1883 . . . the pattern was more than reversed; extremist challenges to party unity heavily predominated.'[41] Furthermore, there was a clear difference between the parties:

[38] Richard H. S. Crossman, 'Introduction', to Walter Bagehot, *The English Constitution*, C. A. Watts, London, 1964, 1–57.
[39] Ibid., 36.
[40] Berrington, 'Partisanship and dissidence', 349.   [41] Ibid., 344.

In the Conservative Party, independence in the division lobbies mainly took the form of crossbench dissidence; in the Liberal Party, of extremist dissidence.   (Berrington, Partisanship and dissidence , 345.)

This is not explained by the fact that in seven of the ten sessions studied the Conservatives were in opposition:

... it was in the nature of the parties, rather than whether they were in government or opposition, which accounted for this difference ... The characteristic Liberal dissident of the nineteenth century House was not the moderate, but the extremist.   (Berrington, 'Partisanship and dissidence', 346 and 348–9.)

Berrington concludes that

... scrutiny of the issues which provoked backbench disaffection suggest that the romantic picture of crusading knights fighting for the rights of the legislature against executive tyranny is a crude if unwitting distortion. Most of the intra-party disputes took the form of sectional conflict—the continuing struggle within the Liberal Party, of radical and moderate; most of the revolts took the form of extremist rebellions against the dominant centre—not of 'moderate' challenges to an extreme and partisan executive ... the consequences of backbench independence have been grossly exaggerated by some commentators. Governments were sometimes defeated on the floor of the House; set against the bald figures of non-party votes, the number of defeats is surprisingly small ...

   The surface fluidity of politics during the middle part of the nineteenth century concealed a basic stability—a stability which rested on a widespread consensus.   (Berrington, 'Partisanship and dissidence', 359–60.)

Although party cohesion began to grow again after 1867, for Berrington the crucial divide is 1886, with the split in the Liberal Party over Home Rule; this solved the continuing Liberal dilemma of Whigs versus Radicals, for most of the former left the party, leaving the field to the latter. This leads him to sum up the *partisan* role of the nineteenth century Member of Parliament as follows:

Until 1886, the relationship between the government and its party followers, and the government and the opposition, were ambivalent. Governments depended on the support of their party to stay in office; to pass legislation or repel criticism, they shifted alternately from the support of the opposition to the support of their own party ...

   ... [After 1886 it was no longer] possible for ministers to rely on the support of opposition leaders to carry through government legislation ...

Party leaders were compelled to find a new basis for legislative support—and they found this in their backbench followers. (Berrington, Partisanship and dissidence , 370–1.)

This view that the classical age of parliamentary government is a myth is strongly supported by Jenkins. His detailed analysis of Victorian parliamentary and party politics is summarily dismissive of the Crossman view:

It would be misleading . . . to suggest that there was ever a golden age of the private Member of Parliament of the sort imagined by Richard Crossman in the 1960s . . . almost all MPs were affiliated to one or other of the parties, in spite of their rhetoric of 'independence'. (Jenkins, 'The whips in the early Victorian House of Commons', 80 –1.)

He goes on to ask,

. . what sort of golden age of the private Member it was when, in the 1854 session, 342 out of 646 MPs did not open their mouths once, or when, as in the 1856 session, only one MP voted in all 198 divisions, fifteen missed up to fifty divisions, another seventy-nine were absent from up to a 100 divisions, 551 were absent from over 100 divisions, and seven did not vote at all.   (Jenkins, 'The whips in the early Victorian House of Commons', 82.)

Gladstone was nearer the mark than Campion: neither believed that parliamentary government meant government by Parliament, but Campion was mistaken in his belief that 'power was reasonably balanced between the executive and the legislature'; it was rather that the fluid party situation meant that governments could not be more or less certain of their survival, nor of the passage of their legislative proposals. Crossman's belief that 'the Commons was the place where the most vital decisions were made' is totally at odds with the reality: once in power, it was ministers who made decisions, it was ministers who mainly took the initiative in public legislation, and most of the time ministers got their way.[42] This did not prevent individual MPs or the House of Commons collectively, from questioning the government and calling it to account. The

---

[42] Interestingly, but not surprisingly, no one suggests that the House of Lords shared in 'the golden age of Parliament', yet the upper house played an important part in nineteenth century politics, not least because of its in-built and overwhelming Conservative majority, but it did not escape the fluidity of party allegiances that characterized the middle of the century.

debate in which Gladstone stated what he believed to be the role of the House of Commons ended in the government's defeat and resignation, but that was the exception to the general rule that governments usually survived, both then and now. Between 1846 and 1868 most governments eventually fell because of an adverse vote in the Commons, but had usually survived many other attempts to eject them from office; nowadays governments are almost always forced from office by adverse votes in a general election. In the meantime, there is much parliamentary scrutiny, but scrutiny is inextricably entwined with the partisan role. Analytically, they can be separated, in practice much parliamentary scrutiny is subordinated to partisan considerations.

Partisan Scrutiny

What did change between the so-called 'golden age' and the latter part of the twentieth century is the nature and extent of the scrutiny role. Here, a distinction needs to be drawn between the role of the opposition, frontbenchers and backbenchers, and that of the individual backbencher, government or opposition, as forms of scrutiny. As the government's grip on parliamentary business tightened, so the role of the opposition became more clearly-defined. In the nineteenth century governments were markedly more organized than the opposition. When the Prime Minister was a member of the House of Lords, there was a clearly-designated leader in the House of Commons, though not necessarily someone who would become Prime Minister in the event of the post becoming vacant. In opposition, however, there was often a split between Lords and Commons and it was by no means clear who would be invited to form the government if and when such an eventuality materialized. Gradually, oppositions became much more organized, until they became 'shadow' governments, ready and waiting to take office should the opportunity arise. Organized scrutiny therefore became increasingly concentrated in the hands of the official opposition, with its control of a designated amount of parliamentary time and its recognition as the principal challenger of the government. Resting as it does on party, opposition scrutiny becomes *partisan* scrutiny. This does not mean it is of no value, rather that is a particular, even peculiar form of parliamentary scrutiny, exposing the government to largely ideological criticism, invariably resulting in the government responding in a similar ideological fashion.

The data presented in Chapter 6 shows clearly the extent to which scrutiny by the opposition has become part of parliamentary activity. Opposition frontbenchers have long been active participants, but increasingly opposition backbenchers became active and, until relatively recently, were more active than government backbenchers. It is, however, not merely the levels but the nature of participation that it is important in the context of scrutiny. Winston Churchill put it succinctly as long ago as 1906:

Even in a period of political activity there is small scope for the supporter of a government. The whips do not want speeches, but votes. The ministers regard an oration in their praise or defence as only one degree less tiresome than an attack. The earnest party man becomes a silent drudge, tramping through the lobbies to record his vote and wondering why he came to Westminster at all.   (Winston Churchill, *Lord Randolph Churchill*, Macmillan, London, 1906, Vol. 1, 69.)

This also became increasingly the case as more standing committees were used for the committee stage of many bills. As already noted, here the government whips want MPs who will 'turn up and shut up' and, at least on bills they strongly oppose, the opposition whips want MPs who will 'turn up and speak up'. No wonder that Arthur Griffith-Boscawen notes in his memoirs that 'Supporting a government of your own party as a private Member is the dullest life a Member can have. Opposition is real fun, and I thoroughly enjoyed myself from 1892 to 1895'.[43] He later quotes Churchill who, tongue in cheek, a few months after leaving the Conservative benches and joining the Liberals, expressed concern at rumours that Balfour's government was going to resign: 'Because if they do, it will be very awkward for me. I joined the Liberals to have some fun in opposition and now it will be all over!'[44]

Important as partisan scrutiny is, not only as a basis for ideological challenge, but also simply as a major means of forcing the government to defend and explain its policies, in the absence of which the neither the House of Commons, nor individual

[43] Sir Arthur Griffith-Boscawen, *Memories*, John Murray, London, 1925, 33.
[44] Ibid., 52.

Members could be said to fulfilling the scrutiny role adequately. A much broader and, in many respects, much more mundane area of scrutiny remains largely untouched by the partisan role—testing the efficacy and effectiveness of policy and administration. And that area of the scrutiny role lies largely in the hands of the individual backbencher, whether on the government or the opposition benches, or, for that matter, representing a third party.

Backbench Scrutiny

The scope for backbench scrutiny is considerable—various types of debates, the tabling of motions, the introduction of Private Members' bills, the asking of parliamentary Questions, and committee activity all play their part. Their use, of course, is not entirely in the hands of backbenchers—participation in debates depends on being called, the time allocated to Private Members' bills is severely limited—quite apart from other obstacles in their way—there are limits on the asking of Questions for oral answer, and membership of committees is essentially in the hands of the parties. On the other hand, there is a wide variety of opportunities to participate in debates, few restraints on the tabling of motions— especially Early Day Motions (EDMs), which are effectively expressions of opinion—and the asking of Questions for written answer is virtually unrestricted. Furthermore, the use of committees has increased enormously, affording backbenchers considerable opportunity to scrutinize policy and administration. This section will concentrate on two major forms of scrutiny—parliamentary Questions and committees, particularly investigatory committees.

The first recorded parliamentary Question was asked in 1721, not in the Commons but the Lords. However, Questions did not become a regular or frequent part of proceedings in either house until the late eighteenth and early nineteenth centuries.[45] The first recorded Speaker's rulings on Questions were made in 1783, [46] but the number of Questions per sitting day did not reach double

---

[45] See Patrick Howarth, *Questions in the House: The History of a Unique British Institution*, The Bodley Head, 1956; D. Norman Chester and Nona Bowring, *Questions in Parliament*, Clarendon Press, Oxford, 1962; and Mark Franklin and Philip Norton (eds.), *Parliamentary Questions*, Clarendon Press, Oxford, 1993.

[46] Howarth, *Questions in the House*, 43.

figures until 1870, but then doubled in the Parliament of 1880–5 and had doubled again by the turn of the century, as Table 7.3 shows.

In 1902, as part of the Balfour procedural reforms, the practice of giving written answers to Questions was introduced. These answers accompanied the daily Votes and Proceedings and were subsequently printed in *Hansard*. This might have been expected to produce a dramatic increase in the number of Questions tabled, since Questions for written answer offered an opportunity to

TABLE 7.3. *Number of parliamentary Questions tabled per sitting day, 1847–1997, (selected sessions/Parliaments)*[a]

Session/Parliament	No. of Questions on the Order paper	Sitting days	Questions per sitting day
1847	129	121	1.1
1870	1,203	120	10.0
1880–85	18,169	787	23.1
1906–10	48,074	637	75.5
1918–22	53,308	588	90.7
1924–29	49,917	658	75.9
1945–50	79,113	765	103.4
1959–64	67,714	805	84.1
1966–70	99,800	708	141.0
1970–74	97,370	610	159.6
1974–79	165,007	793	208.1
1987–92	258,280	610	423.4[b]
1992–97[c]	220,559	785	281.0

[a] The figures relate to Questions tabled (i.e. on the Order Paper), not the number answered in *Hansard*, since from 1902 starred Questions (i.e. those tabled for oral answer) may not be reached and may be withdrawn, given a written answer, or deferred. The figures therefore represent a more accurate measure of Members' activity.

[b] Further restrictions were placed on the tabling of Questions for oral answer were introduced in 1990–1, dramatically reducing the number of Questions on the Order Paper.

[c] The average number of Questions per sitting day for the two sessions from 1997 to 1999 was 251.2.

Sources: 1847–1900: Chester and Bowring, *Questions in Parliament*, Appendix 4, 316; 1900–97: Butler and Butler, *Twentieth Century British Political Facts*, 190–3.

extract information from the government at minimal cost to the Member. Of course, Questions for oral answer had been used for this purpose, but whatever the nature of the Question, those for oral answer afforded MPs opportunities that those for written answer did not. In particular, Question Time provides the Member with an opportunity, however fleeting, to hold centre stage in the chamber, an opportunity that had been enhanced by the development of supplementary Questions in the mid-nineteenth century, but especially in the 1880s. This was the practice of allowing the Member asking the original Question to ask an additional or supplementary Question—sometimes more than one—which might embarrass the minister or the government generally. Nonetheless, it is misleading to assume that for most of its history Question Time has been dominated by partisanship. Writing in 1962 Norman Chester and Nona Bowring found that, in contrast to debates, there

. . . is much less political content in the majority of Questions. Many are asked purely for the sake of obtaining information and a good proportion of the remainder about constituency matters or concern interests with which the Member is associated. (Chester and Bowring, *Questions in Parliament*, 216.)

Partisanship has always played a part in Question Time, but it is since Chester and Bowring's study that it has become the most partisan of parliamentary occasions, especially the formerly twice-a-week, now once-a-week clash between the Prime Minister and the Leader of the Opposition.

It was therefore Questions for oral answer that are reflected in the increase in the number of Questions tabled shown in Table 7.3, until at least the 1960s. As recently as 1966–7 the number of Questions tabled for oral answer exceeded those tabled for written answer—17,314 compared to 16,951.[47] A major factor in what happened subsequently was that the number of Questions tabled for oral answer that were actually answered during Question Time declined sharply. In 1946–7 the mean number of oral Questions answered was 41.4 and it was still as high as 34.4 in 1966–7, but by

---

[47] Helen Irwin, Andrew Kennon, David Natzler, and Robert Rogers, 'Evolving Rules', in Franklin and Norton, *Parliamentary Questions*, Table 2.1.

1976–7 it had halved to 16.7 and, although there were subsequent fluctuations, eventually levelling out at somewhat below this figure—13.1 in 1992–3, 15.0 in 1994–5, 13.5 in 1996–7, and 14.0 in 1997–8.[48] Conversely, from the mid-1960s the number of Questions tabled for written answer rose considerably: in 1946–7 it was twenty-two per day; by 1966–7 it was sixty-nine, in 1976–7 168, and by 1989–90 326. However, these figures mask some variations: the daily average for the 1987–92 Parliament was 291 and for 1992–7 277, but the highest number per sitting day was 386 in 1995–6.[49] Such variations apart, Questions for written answer have become a major means of extracting information from the government, although it is somewhat curious that their extensive use for this purpose is such a recent phenomenon. In 1902 the average per sitting day was seventeen and it did not rise markedly from this figure for well over sixty years.[50] That written Questions are now seen very much as an information-extracting procedure is shown by a survey of MPs conducted by Franklin and Norton: the three most important reasons for using oral Questions were seen as 'holding ministers accountable', 'defending or promoting constituency interests', and 'influencing government policy'; whereas the three most important reasons for using written Questions were seen as 'discovering information that might be hard to get elsewhere', 'getting the government to make a formal statement', and 'making ministers aware of points of concern to constituents'. [51] In terms of effectiveness, however, Questions generally were regarded as least effective in 'influencing government policy and actions', 'getting hard-to-obtain information', and 'holding ministers accountable'; and most effective in 'publicising backbench MPs and their concerns', 'evaluating parliamentary performance', 'taking up

[48] Adapted from ibid. for 1946–7 and from *House of Commons Sessional Returns* for 1992–8.

[49] The averages for 1997–8 and 1998–9 were 219 and 216 respectively, which may reflect the large number of government and the much smaller number of opposition backbenchers.

[50] See Chester and Bowring, *Questions in Parliament*, table, 87–8. The highest average between 1902 and 1959–60, apart from the short four-day session of 1948, was thirty in 1945–6; in a further nineteen sessions it exceeded twenty, but was in single figures in the three session from 1932 to 1935, a period with an even smaller number of opposition backbenchers than the 1997 Parliament.

[51] Mark Franklin and Philip Norton, 'Questions and Members' in Franklin and Norton, *Parliamentary Questions*, Table 4.2.

TABLE 7.4. *The number of active committees, 1871–1995*

Session	Legislative committees		Investigatory committees		Total[a]	
	No. of comms.	No. of meetings	No. of comms.	No. of meetings	No. of comms.	No. of meetings
1871	17	73	18	237	35	310
1887	15	100	16	204	31	304
1901	6	60	7	63	13	123
1913	20	62	10	173	30	235
1928	26	88	5	63	31	151
1947–8	21	140	2	38	23	178
1961–2	33	216	3	40	36	256
1976–7	58	353	13[b]	376	71	729
1994–5	50	529	19	655	69	1,184

[a] The totals for numbers of meetings includes meetings of sub-committees.
[b] In 1976–7 there were eight investigatory committees, but the Select Committee on Expenditure operated through six sub-committees, one general and five specialized. For comparative purposes it has been treated as six committees, giving a total of thirteen.

Source: standing and select committee returns for each session.

constituency interests', and 'getting information on policy, the work of the government etc.'[52]

Chester and Bowring also found that opposition backbenchers asked more Questions than government backbenchers and this is confirmed by the figures in Table 6.10, but whereas there is little difference between the number of oral Questions asked by opposition frontbenchers and backbenchers, whether government or opposition, backbenchers ask far more Questions for written answer. In 1994–5, for example, the mean numbers of Questions for oral answer asked by opposition frontbenchers and government and opposition backbenchers were 10.5, 10.2, and 9.5 respectively, whereas those for written answer showed a marked contrast—26.5, 137.1, and 101.7 respectively.

Clearly, parliamentary Questions constitute a major means of scrutiny. However, those for oral answer are now largely within the sphere of partisan scrutiny, whereas those for written answer have become increasingly important as a means of extracting information from the government, often information which is not otherwise or readily available.

The other area in which there has been a considerable expansion of activity is in use of committees, but here a distinction needs to be drawn between committees used to scrutinize legislation, especially the committee stage of government bills, and those used to investigate policy and its administration.

It is clear from Table 7.4 that the House of Commons has made and continues to make extensive use of committees for legislative purposes. Originally, such committees dealt with various aspects of bills, mostly public bills and increasingly the committee stage of bills. From 1944, however, committees began to be used to examine delegated legislation, although until recently their role has been confined to the legal and technical aspects of such legislation. Similarly, since 1974 secondary legislation emanating from the European Commissions in Brussels has been subject to scrutiny by both Lords' and Commons' committees. However, the most important legislative committees are the standing committees[53] that deal

[52] Franklin and Norton, Table 4.2.

[53] Except for the 1887 and 1901 sessions the term 'standing committee' is a misnomer, since standing committees are reconstituted for each bill referred to them, and this is taken into account in calculating the number of legislative committees in all other sessions in Table 7.4.

with the committee stage of 50 to 60 per cent of government bills each session. In effect, these are miniatures of the whole house, not only in composition but procedurally, and reproduce the adversarial arrangements found in the chamber, in that government and opposition face each other and are lead by ministers and opposition frontbenchers respectively. They are therefore simply a device for dealing with the committee stage of several bills simultaneously and, as such, are subject to the full rigours of the whipping system. In short, they are largely a form of partisan scrutiny.

Standing committees were first used in 1883 and were a response to the growing volume of government legislation, but it was not until 1906 that they became a significant feature of the legislative process. Select committees, however, have a much longer history and were used for a variety of purposes, including, on occasion, dealing with legislation or proposed legislation. However, domestic committees, such as Privileges, aside, the only permanent[54] select committee before 1912 was the Public Accounts Committee (PAC), established by Gladstone in 1861. Its task is, with the assistance of the Comptroller and Auditor-General, to audit public expenditure. All other select committees were set up to deal with a particular matter and, once their task was complete, they were disbanded. The second edition of Todd's *Parliamentary Government in England* cites nine such cases between 1841 and 1874,[55] but it was not until 1912 that a second permanent investigatory committee was created. This was an Estimates Committee to examine proposals for public expenditure. No further permanent investigatory committees were set up until 1956, with the appointment of a Select Committee on Nationalized Industries. The 1960s and 1970s were a period of experimentation, culminating in the creation of the departmental select committees in 1979. Thus, it is only since 1979 that the House of Commons has had a comprehensive investigatory committee *system*, rendering virtually the whole range of governmental activity subject to parliamentary scrutiny.[56]

---

[54] 'Permanent' in this context means committees established either by standing order—for example the Public Accounts Committee and the departmental committees since 1979—or sessional or annual order, as distinct from *ad hoc* committees.

[55] Todd, *Parliamentary Government*, Vol. 1, 428–39.

[56] For a brief account of these developments see Philip Giddings, 'Select Committees and parliamentary scrutiny: plus ça change', *Parliamentary Affairs*, 47,

These developments are reflected in the figures in Table 7.4, which show extensive use of investigatory committees in 1871 and 1887, but thereafter a decline to the point that, in 1947–8, only the PAC and the Estimates Committee were appointed, followed by a subsequent revival in their use. Not surprisingly, the use and development of committees for both legislative and investigatory purposes are manifested in the committee activity of government and opposition backbenchers, as shown in Table 7.5.

The growth in the use of legislative committees is such that the overwhelming majority of backbenchers are now involved and attendance levels for government and opposition backbenchers are very similar, a reflection of the effectiveness of the whips. Although less than half of backbenchers were involved in investigatory committees in 1994–5, this is a considerable increase on 1976–7, when the proportion was less than a third. Attendance levels are comparable to those for legislative committees, resulting, however, not so much from whipping as from a desire to attend. Select committees generally are far less partisan in their operation and this can be illustrated by noting that, in 1995–6, investigatory committees conducted 174 enquiries and produced 131 reports, but formally divided—not always on party lines—on only thirty-four occasions, a ratio of 0.05 divisions per meeting. The comparable figures for the 1998–9 session were 244 enquires, 183 reports, but significantly more divisions: 147. However, the latter amounted to a ratio of 0.17 divisions per meeting, concentrated largely in four committees and a limited number of investigations on which there were party disagreements. The extent of parliamentary scrutiny via the departmental committees is illustrated by Table 7.6.

The figures shown in the table can be placed in a broader perspective by noting that in 1956–7 the number of meetings held by investigatory committees was 0.8 per sitting day compared with 2.2 in 1968–9, 2.7 in 1977–8, 3.2 in 1985–6, 4.3 in 1995–6, and 5.7 in 1998–9.

1994, 669–704. For a more extensive account and assessment see Gavin Drewry (ed.,), *The New Select Committees: A Study of the 1979 Reforms*, Clarendon Press, Oxford, 2nd ed., 1989.

TABLE 7.5. *Attendance at legislative and investigatory committees by government and opposition backbenchers, 1971–1995*

A. Legislative Committees					
	Government backbenchers			Opposition backbenchers		
Session	% partic.	Mean no.	% 20 +	% partic.	Mean no.	% 20 +
1871	15.5	0.9	0.3	17.1	0.7	0.0
1887	16.8	1.3	1.4	17.9	1.4	2.4
1901	28.1	1.6	0.0	34.4	1.8	0.0
1913	51.8	3.6	3.1	36.2	2.0	0.4
1928	56.3	4.8	5.0	56.6	5.1	4.9
1947–8	62.7	8.4	15.8	66.5	7.4	12.5
1961–2	64.9	9.6	19.9	59.9	8.7	17.5
1976–7	79.8	7.6	10.1	77.9	6.9	8.4
1994–52	90.2	13.4	28.2	69.3	12.6	27.8

B. Investigatory committees

	Government backbenchers			Opposition backbenchers		
Session	% partic.	Mean no.	% 20 +	% partic.	Mean no.	% 20 +
1871	24.8	3.9	5.6	29.9	3.4	7.2
1887	26.1	2.9	3.7	31.5	3.1	5.4
1901	18.5	1.4	0.0	21.5	1.9	1.2
1913	18.9	3.1	7.0	15.8	2.1	4.2
1928	12.3	1.3	0.0	7.7	0.7	0.7
1947–8	7.1	0.8	1.2	6.5	0.7	1.0
1961–2	14.5	1.5	2.9	12.4	1.4	0.9
1976–7	29.8	4.9	9.7	26.5	5.2	12.8
1994–5	47.8	11.7	31.0	47.2	8.2	37.5

Notes: % partic. = the percentage of backbenchers participating in committees; Mean no.= the mean number of committees attended; % 20 + = the proportion of backbenchers attending 20 or more committee meetings.

In *quantitative* terms the extent to which government policy and its administration are subject to backbench scrutiny has increased enormously since the middle of the nineteenth century, if backbench

TABLE 7.6. *Number of meetings held and reports presented by departmental select committees, 1979–1997*

	Parliament			
	1979–83	1983–7	1987–92	1992–7
Meetings[a]	2,140	1,789	1,968	2,748
Reports[b]	193	218	323	366

[a] Meetings include sub-committee meetings.
[b] Reports exclude special reports, which are mostly government responses to substantive reports.

Source: House of Commons Sessional Returns.

activity generally is used as a measure. If the tabling of Questions for written answer and involvement in investigatory committees are used in particular, that extension of scrutiny is much more recent. A *qualitative* judgement is much more difficult to make: measuring the *impact* of parliamentary activity, other than where divisions determine the outcome, is at best a labyrinthine, at worst an impossible task. Certainly, anecdotal evidence can be brought to bear: no one doubts, for example, that the dramatic reduction in the normal Conservative majority on 8 May 1940 was a crucial factor in the subsequent resignation of Neville Chamberlain as Prime Minister. On a more mundane level the influence of the PAC as a check on financial probity and value for money in public expenditure has long been acknowledged, but particular select committee reports have been linked directly with subsequent government decisions. For instance, John Griffith and Michael Ryle, in their major study, *Parliament*, suggest twelve 'claimed successes' for the departmental committees[57] and other, similar successes, have been claimed by the Procedure Committee.[58] There is also little doubt that critical reports from select committees have contributed to important changes in the operation of the Child Support Agency. An alternative, more systematic approach, is to calculate the proportion of committee recommendations accepted by the government: studies

[57] John A. G. Griffith and Michael Ryle, *Parliament: Functions, Practice and Procedures*, Sweet and Maxwell, London, 1989, 430–3.
[58] Select Committee on Procedure, *Second Report*, HC 19-I, 1989–90, para. 358.

of the former Education, Science, and Arts and the Social Services Committees found that 26.5 and 35.1 per cent respectively of the recommendations made by the two committees in the 1979–83 Parliament were accepted, compared with the rejection of 27.1 and 19.7 per cent of recommendations. The remaining 46.4 and 45.2 per cent of recommendations were kept under review, which is in most cases what the committees had asked.[59] Such evidence is at best indicative rather than conclusive, and the impact of investigatory committees on policy is an area in need of further research.

In terms of the scrutiny role of the Member of Parliament, however, what is absolutely clear is that the involvement of back-benchers is now greater than it has ever been. The 'golden age' may be a myth, but it was nonetheless a period when the executive was far less dominant, when MPs had more scope for fulfilling the scrutiny role than for most of the period since. Yet the growth of parliamentary Questions, the creation of a comprehensive system of investigatory committees, and other changes, such as much-improved services and facilities, may not have shifted the balance between the executive and the legislature, but they have enhanced the scrutiny role far beyond what it was at the time of the Balfour reforms or, indeed, at the time of the 'golden age'. Governments are now subject to broader and deeper scrutiny than ever before; how effective it is remains a matter of opinion, but it means that the scrutiny role has become one of the major roles performed by the Member of Parliament.

The Constituency Role

In his book *Westminster Man*, Austin Mitchell (Labour MP for Grimsby since 1977) paints a portrait of the MP from the inside, but also brings to it the insights of a former academic and continuing journalist. The most frequently-quoted passage in the book is almost certainly that in which he describes the experience of one newly-elected Labour MP in 1950 returning to his constituency for the first time after his election:

[59] Michael Rush, 'The Education, Science and Arts Committee', and 'The Social Services Committee', in Drewry (ed.), *The New Select Committees*, 100 and 249.

A top-hatted stationmaster met him to ask whether he would be following the previous Member in paying his annual visit at that time of the year. A. V. Alexander [Labour MP for Sheffield-Hillsborough 1922–31 and 1950] hardly ever visited his Sheffield constituency during or after the war, producing such disgruntlement that his successor George Darling [Labour MP for Sheffield-Hillsborough 1950–February 1974] was selected on the radical promise of quarterly visits. When he was later appointed PPS to Arthur Bottomley, the constituency wrote to absolve him from that promise 'in the light of his heavy duties'.   (Austin Mitchell, *Westminster Man*, 183.)

Other references to annual visits to the constituency can certainly be found: a former Speaker, Viscount Ullswater, for example, recalls his 'annual visit to my constituents' in 1895.[60] He also recalls the case of C. H. Warton who, from the day of his election in 1880, 'never visited his constituents' in all the six years he was Member for Bridport.[61] That some MPs neglected their constituents, let alone seldom visited them, is not in dispute, but a more typical case is that of Sir Charles Dilke, when he was MP for the Forest of Dean (1892–1911): '. . . he usually went there three times a year: for a holiday at Whitsun; to work on the parliamentary register when the Revision Courts were in session in the autumn . . .; and to attend political meetings and the miners' rallies in winter'.[62] Certainly, Dilke acted in the interests of his constituents in promoting and supporting several attempts to pass the Miners (Eight Hours) Bill.[63] This relatively remote relationship with the constituency can also be found much more recently with Roy Jenkins and two of the constituencies he represented, the Stechford division of Birmingham (1950–77) and Glasgow-Hillhead (1982–7):

Looking back, I suppose that I was by modern standards . . . an old-style Member. I descended on the constituency for what was at first a weekend a month (although latterly it became more like a day a month), with one or sometimes two supplementary visits to fulfil specific engagements, and for a week in each September. But I was always careful not to cancel an

---

[60] Viscount Ullswater, *A Speaker's Commentaries*, Edward Arnold, London, 1925, Vol. 2, 249.

[61] Ibid., Vol. 1, 174.

[62] David Nichols, *The Lost Prime Minister: A Life of Sir Charles Dilke*, The Hambledon Press, London, 1995, 266.

[63] Ibid., 288.

engagement once it was accepted and never to give a blank refusal to a request for a visit, although frequently to juggle it into a time which suited me. I dealt meticulously by correspondence and advice bureaux interviews with individual cases, but I hardly ever raised constituency issues on the floor of the House of Commons. I rarely asked parliamentary Questions (except for an occasional supplementary to the Prime Minister or some other senior minister) or used adjournment debates. But I sometimes (and successfully) went to see ministers on constituency issues ... There [Hillhead] we [he and his wife] tried to spend at least one long weekend a month, as well as a September ten days supplemented by a lot of one-night visits by me alone.   (Roy Jenkins, *A Life at the Centre*, Macmillan, London, 1991, 81 and 571.)

A not dissimilar picture emerges in the case of Jennie Lee (Labour MP for North Lanark 1929–31 and for Cannock 1945–0), but with a crucial difference: 'Jennie visited the constituency [Cannock] every six to eight weeks (though during 1967–68 nine months went by without a visit to Cannock). In the late 1940s and 1950s, this was acceptable. Quarterly visits were not uncommon. However, expectations rose.'[64] But 'Jennie's ministerial work [as Minister for the Arts] was absorbing, her party work demanding. In consequence, she neglected Cannock. *She had never been an assiduous constituency MP*—in that respect she was not so very different from many MPs of her generation.'[65]

The most important part of these two accounts is not how often Roy Jenkins and Jennie Lee visited their constituents, but how much *attention* they paid to them and, crucially, *why*. What were the expectations of constituents? And to what extent have they changed and increased? In speaking in favour of the Irish Trade Bill in 1778, Edmund Burke went to considerable lengths to explain to his Bristol constituents, a number of whom opposed the bill, why he supported it.[66] This was not a Member ignoring his constituents, but responding to them, even though he disagreed with them. Burke was far from unusual in being faced with demands from constituents. Following food riots in Exeter in 1766, for instance, the City Chamber appealed to the city's two MPs 'to make strenuous efforts in Parliament to pursue "an

---

[64] Patricia Hollis, *Jennie Lee: A Life*, Oxford University Press, 1997, 373.
[65] Ibid., 371 (added italics).
[66] See *Parliamentary History*, T. C. Hansard, London, 1814, XIX, cc. 1100–24.

adequate remedy" '[67] Similarly, Bamber Gascoyne and his brother, Isaac Gascoyne, MPs for Liverpool from 1780 to 1796 and 1796 to 1831 respectively, regularly spoke and acted on behalf of their constituents, particularly in opposing the abolition of the slave trade and other matters relating to trade and commerce.[68] An earlier Liverpool MP, Sir Thomas Johnson (1701–23), 'especially watched Liverpool's interests in the Virginia tobacco trade.'[69] Porritt also cites the case of Birmingham in 1780:

Its manufacturers appealed to the Earl of Dartmouth, then Lord Keeper of the Privy Seal, and long connected with the County of Warwick, to help them in electing Sir Robert Lawley as one of the knights of the shire, because he was familiar with the industrial and commercial interests of Birmingham.   (Porritt, *The Unreformed House*, 263.)

Porritt later quotes Lord North, when Prime Minister: 'The representatives of the trading towns and manufacturing counties are fully apprised of the sentiments and wishes of their constituents.'[70] Indeed, MPs ran the risk that their constituents might be dissatisfied with their efforts: '. . . in 1818, William Hanbury, who had been one of the Members for Northampton in the two preceding Parliaments, was compelled to retire at the general election because he had not supported a Northampton petition against the Corn Bill.'[71]

MPs frequently promoted private bills on behalf of constituency interests. Townsend, for example, cites Isaac Gascoyne as claiming that he promoted two hundred such bills on behalf of Liverpool[72] and in 1832, in response to a cholera epidemic, the local Improvement Commission in Exeter sought new powers through a

[67] Robert Newton, *Eighteenth Century Exeter*, University of Exeter Press, Exeter, 1984, 73.

[68] See Sir Lewis Namier and John Brooke, *The History of Parliament: The House of Commons, 1754–1790*, HMSO for the History of Parliament Trust, London, 1964, Vol. 1, 492; and R. G. Thorne, *The History of Parliament: The House of Commons, 1790–1820*, Secker and Warburg for the History of Parliament Trust, London, 1980, Vol. 4, 9–13.

[69] Edward Porritt, *The Unreformed House of Commons: Parliamentary Representation Before 1832*, Cambridge University Press, Cambridge, 1909, Vol. 1, 262.

[70] Ibid., 278.

[71] Ibid., 277.

[72] Townsend, *History of the House of Commons: From the Convention Parliament of 1688 to the Passing of the Reform Bill in 1832*, Henry Colburn, London, 1843., Vol. 2, 380.

private bill, which 'was passed with the assistance of the city's two Members of Parliament'.[73] Constituency interests and considerations undoubtedly played an important part in voting behaviour in the mid-nineteenth century, although often coinciding with party interests as well.[74]

Another area in which constituents made demands of MPs was for jobs, sinecures, and pensions in the gift of the government. In a letter written after the repeal of the Corn Laws in 1846, in which he had been prominently involved, Richard Cobden (Liberal MP for Stockport) complained, 'I thought I should be allowed to be forgotten after my address to my constituents. But every post brings me twenty or thirty letters—and such letters! I am teased to death by place-hunters of every degree . . .'[75] The publication of the Northcote–Trevelyan Report on the civil service in 1854 and the consequent appointment of a Civil Service Commission in 1855, began the process of removing patronage as the principal means of recruiting civil servants, although ministerial patronage remained the norm until open competition was introduced in 1870.

That MPs should be faced with demands from their constituents and respond to them is hardly surprising: the tradition of territorial representation is directly related to the origins of Parliament and, however much it may have been shaped by the limits of the franchise and distorted by electoral corruption, it remained for many MPs a significant factor. Moreover, significant proportions of MPs—a majority, in fact, in the middle of the nineteenth century— had direct connections with the constituencies they represented, often sharing economic interests with many of their constituents.[76]

[73] Newton, *Eighteenth Century Exeter*, 162.
[74] See William O. Ayedelotte, 'Voting patterns in the British House of Commons', *Comparative Studies in Society and History*, 2, 1963, 134–63; and William O. Ayedelotte, 'Constituency Influence in the British House of Commons', in Ayedelotte (ed.), *The History of Parliamentary Behaviour*, 225–46.
[75] Quoted in Michael MacDonagh, *Parliament: Its Romance, Its Comedy, Its Pathos*, T. Fisher Unwin, London, 1904, 68. For a more detailed account of patronage see Porritt, *The Unreformed House*, Vol. 1, ch. 15.
[76] Porritt says, for example, that '[k]nights of the shire all through the history of the old representative system were resident in the counties for which they were elected, or were prominently identified with the counties they served.' *The Unreformed House*, Vol. 1, 261. Local connections in boroughs were less common, especially in 'pocket' or 'rotten' boroughs.

TABLE 7.7. *Incidence of direct constituency connections among MPs in selected years, 1868–1997 (%)*

Election	Cons.	Lab.	Lib./LD	All
1868	66.9	—	48.3	56.5
1874	61.2	—	45.3	54.1
1880	60.7	—	47.8	52.2
1885	47.6	—	42.0	44.1
1900	31.2	0.0	25.7	30.1
1918	28.2	46.4	31.8	31.1
1945	25.1	30.7	25.0	28.6
1979	14.2	36.2	45.5	24.8
1997	9.1	56.9	65.2	45.0

Note: Direct connections are defined as being born, educated, living, or working in the constituency; having property interests or serving or having served as a member of a local government body in the constituency, or, in the case of towns or cities divided into two or more constituencies, with the town or city within which the constituency lies.

The figures in Table 7.7 show several interesting patterns, especially the very high proportion of Conservative MPs with direct constituency connections between 1868 and 1880, followed by a dramatic fall in 1885, almost certainly largely the consequence of the severe agricultural depression of the 1880s and beyond. The lower but still high proportion of Liberal MPs with direct connections in the same period in part reflects landed interests, but it also reflects considerable local industrial and commercial interests in the towns and cities represented by Liberals. By the turn of the century direct connections had fallen below a third overall and gradually fell to about a quarter, although they remained higher among Labour MPs. The incidence of direct constituency connections is a function of political recruitment and, while it does not delineate the constituency role, the latter often plays an important part in the selection of candidates. In choosing candidates, local parties have become increasingly mindful of the constituency role and would-be candidates with a direct constituency are often seen as an advantage, both electorally and once elected. This can be seen in periodic Liberal/Liberal Democrat revivals and by-election successes from the mid-fifties onwards, which have tended to bring in more Members with direct connections—although the numbers involved were small until 1997—predicated in part in the belief that a local candidate will attract electoral support and make a 'good constituency Member'. Of greater interest, however, is the marked increase in the proportion of Labour MPs with direct connections in 1979 and since. The proportion rose throughout the 1980s and beyond, peaking between 1987 and 1992—excluding the 1992 general election—when no fewer than 69 per cent of those first elected in that period had direct connections. In many cases these were individuals with local government experience in the constituency, which, it is likely, local selectors thought would be valuable in dealing with constituency issues once elected to Parliament.

What, then, has changed with the constituency role? The answer is, in two important respects—in scale and scope. Some measure of this can be seen by examining the extent to which constituency issues are raised in debates or through parliamentary Questions.

The data shown in Table 7.8 must necessarily seen as indicating *minimum* levels of constituency activity by backbench MPs, since raising constituency issues in Parliament is, for most MPs, not the commonest way of dealing with such matters. Contact with ministers, formal or informal, and with government departments has long been the normal practice. Indeed, the figures are evidence of this in that, apart from 1871 and 1994–5, a higher proportion of opposition than government backbenchers raised constituency issues in Parliament. More generally, the data are incontrovertible evidence of Members dealing with constituency matters, that the practice was already widespread by latter part of the nineteenth century, and that for all intents and purposes has become universal. That it has become universal is supported by the fact that virtually all MPs hold regular 'surgeries' to enable constituents to raise matters personally with them: in 1963 Robert Dowse found that 84.1 per cent of MPs, including ministers, held constituency surgeries;[77] and a replication of this research by Barker and Rush found that 90.7 per cent of MPs, excluding ministers, held surgeries, with most others seeing constituents by appointment.[78]

---

[77] Robert E. Dowse, ' The MP and his surgery', *Political Studies*, 11, 1963, 334.
[78] Barker and Rush, *The MP and His Information.*, Appendix 3, Table 18.

TABLE 7.8. Proportion of backbench MPs raising constituency issues in Parliament, 1871–1997 (%)

Party	1871	1887	1901	1913	1928	1946–7	1961–2	1976–7	1994–5
Cons.	9.6	31.8	34.8	47.5	45.6	84.5	75.4	89.3	85.7
Lib/LD	11.7	43.5	55.2	44.5	55.8	65.0	85.7	100.0	100.0
Lab.	–	–	100.0	60.0	76.2	75.2	88.9	84.4	86.9
Irish N.	100.0	89.4	89.0	61.9	–	–	–	–	–
All	11.2	45.2	50.1	49.8	54.5	78.2	81.2	87.3	86.6

Source: Hansard indexes for each year.

Two other measures illustrate the change in scale of the constituency role—the number of letters MPs receive from their constituents and the consequent correspondence MPs have with ministers. Writing in 1958, Peter Richards suggested that the average number of letters received by a Member on *all* matters was between twelve and twenty a week;[79] in 1967 Barker and Rush found that 45.5 per cent of MPs received fifty or more letters a week from constituents, with nearly a fifth receiving seventy-five or more;[80] in 1986 a Letter Writing Bureau survey 'found that the typical MP received between twenty and fifty letters *a day*, with more than half coming from constituents.'[81] And Philip Norton notes that in 'the mid-1960s, 10,000 items of mail arrived at the Palace of Westminster every week. By the mid-1990s, the number was 40,000 *per day*.'[82] Correspondence between ministers tells a similar story: Chester and Bowring estimated that in 1908 Members' letters to ministers amounted to no more than 'a few thousand', whereas in 1947–8 'well over 100,000 Members' letters were handled by ministers';[83] in 1990 the Cabinet Office Efficiency Unit 'found that ministers answered 250,000 letters a year, most of them from MPs.'[84]

The enormous expansion of the constituency role cannot be doubted, but there has also been an enormous change in its scope. Leaving aside pleas for jobs and the like, it would be misleading to suggest that MPs in the nineteenth century and earlier did not receive requests or demands from individual constituents. The nineteenth century *Hansard* indexes show cases being taken up by MPs. These involved a wide variety of matters, such as dismissal from posts in the public service, the provision of pensions to particular individuals, taxation disputes, various cases involving members of the army and navy, and frequently, criminal cases. The Irish Nationalists were particularly active in raising the latter, but

[79] Peter Richards, *Honourable Members: A Study of the British Backbencher*, Faber, London, 1959, 171.

[80] Barker and Rush, *The MP and His Information*, Appendix 3, Table 15.

[81] Cited by Griffith and Ryle, *Parliament*, 72.

[82] Philip Norton, 'The individual Member in the British House of Commons', *The Journal of Legislative Studies*, 5, 1999, 55.

[83] Chester and Bowring, *Questions in Parliament*, 105.

[84] Philip Norton, 'The growth of the constituency role of the MP', *Parliamentary Affairs*, 47, 1994, 711.

they were far from alone. More generally, however, the most common issues at this time arose from *collective* constituency interests, related to trade, industry, commerce, agriculture, and employment. With the development of postal, telegraph, and telephone services, these too figured prominently in the constituency matters raised by Members. However, even during the last quarter of the nineteenth century, some constituencies made few demands on their MPs: St John Brodrick (Conservative MP for Surrey West 1880–5 and Surrey South-West of Guildford 1885–1906, later Earl of Midleton) says of Arthur Balfour's early years in Parliament, 'His constituency was negligible, while many MPs were pressed for wearisome functions on every free evening.'[85] The experience of other MPs was different: Sir Alfred Pease, when Liberal MP for York in 1890, recalls, 'I made it a rule to answer with my own pen every letter from my constituents, and on occasion had some forty to write a day, these extra duties were a trial'[86] and Brodrick himself remarks that, in April 1901 when he was Under Secretary of State for War, '. . . as I went through the division lobby . . . [there were] . . . ten or twelve MPs waiting in a queue to buttonhole me on personal questions connected with their constituents or local corps in South Africa, on which they desired some action taken.'[87] It is also worth noting that both St John Brodrick and James Lowther believed that their attention to constituency demands helped in securing their re-election and, in Brodrick's case, to his defeat in 1906 because the demands of his later Cabinet post led to 'the necessary curtailment of such duties'.[88] In this context, whether it did or not is less important than that they believed it.

[85] The Earl of Midleton, *Records and Reactions, 1856–1939*, John Murray, London, 1939, 113. Balfour's first constituency was Hertford (1874–85), then largely under the control of his uncle, Lord Salisbury, who owned many of the houses in the constituency and whose influence would have obviated constituency demands on the Member. In 1874 it had only 1,041 constituents and in 1880 1081 (F. W. S. Craig, *British Parliamentary Elections Results 1832–1885*, Macmillan, London, 1977, 153).

[86] Sir Alfred E. Pease, *Elections and Recollections*, John Murray, London, 1932, 257.

[87] Midleton, *Records and Reactions.*, 127. It is worth noting that this led Joseph Chamberlain to remark, 'How can you administer the War Office and reply in the House, if you waste time on such trifles', to which Brodrick replied, 'I pointed out that . . . my Parliamentary Private Secretary . . . dealt with scores of such questions, but some MPs declined to accept anything unless the minister himself gave it attention.'

[88] Midleton, *Records and Reactions*, 46–7; and Ullswater, Commentaries, Vol. 2, 16.

However, it was growing government intervention that had the most significant impact on the constituency role, intervention that affected particular collective interests, but more especially intervention that impinged directly on the individual. In particular, the introduction of the old age pension in 1909 and sickness and unemployment benefits in 1911 resulted in MPs taking up individual cases with ministers. The 1909 *Hansard* index contains 157 named pension cases, that of 1910 251, falling to fifty-three in 1913. The national insurance benefits produced similar listings and the number of cases increased yet further during and after the First World War. Soon after his election in 1918 as MP for Watford, Sir Denis Herbert (later Lord Hemingford) found that '[I]ndustrial troubles, and demobilisation matters, kept me busy in the constituency. In the House, I contented myself mostly with a few Questions, usually resulting from affairs in the constituency.'[89] Further intervention in the interwar period, increasingly including housing matters, added to constituency demands, which grew yet more with the creation of a fully-fledged welfare state. The scale and scope of the constituency role were now beyond the imaginings of the nineteenth or earlier twentieth century MP. And it created a dilemma for many Members, well-illustrated by the advice given to Jennie Lee soon after she was first elected for North Lanark in 1929:

[James] Maxton [ILP MP for Glasgow-Bridgeton 1922–46], seeing her struggling with a huge pile of letters, told her she had better make up her mind whether she was going to be a socialist MP or 'another bloody welfare worker'. That was bad advice (and advice Jennie passed on many years later to the young Joan Lestor, who had the sense to ignore it). It fuelled suspicions in North Lanark that she was more interested in building a national career for herself than in looking after the constituency. Many years later the same allegation was to cost her Cannock.[90]

Patricia Hollis later elaborates on Jennie Lee's attitude towards the constituency role:

Constituency work she regarded as drudgery, a political version of housework, which she also ignored. Although Jennie happily, and effectively on behalf of Cannock, engaged in the parliamentary bills and debates on coal,

---

[89] Lord Hemingford, *Backbencher and Chairman: Some Parliamentary Reminiscences*, John Murray, London, 1946, 13.
[90] Hollis, *Jennie Lee*, 37.

a not undemanding territory, she took no pleasure from her constituency work and cut corners when she could.   (Hollis, *Jennie Lee*, 133.)

The constituency role, especially its 'welfare officer' element, is now taken for granted by Member and constituent alike, but Jennie Lee was far from being the first MP to resent it and find it irksome. In the middle of the nineteenth century Todd noted that,

ministers of the Crown have generally preferred to represent small boroughs, on account of the comparative immunity thereby obtained from the incessant demands upon their time and attention on behalf of their constituents, which are so great a tax upon Members who represent populous constituencies.   (Todd, *Parliamentary Government*, Vol. 1, 14.)

On a more idiosyncratic note, according to his PPS, Sir Michael Hicks-Beach (then Chancellor of the Exchequer and MP for Bristol West) 'had a peculiar hatred for his constituents' and refused to see any that came to Westminster.[91] Some thirty or so years later, Henry Snell (Labour MP for Woolwich East 1922–9, later Lord Snell) complained in his memoirs:

One of the chief torments of a Member's life is the answering of letters, most of which should never have been written . . . No inconsiderable number of the British public appear to think that the chief duty of a Member of Parliament is to attend to their personal claims, and that he should always place these before the needs of the nation.   (Lord Snell, *Men, Movements and Myself*, J. M. Dent, London, 1936, 213.)

Even more recently, Barker and Rush found 11.9 per cent of their respondents agreeing with the view 'the "welfare officer role" has been taken too far'.[92] There are doubtless those who still resent, if not the demands of constituents, certainly the pressures that the constituency role creates.

A final measure of the growth of the constituency role can be found in the surveys conducted on behalf of the TSRB/SSRB between 1971 and 1996—see Tables 5.2 and 5.3. The 1971 survey found that during the parliamentary session constituency work accounted for rather less than a fifth of the hours worked by MPs (17.9 per cent); in 1982 it was nearly a fifth (19.4 per cent)—it had been 21.5 per cent in 1978; but by 1996 it had increased to two-

---

[91] Sir Arthur Griffith-Boscawen, *Memories*, 39–40.
[92] Barker and Rush, *The MP and His Information*, Appendix 3, Table 22.

fifths during the session and to as much as three-fifths during recesses. A survey conducted by members of the SPG suggests that constituency work now occupies more of a Member's time than any other single activity.[93]

Whatever else may be said about it, the constituency role looms large, but, as one of the roles performed by MPs, it should not be seen as a recent phenomenon. It was present before the Reform Act of 1832, it was by no means insignificant during the rest of the nineteenth century, and grew considerably as government intervention increased in range and volume, as a result of which the demands of individual constituents—the 'welfare officer role'—grew apace, not displacing but adding to the collective demands of the constituency.

Conclusion

The partisan, scrutiny, and constituency roles have all developed and changed since the middle of the nineteenth century. Each recognizably existed then, as now. Some Members may be more active in one role than another—and, indeed, have preferences for one more than another—virtually all Members are engaged in each role. A few may spend all or most of their political careers as MPs on the frontbench, in government or opposition—that has long been so. Moreover, the opportunities to serve on the frontbench have increased markedly, but most serve either exclusively as backbenchers or have careers divided between frontbench and backbench. They may see their roles as Members of Parliament differently at different stages of their careers and change their views in the light of experience. How they see the balance between the partisan, scrutiny, and constituency roles and whether they are perceived as complementary, separate, or conflicting is the subject of the final chapter.

---

[93] Unpublished research by the Study of Parliament Group, supported by ESRC Award No. R000222470.

8

From Gentlemen to Players: Complementary, Separate or Conflicting Roles?

From Gentleman to Players

The gentlemen have become players. From being an unpaid and, for the overwhelming majority, part-time job, the position of Member of Parliament has become fully-paid and full-time. Those who held ministerial posts or positions on the opposition front-bench in the nineteenth century and for much the twentieth were, at least as long as they held such positions, full-time politicians in the sense that it was their principal activity. This was also true of some backbenchers, but, in terms of demands, being a backbench MP was not a full-time occupation. However, increasingly it became their principal activity, with other work being in addition to their parliamentary duties, often as a necessary means of supplementing their income. But for most early Labour Members being an MP was their only occupation and it was eventually for them that the payment of MPs was introduced. Before 1912 private wealth, an occupational compatible with the demands of member-ship of the House of Commons, the financial support of a party—as in the case of the Irish Nationalists and some ILP Members—or a trade union, or earlier, of a wealthy patron, were a necessity. Even after 1912, MPs with no other source of income did not find it financially easy, not least because, until the late 1960s, the absence of a clear distinction between the parliamentary salary and the expenses of carrying out parliamentary duties meant that much of the cost of being a Member of Parliament could, at best, only be set against tax.

As governmental activities expanded, so the demands on Parliament and therefore MPs grew. The House of Commons adapted its procedures and political parties became more organised inside and outside Westminster, processes which were virtually complete by the beginning of the twentieth century—Labour MPs and the Labour Party simply adapted to the norms they found on their arrival on the parliamentary scene. Inside Westminster this meant increasing party cohesion: MPs were expected and them-selves expected to support their parties in the division lobbies. For government backbenchers the partisan role increasingly demanded their presence more than their participation; for most opposition frontbenchers and backbenchers much of their parliamentary activity consisted of a partisan critique of the government. In this sense the partisan role can be said to be the dominant role. As such, it demands relatively little in the way of resources, particularly for individual backbenchers, although for opposition frontbenchers and, to a lesser extent, opposition backbenchers, the importance of information with which to combat the massive resources available to ministers cannot be underestimated.

As the partisan role grew, so the scrutiny role declined. In the second half of the nineteenth century ministers were subject to much parliamentary scrutiny through debates and select commit-tees and, increasingly, parliamentary Questions, but it was haphaz-ard and unsystematic, depending on the whim of the opposition frontbench and individual backbenchers. That it could be focused and systematic was vividly illustrated by the activities of the Irish Nationalists and the Fourth Party, but neither acted in the name of parliamentary scrutiny: the former used the House of Commons as a legitimate—some would say illegitimate—means to a political end and the latter were fulfilling a partisan role that they believed their leaders in the Commons were performing inadequately.

The use of parliamentary Questions, particularly those for writ-ten answer, as a means of scrutiny, developed remarkably slowly and Question Time, especially Prime Minister's Questions, became more and more part of the partisan role. This is not to dismiss parti-san scrutiny as unimportant—exposing the government to ideo-logical criticism has long been part of representative government in general and parliamentary government in particular—but to high-light the extent to which the calling of the government to account

became increasingly subordinated to the demands of governments
supported by single-party majorities in the House Commons—the
essence of the partisan role. To be sure, committee activity increased,
but it was largely in the form of legislative committees, dominated
by party; investigatory committee activity actually declined and was
not revived until demands for more effective parliamentary scrutiny
began to surface in the late 1950s and early 1960s. These elicited a
tentative and cautious response that did not culminate in a comprehensive system of investigatory committee until 1979.

It was, not surprisingly given the growth of government, the
constituency role that saw the most dramatic increase in the
demands on MPs. But even here there was a time lag, both of
constituents' demands and, more particularly, of the extent to
which MPs responded to them. Members have long taken up the
collective interests of their constituents and dealing with the
demands of individual constituents, Cobden's place-hunters aside,
was by no means unusual in the later nineteenth century, but it is
the sheer scale and scope of the constituency role that has changed.

There can be no doubt that the demands of the constituency role
and widespread belief among many MPs that their ability, both
individually and collectively, to subject the executive to effective
parliamentary scrutiny was seriously curtailed, were important
factors in bringing about improvements in pay and resources. The
separation of pay from expenses and the introduction of much-
improved services and facilities have professionalised the role of
the Member of Parliament. Successive surveys conducted on behalf
of the TSRB/SSRB have shown that British MPs are in the middle of
the international legislative league in terms of pay and resources,
but, more importantly, that the general tendency is towards full-
time, professional legislatures, a trend which is also widely true of
sub-national legislatures.[1]

---

[1] See Michael Rush, 'The pay, allowances, services and facilities of legislators in
eighteen countries and the European Parliament' and Tom Stark, 'International
comparisons of the remuneration of Members of Parliament' in Senior Salaries Review
Body, *Report No. 38: Review of Parliamentary Pay and Allowances*, Vol. 2: Surveys and
Studies, Cm. 3330-II, July 1996, 38–59, and 60–68 respectively. See also Michael Rush,
'The pay, allowances, services and facilities of legislators in sub-national legislatures' in
Senior Salaries Review Body, *Report No. 47: Initial Pay, Allowances, Pensions and Severance
Arrangements for Members of the Scottish Parliament, National Assembly of Wales and
Northern Ireland Assembly*, Cm. 4188, March 1999, 87–105.

The Member's View

Research conducted by the Study of Parliament Group throws some light on how Members see their various roles.[2] Who do MPs see themselves as representing? In order to answer this question MPs were asked: 'In carrying out your role as a representative, which of the following do you think are the more important—the nation as a whole, my constituents, my party?'—and asked to place them in rank order.

An initial interpretation of Table 8.1 might suggest that the Burkean concept of the Member of Parliament as representing the interests of the nation is not widely subscribed to by the modern MP, especially Labour MPs, but this is to take the figures too literally. Certainly, they suggest that the Burkean view is more strongly held by Conservative—and members of other parties—than by Labour MPs; nor, given their respective party histories, is it surprising to find that representing the party is more strongly felt by Labour Members. However, they do not necessarily mean that the views of constituents prevail over the national interest, since in the mind of the individual MP they may more often coincide than conflict, as, indeed, may nation, constituency and party.[3] What is of particular interest in assessing Members' views of their role is the prominence of representing constituents, on the one hand, and the widespread recognition that nation and party are an integral part of the spectrum of representation.

A further question then sought to explore which of various aspects of the job of being an MP respondents thought the most important. These were:

---

[2] Questionnaires sent to MPs in 1994 and 1999 as part of an SPG study of the socialisation of MPs, supported by the Nuffield Foundation Small Grant Scheme and the ESRC (Award No. R000222470). The main focus of the research is on MPs first elected in 1992 and 1997, to whom a series of questionnaires have been sent at intervals. However, the responses reported here relate to questionnaires sent to the 1992 intake in 1994 and the 1997 intake in 1999, together with a questionnaire sent to control groups of longer-serving MPs in each year. The response rates for the four questionnaires were 49.6 per cent, 31.2 per cent, 56.0 per cent, and 30.1 per cent respectively. No distinction is drawn here between either group of MPs, newly-elected or longer-serving, and none of those surveyed in 1994 were involved in the 1999 survey.

[3] For a discussion of the Burkean concept and the modern MP see David Judge, 'Representation in Westminster in the 1990s: the Ghost of Edmund Burke, *Journal of Legislative Studies*, 5, 1999, 12–34.

TABLE 8.1: *MPs' views of their representative role, 1994 and 1999*

A. *Rank order*

| Represent | 1994 | | | 1999 | | |
	Cons.	Lab.	All	Cons.	Lab.	All
Nation	2	3	2	2	3	2
Constituents	1	1	1	1	1	1
Party	3	2	3	3	2	3

B. *% ranking first*

| Represent | 1994 | | | 1997 | | |
	Cons.	Lab.	All	Cons.	Lab.	All
Nation	40.4	11.1	21.7	40.0	9.3	16.3
Constituents	48.9	63.5	64.2	55.0	71.3	68.4
Party	2.1	14.3	8.3	2.5	12.4	9.7
N	47	63	122	40	129	196

Note: The rank order was calculated by summing the preferential scores for each respondent.

(1) 'scrutiny or keeping a check on the government and the civil service';
(2) 'supporting my party and helping it achieve its policy objectives';
(3) 'influencing or changing my party's policy' and
(4) 'helping constituents with their problems/dealing with constituency issues'.

Again, respondents were asked to place these in rank order.

The constituency role again looms large in Table 8.2—ranked first by all MPs in both 1994 and 1999, though dropping to second among Conservatives in 1999, but this reflects a shift in Conservative views on the scrutiny role. Similarly, as with the representative role, the partisan role is more strongly supported by Labour than Conservative MPs, but it is notable that the proportion of

TABLE 8.2: *The most important part of the job of being an MP, 1994 and 1999*

A. *Rank order*

Pt. of job	1994			1999		
	Cons.	Lab.	All MPs	Cons.	Lab.	All MPs
Constit.	1	1	1	2	1	1
Influ. pol.	2	4	4	4	4	4
Supp. pty.	3	2	2=	3	2	3
Scrutiny	4	3	2=	1	3	2

B. *% of MPs ranking helping constituents/dealing with constituency issues first or second*

Party	1994	1999
Conservative	60.5	76.9
Labour	71.2	78.6
All MPs	64.7	80.2

C. *% of MPs ranking supporting their party first or second*

Party	1994	1999
Conservative	42.9	30.8
Labour	54.9	61.5
All MPs	48.7	50.5

D. *% of MPs ranking parliamentary scrutiny first or second*

Party	1994	1999
Conservative	31.7	82.0
Labour	45.8	35.0
All MPs	42.5	50.5

Conservatives placing party first or second is lower in 1999 compared with 1994 and, conversely, higher among Labour Members in 1999 than in 1994. This may well be an example of the government-opposition dichotomy, rather than a simple party difference. This view is reinforced by that fact that the scrutiny role was ranked fourth by Conservatives in 1994, but first in 1999, with a massive difference between those placing it first or second. In contrast, although the difference is less dramatic, Labour respondents showed less support for the scrutiny role in 1999. One difference that may be the product of events at the time is the second ranking of seeking to influence or change party policy among the 1994 respondents – possibly a reflection of divisions over Europe that wracked the Conservative Party in the 1992–97 Parliament.

The third question in the SPG survey that throws some light on Members' views of their role asked respondents, 'In deciding how to act and vote in Parliament are you strongly influenced by

(1) the advice of your party leadership?
(2) your own personal opinions?
(3) constituency opinion?
(4) representations from interest or pressure groups?

The data in Table 8.3 provide a crucial context to the responses to the three earlier questions. Not surprisingly, pressure groups play very little part in influencing Members' behaviour, but what stands out most sharply is that constituency opinion falls far behind personal and party opinion. Furthermore, although MPs do not always agree with their parties, their personal opinions are, nonetheless, likely to be broadly in line with those of the party. In short, the responses support the analysis of the partisan, scrutiny and constituency roles presented in Chapter 7: that the partisan role explains much of the parliamentary activity of Members, with the scrutiny role playing a secondary but still important part, leaving the constituency role as a distinct and often separate role.

Complementary, Conflicting or Separate Roles?

Even analytically it is not always possible to say which of the three major roles performed by MPs is actually being carried out. Voting, apart from free votes and the occasional rebellion, is the partisan

TABLE 8.3: *Influences on MPs' parliamentary behaviour, 1994 and 1999*

A. *Rank order*

Influenced by	1994			1997		
	Cons.	Lab.	All MPs	Cons.	Lab.	All MPs
Leadership	1	1	1	2	1	1
Personal opinion	2	2	2	1	2	2
Constit. Opinion	3	3	3	3	3	3
Pressure groups	4	4	4	4	4	4

B. *% replying 'nearly always' or 'usually'*

Influenced by	1994			1997		
	Cons.	Lab.	All MPs	Cons.	Lab.	All MPs
Leadership	85.1	82.9	83.2	72.5	89.9	86.5
Personal opinion	63.8	67.1	67.9	77.5	80.6	81.3
Constit. Opinion	38.3	41.4	41.2	40.0	44.2	42.5
Pressure groups	4.2	1.4	0.8	0.0	6.2	5.2
N	47	70	131	40	129	193

role in its purest form, but even fulfilling the constituency role may be influenced by partisan considerations in terms of the issue taken up and the vigour with which particular cases or issues may be pursued. Nevertheless, it is the constituency role that is the most distinct or separate. For the most part, MPs deal with constituency issues and cases in a non-partisan manner, seeing themselves as Members of Parliament rather than members of a party. Constituency matters, especially individual cases, are most commonly dealt with in private rather than public and impinge on Members' overt parliamentary activity only to a limited extent. Aspects of the scrutiny role, notably much select committee activity, are also conducted in a largely non-partisan fashion. Conversely, some scrutiny is highly partisan in form and context, most obviously at Question Time, whether ideologically critical or sycophantic, but much partisan scrutiny also complements rather than conflicts with non-partisan scrutiny. The constituency role may operate largely separately, but it complements both the partisan and scrutiny roles by keeping Members in touch with what is happening outside Westminster and, particular, where the policy shoe pinches.

Yet there is also an inevitable conflict between the three roles. This conflict takes three distinct forms. First, there is a practical conflict stemming from the constituency role, the demands of which have increased to an extent that it can be argued that MPs spend so much time dealing with constituency casework that they neglect, if not the partisan, certainly the scrutiny role. British MPs are not alone in having to deal with demands from those they are elected to represent, but it is a burden that varies from one political system to another. This is partly because of different traditions of representation and types of electoral system and partly because it tends to be heavier in single-member rather than multi-member constituencies. There is, however, another dimension—the extent to which there are two or more levels of representation. All liberal democracies have at least two levels of elected representatives—the national and the local, but some have an intermediate or regional level. Most of these are federal systems, but there has also been a growth in the number of political systems that are not formally or constitutionally federal, but do have some form of elected regional representation.

Proposals have been made for a reduction in the number of MPs in the Westminster Parliament, usually with a concomitant proposal that the resources thus released be used to provide better services and facilities for the smaller number of MPs. For instance, in 2000 the Conservative Party Commission to Strengthen Parliament suggested this should be a longer-term objective, after its specific recommendations had been implemented. It also made a specific recommendation that the number of MPs appointed to ministerial office should be reduced.[4]

Historically, the number of MPs was determined by the medieval formula of two Members per county and two Members per city or

---

[4] Conservative Party, *Report of the Commission to Strengthen Parliament*, London, July 2000, 57–8 and 64. See also Peter Riddell, *Parliament Under Blair*, Politico's Books, London, 2000, 225–6.

borough. Subsequently, more boroughs acquired the right to return MPs, sometimes two Members, sometimes one, but this was a haphazard process, sometimes simply being granted by the Crown as a means of raising money. Representation was not therefore linked proportionately to population, nor, except for two extra seats being given to Yorkshire in 1826, was any account taken of population movements until the redistribution of constituencies associated with each of the Reform Acts, starting in 1832. As early as the end of the reign of Elizabeth I, in 1603, the House of Commons had a membership of 460,[5] with more Members being added following the union with Scotland in 1707 and Ireland in 1800, realising a total of 658. Since then the number has varied between 615 and 670, the current number being 659.[6] Thus, whereas the population of the UK grew from nearly sixteen million in 1801 to more than fifty-nine million in 1998, the number of MPs has changed little over the same period. A similar phenomenon can be found in other countries. The United States' House of Representatives, for example, originally increased in size as the population increased, but since 1929 the number of Representatives has been fixed at 435. However, a direct comparison with the House of Commons is misleading, since it takes no account of the fact that the United States is a federal system, with extensive elected representation being provided through the state legislatures. If, where appropriate, account is taken of intermediate or regional levels of representation then, in comparison with many other countries, the British population is under-represented in terms of population per legislator. Compared therefore with other members of the European Union and with countries like Australia, Canada, New Zealand, Japan and the United States, only the Japanese are worse off than

[5] At the end of the reign of Edward I (1307), the House of Commons had 234 Members; on the death of Edward IV (1483), there were 296 and there was no increase under Richard III (1483–85) or Henry VII (1485–1509). However, between 1509 and 1603, there was an increase of 55.4 per cent, making the Tudor period that of greatest expansion—see Ken Powell and Chris Cook, *English Historical Facts 1485–1603*, Macmillan, London, 1977, 83–5. See also Chris Cook and John Stevenson, *British Political Facts 1688–1760*, Macmillan, London, 1988, 96–7.

[6] This excludes the short period between 1918 and the partition of Ireland, when the total was 707, but, following the general election of 1918, the 69 Sinn Fein MPs refused to take their seats.

the British.[7] Of course, the setting up of the Scottish Parliament and the National Assembly for Wales and the restoration of the Northern Ireland Assembly has improved the level of representation in the UK, but only for those parts of the UK concerned and taking no account of the fact that, proportionately, Scotland and Wales are already over-represented at Westminster.

Although there is nothing sacrosanct about the number of MPs, a reduction in their number would mean the same burden of work being shared among fewer Members. Of course, as people, especially in Scotland and Wales, get used to devolution, that burden may lessen, but not for MPs representing English constituencies and the logic of devolution is for there to be fewer Scottish and Welsh Members, not fewer generally. Additional resources would undoubtedly help, but may in turn be offset by a further growth in demands from constituents, which show no signs of decline. Either way, fewer MPs or better resources, it might make the use of resources more efficient if, as is the case in a number of countries, a proportion of them were specifically allocated to support the constituency role. These electorate allowances have the advantage of being directed at particular needs and the added flexibility of being proportionate to the number of electors represented. A case can also be made for an additional electorate allowance for MPs with a higher than normal constituency caseload resulting from the nature of the constituency. What is surely clear is that, unless offset by improved resources, an increase in the constituency burden will undermine the ability of Members to fulfil the scrutiny role.

There is a second practical conflict that affects the scrutiny role: by definition, ministers cannot be expected to act as a check on the executive, as scrutinisers of the exercise of their ministerial responsibilities. This is why reducing the number of ministers has its attractions: it would reduce in size the 'payroll vote' of MPs bound to the partisan role by collective responsibility; it would make more Members available to share the scrutiny role, especially in manning select committees—one of the disadvantages of an overall reduction

---

[7] See Michael Rush, 'The Pay, Allowances, Services and Facilities of Legislators in Eighteen Countries and the European Parliament: A Comparative Survey' in Senior Salaries Review Body, *Report No. 38*, Cm. 3330-II, July 1996, paras. 7–11 and Annex, Table 1.

in the number of MPs); and it would release resources that could be used to improve services and facilities for backbench MPs. This process would be further assisted if the number of Parliamentary Private Secretaries, the MPs who act as unpaid aides to ministers were also significantly reduced: in 1900 a mere nine MPs were PPSs, in 1999 the number was 47.

The third type of conflict is more generic than practical: ultimately the partisan and scrutiny roles are incompatible. If all backbench activity in Parliament is focused on the partisan role, then effective scrutiny becomes impossible; if all backbench activity in Parliament is devoted to the scrutiny role, the myth of 'the golden age' of Parliament might become a reality, but government a virtual impossibility. There has to be a balance between the partisan and scrutiny roles, between the need to establish and sustain a government in office and the need to render that government accountable to the electorate between elections. This, in turn, depends on the attitudes of Members of Parliament: 'my party might or wrong' is fatal to accountability, but governments must be able to govern; MPs must be prepared to use their undoubted powers of scrutiny, but not to the point of destruction. There is another side to this coin—the attitude of the government. A government supported by a party majority is not only normally secure in office from one election to the next, but can normally secure the passage of its programme through Parliament—the House of Lords notwithstanding). The reality of parliamentary government is that the government normally controls Parliament and the effectiveness of parliamentary scrutiny therefore rests as much on the attitude of the goverbnment as it does on backbench MPs. Organisational and procedural changes may help, but ultimately it is a matter of attitude and the eloquent and succinct words of Bernard Crick remain as true now as they did when he first penned them in 1963:

Control means influence, not direct power; advice, not command; criticism, not obstruction; scrutiny, not initiation, and publicity, not secrecy. (Bernard Crick, *The Reform of Parliament: The Crisis of British Government*, Weidenfeld and Nicolson, London, 2nd ed., 1968, 80.)

APPENDIX

Notes on the Socio-Economic Backgrounds of MPs

The categories used in analysing the socio-economic backgrounds of MPs were as follows:

1. *Education*
   (a) *Public school education*: attendance at school listed as a member of the Headmasters' Conference, the Association of Governing Bodies of Public Schools, together with the list of overseas public schools and the list of principal girls' schools published annually in *Whitaker's Almanac*. These were further subdivided into those who had attended one of the nine 'Clarendon' schools—as defined by the Royal Commission on Public Schools, 1864, chaired by Lord Clarendon, that is, Eton, Harrow, Winchester, Charterhouse, Shrewsbury, Rugby, Westminster, St Paul's, and Merchant Taylors'—and those who did not.
   (b) *Graduates*: graduated from a university, former polytechnic, or service college in the UK or overseas, further subdivided into those who had attended either Oxford or Cambridge and those who had attended other institutions.
   (c) *Elementary*: those whose full-time education terminated at elementary school, including those who had further education in evening classes, adult education etc.
2. *Occupation*
   (a) *Professions*: lawyers, doctors, dentists, school, further education, university and adult education teachers, officers of the armed forces, and all recognized professions.
   (b) *Business*: all employers, directors of private and public companies, business executives, stockbrokers, farmers and working landowners, and small businessmen.
   (c) *Workers*: blue and white-collar workers, including all full-time trade union officials.
   (d) *Miscellaneous*: housewives, professional politicians, welfare workers, local government officers, insurance agents and estate valuers, journalists, party publicists, professional party organizers, and miscellaneous administrators.

(e) *Private means*: those who lived from unearned income, for example from investments, shares and dividends, rents, or income from landed estates.

With exception of (e), these are the categories used by David Butler and his co-authors in the Nuffield Election Studies and by Samuel E. Finer, Hugh B. Berrington, and D. Bartholomew *Backbench Opinion in the House of Commons, 1955–59*, Pergamon Press, London, 1961, but following the latter's practice of classifying by the subject's occupation on election, rather than the former's practice of using the earliest or formative occupation.

3. *Direct Local Connections*

Born, educated, living or working in the constituency; having property interests or serving or having served as a member of a local government body in the constituency, or, in the case of towns or cities divided into two or more constituencies, with the town or city within which the constituency lies.

BIBLIOGRAPHY

Official Documents

Committee on the Remuneration of Ministers and Members of Parliament (the Lawrence Committee), Cmd. 2516, November 1964.

Conference on the Reform of the Second Chamber (the Bryce Commission), *Report* Cmd. 9038, 1918.

House of Commons Commission, *Annual Reports*.

House of Commons Debates.

House of Commons Library, *Factsheets*.

House of Commons, *Sessional Returns*.

House of Commons, *Standing Orders on Public Business*, HC 7, 1994–5.

House of Commons, Liaison Committee, *First Report: Shifting the Balance— Select Committees and the Executive*, HC 300, 1999–2000 (Government response: Cm. 4737, May 2000).

—— *Second Report: Independence or Control?*, HC 748, 1999–2000.

House of Commons, Select Committee on Procedure, *Reports*.

House of Commons, Select Committee on the Library (House of Commons), *Second Report*, HC 99, 1945–46.

House of Commons, Services Committee, *Third Report: Accommodation in the New Parliamentary Building*, HC 295, 1968–9.

House of Commons, Standing Committee appointed to assist Mr Speaker on the Direction of the Library, *Report*, HC 104, 1835.

House of Lords, *A Brief Guide to the Procedures and Practices of the House of Lords and the Companion to Standing Orders*, HL 9, 1994–5.

House of Lords, *Standing Orders on Public Business*, HL 15, 1994–5.

Independent Commission on the Voting System (the Jenkins Commission), *Report*, Cm. 4090, October 1998.

Parliamentary History (debates).

Royal Commission on the Constitution (the Kilbrandon Commission), *Report*, Cmd., 5640, October 1973.

Royal Commission on the House of Lords, *A House for the Future* (the Wakeham Report), Cm. 4534, January 2000.

Senior Salaries Review Body, *Report No. 38*, Cm. 3330, July 1996

—— *Report No. 47*. Cm. 4188, March 1999.

The Cabinet Office, *Modernising Parliament: Reform of the House of Lords*, Cm. 4183, January 1999.

Top Salaries Review Body, *First Report: Ministers of the Crown and Members of Parliament*, Cmd. 4836, December 1971.

—— *Report No. 8*, Cmd. 6574, July 1976.

—— *Report No. 12*, Cmd. 7598, June 1979.

—— *Report No. 20*, Cmd. 8881, May 1983.

—— *Report No. 24*, Cmd. 131, April 1987.

—— *Report No. 32*, Cmd. 1943, July 1992.

Autobiographies, Memoirs, and other Contemporary Sources

Anson, Sir William, *The Law and the Constitution*, Clarendon Press, Oxford, 1st ed. 1886.

Asquith, Margot, *The Autobiography of Margot Asquith*, ed. Mark Bonham Carter, Weidenfeld and Nicolson, London, 1995 (originally published in two volumes, 1920 and 1922).

Bagehot, Walter, *Collected Works: The English Constitution*, ed. Norman St. John Stevas, *The Economist*, London, 1974 (originally published 1865–7).

Baker, Arthur, *The House is Sitting*, Blandford, London, 1958.

Ball, Stuart (ed.), *Parliament and Politics in the Age of Baldwin and Macdonald: the Headlam Diaries, 1923–1935*, The Historians' Press, London, 1992.

Bentham, Jeremy 'First Principles Preparatory to Constitutional Code', [1830] in *Collected Works of Jeremy Bentham*, ed. Philip Schofield, Clarendon Press, Oxford, 1989, 96–100.

—— 'An Essay on Political Tactics', in Michael James, Cyprian Blamires, and Catherine Pease-Watkins (eds.), *The Collected Works of Jeremy Bentham: Political Tactics*, Clarendon Press, Oxford, 1999 (originally published 1791).

Blackstone, Sir William, *Commentaries on the Laws of England*, London, 1765.

Brandreth, Gyles, *Breaking the Code: Westminster Diaries*, Phoenix, London, 2000.

Bright, John, *The Public Letters of the Rt. Hon. John Bright*, ed. H. J. Leech, Sampson Low, London, 1885.

Burke, Edmund, 'Letter to the Electors of Bristol', *Collected Works*, Vol. 1, George Bell, London, 1883.

—— 'Thoughts on the Present Discontents', *Collected Works*, Vol. 1, George Bell, London, 1883.

Charter 88, *Reinventing Westminster*, Charter 88, London, 1998.

Churchill, Winston, *Lord Randolph Churchill*, Macmillan, London, 1906.

Clarke, Sir Edward, *The Story of My Life*, John Murray, London, 1918.

Conservative Party, *Report of the Commission to Strengthen Parliament*, London, July, 2000.

Dicey, A. V., *An Introduction to the Law of the Constitution*, Macmillan, London, 1st ed. 1885.

Elsynge, Henry (ed.), *The Manner of Holding Parliaments in England*, reprinted Irish University Press, Dublin, 1972.

Lord Ernle, *From Whippingham to Westminster*, John Murray, London, 1918.

(Viscount) Gladstone, Herbert, *After Thirty Years*, Macmillan, London, 1928.

Gray, Frank, *Confessions of a Candidate*, Martin Hopkinson, London, 1925.

Earl Grey, *Parliamentary Government considered with reference to a Reform of Parliament*, London, (publisher not listed), 1st ed. 1858.

Griffith-Boscawen, Sir Arthur, *Memories*, John Murray, London, 1925.

Grimond, Jo, *Memoirs*, Heinemann, London, 1979.

Lord Hamilton, George, *Parliamentary Reminiscences and Reflections 1868–1885*, John Murray, London, 1916.

Hatsell, John, *Precedents of Proceedings in the House of Commons*, London, 1781.

Hattersley, Roy, *Who Goes Home? Scenes from Political Life*, Little Brown, London, 1995.

Lord Hemingford (Sir Denis Herbert), *Backbencher and Chairman: Some Parliamentary Reminiscences*, John Murray, London, 1946.

Hill, Anthony, and Whichelow, Anthony, *What's Wrong with Parliament?*, Penguin, London, 1964.

Hollis, Christopher, *Can Parliament Survive?*, Hollis and Carter, London, 1949.

Holyoake, G. J., *Working Class Representation*, Birmingham, 1868.

Hyland, Stanley, *Curiosities from Parliament*, Allan Wingate, London, 1955.

Hutchinson, Horace G., (ed.), *The Private Diaries of Sir Algernon West*, John Murray, London, 1922.

Ilbert, Sir Courtenay, Supplementary Chapter in Josef Redlich, *The Procedures of the House of Commons* (trans. A. Ernest Steinthal), London, Constable, 1908, Vol. 3, 202–23.

Jenkins, Roy, *A Life at the Centre*, Macmillan, London, 1991.

Jennings, G. H., *An Anecdotal History of the British Parliament*, Appleton & Co., New York, NY, 1881.

Lindsay, T. F., *Parliament From the Press Gallery*, Macmillan, London, 1967.

Lucy, Henry W., *A Diary of Two Parliaments: 1—The Disraeli Parliament, 1874–1880; 2—The Gladstone Parliament, 1880–1885*, Cassell, London, 1885.

—— *A Diary of the Salisbury Parliament, 1886–1892*, Cassell, London, 1892.

—— *Later Peeps at Parliament: Taken from Behind the Speaker's Chair*, George Newnes, London, 1905.

—— *The Balfourian Parliament, 1900–1906*, Hodder and Stoughton, London, 1906.

Lyttleton, Oliver (Viscount Chandos), *The Memoirs of Lord Chandos*, The Bodley Head, London, 1962.

Lord Macaulay (Thomas Babington), *History of England from the Accession of James II*, Longman, Brown, Green and Longmans, London, 3rd ed. 1849.

MacDonagh, Michael, *Parliament: Its Romance, Its Comedy, Its Pathos*, T. Fisher Unwin, London, 1904

—— *The Pageant of Parliament*, T. Fisher Unwin, London, 1921.

Mackay, T., *The Reminiscences of Albert Pell*, John Murray, London, 1908.

Mackintosh, Sir Alexander, *From Gladstone to Lloyd George: Parliament in Peace and War*, Hodder and Stoughton, London, 1921.

—— *Echoes of Big Ben: A Journalist's Parliamentary Diary, (1881–1940)*, Jarrolds, London, 1946.

Maitland, F. W., *The Constitutional History of England: A Course of Lectures Delivered by F. W. Maitland in 1887 and 1888*, Cambridge University Press, Cambridge, 1st ed, 1908.

May, Thomas Erskine, *Treatise on the Law, Privileges, Proceedings and Usage of Parliament*, Charles Knight, London, 1st ed. 1844.

—— *Remarks and Suggestions with a View to Facilitating the Despatch of Public Business in Parliament*, James Ridgway, London, 1849.

The Earl of Midleton, *Records and Reactions, 1856–1939*, John Murray, London, 1939.

Mill, John Stuart, *Representative Government*, J. M. Dent, London, 1910 (originally published 1861).

Mitchell, Austin, *Westminster Man: A Tribal Anthropology of the Commons People*, Thames Methuen, London, 1982.

Morley, John, *Life of Gladstone*, Macmillan, London, 1903.

Morris-Jones, Sir Henry, *Doctor in the Whips' Room*, Robert Hales, London, 1955.

Mowbray, Sir John, *Seventy Years at Westminster*, ed. Edith Mowbray, Blackwood, London, 1900.

Nicolson, Nigel, *People and Parliament*, Weidenfeld and Nicolson, London, 1958.

O'Brien, Barry, *The Life and Times of Charles Stewart Parnell*, Smith, Elder and Co., London, 1898.

O'Connor, T. P., *Gladstone's House of Commons*, Ward Downey, London, 1885.

O'Donnell, F. H., *A History of the Irish Parliamentary Party*, Longman Green, London, 1910.

Ostrogorski, M. I., *Democracy and the Organisation of Political Parties, Vol. I—England, Vol. II—United States* (ed. and abridged S. M. Lipset) Quadrangle Books, Chicago, Ill., 1964 (originally published in English 1902).

Palgrave, Sir Reginald, *The House of Commons: Illustrations of its History and Practice*, Macmillan, London, 1878.

Pease, Sir Alfred, *Elections and Recollections*, John Murray, London, 1932.

Redlich, Josef, *The Procedures of the House of Commons* (trans. A. Ernest Steinthal), London, Constable, 1908 (originally published 1905).

Redmond, John, 'Fifteen Years in the House of Commons', lecture given in New York, 29 November 1896, in Christopher Sylvester (ed.), *The Literary Companion to Parliament*, Sinclair Stevenson, London, 1996, 28–30.

Rogers, James E. Thorold, *Cobden and Modern Public Opinion*, Macmillan, London, 1873.

(Lord) Snell, Henry, *Daily Life in Parliament*, Routledge, London 1930.

—— *Men, Movements and Myself*, J. M. Dent, London, 1936.

Thomas, George, *Mr Speaker*, Century Publications, London, 1985.

Thomas, J. H., *The Story of My Life*, Hutchinson, London, 1937.

Todd, Alpheus, *On Parliamentary Government in England: Its Origins, Development and Operation*, Longman, London, 2nd ed. (ed. A. H. Todd), 2 vols., 1887 and 1889 (originally published 1867 and 1869).

Townsend, Charles, *History of the House of Commons: From the Convention Parliament of 1688 to the Passing of the Reform Bill in 1832*, Henry Colburn, London, 1843.

Viscount Ullswater (J. W. Lowther), *A Speaker's Commentaries*, Edward Arnold, London, 1925.

White, William, *The Inner Life of the House of Commons*, ed. Justin McCarthy, T. Fisher Unwin, London, 1898.

Earl Winterton, *Orders of the Day*, Cassell, London, 1953.

—— *Fifty Tumultuous Years*, Hutchinson, London, 1955.

Secondary Sources

Ayedelotte, William O., 'Voting patterns in the British House of Commons', *Comparative Studies in History and Society*, 2, 1963, 134–63.

—— (ed.), *The History of Parliamentary Behaviour*, Princeton University Press, Princeton, NJ, 1977.

—— 'Constituency Influence in the British House of Commons', in William O. Ayedelotte (ed.), *The History of Parliamentary Behaviour*, Princeton University Press, Princeton, NJ, 1977, 225–46.

Barker, Anthony, and Rush, Michael, *The Member of Parliament and His Information*, Allen and Unwin, London, 1970.

Beer, Samuel H., *Modern British Politics: A Study of Parties and Pressure Groups*, Faber, London, 1965.

Berrington, Hugh, 'Partisanship and dissidence in the nineteenth century House of Commons', *Parliamentary Affairs*, 21, 1967–8, 338–74.

—— *Backbench Opinion in the House of Commons, 1945–55*, Pergamon Press, London, 1973.

Best, Heinrich, and Cotta, Maurizio (eds.), *Parliamentary Representatives in Europe 1848–2000: Legislative Recruitment and Careers in Eleven European Countries*, Oxford University Press, Oxford, 2000.

Birch, A. H., *Representative and Responsible Government*, Allen and Unwin, London, 1964.

Blackburn, Robert, *The Electoral System in Britain*, Macmillan, London, 1995.

Bown, Francis, 'The Defeat of the Shops Bill, 1986', in Michael Rush (ed.), *Parliament and Pressure Politics*, Clarendon Press, Oxford, 1990, 213–33.

Brazier, Alex, *Systematic Scrutiny: Reforming the Select Committees*, Hansard Society, London, 2000.

Bromhead, P. A., *The House of Lords and Contemporary Politics*, Routledge and Kegan Paul, London, 1958.

Butler, David, and Butler, Gareth, *Twentieth Century British Political Facts, 1900–2000*, Macmillan, London, 2000.

—— and Kavanagh, Dennis, *The British General Election of 1983*, Macmillan, London, 1984.

—— —— *The British General Election of 1987*, Macmillan, London, 1988.

—— —— *The British General Election of 1992*, Macmillan, London, 1992.

—— —— *The British General Election of 1997*, Macmillan, London, 1997.

Butt, Ronald, *The Power of Parliament*, Constable, London, 1st ed. 1967, 2nd. ed. 1969.

Butterfield, Herbert, *The Whig Interpretation of History*, G. Bell, London, 1931.

Lord Campion (ed.), *Parliament: A Survey*, Allen and Unwin, London, 1952.

Campion, Gilbert, 'Parliament and Democracy', in Lord Campion (ed.), *Parliament: A Survey*, Allen and Unwin, London, 1952, 9–36.

—— 'Parliamentary Procedure, Old and New', in Lord Campion (ed.), *Parliament: A Survey*, Allen and Unwin, London, 1952, 141–67.

Cannadine, David, *The Decline and Fall of the British Aristocracy*, Macmillan, London, 1992.

Carr, Cecil, 'Delegated Legislation', in Lord Campion (ed.), *Parliament: A Survey*, Allen and Unwin, London, 1952, 232–51.

Chester, D. Norman, and Bowring, Nona, *Questions in Parliament*, Clarendon Press, Oxford, 1962.

Cline, Catherine Ann, *Recruits to Labour: The British Labour Party 1914–1931*, Syracuse University Press, New York, NY, 1963.

Coates, R. Morris and Dalton, Thomas R., 'A note on the cost of standing for the British Parliament, 1852–1880', *Legislative Studies Quarterly*, 17, 1992, 585–93.

Cocks, Sir Barnett, *Mid-Victorian Masterpiece: The Story of an Institution Unable to Put Its Own House in Order*, Hutchinson, London, 1977.

Cook, Chris and Keith, Brendan, *British Historical Facts, 1830–1900*, Macmillan. London, 1975.

—— and Stevenson, John, *British Historical Facts, 1760–1830*, Macmillan, London, 1980.

—— ——, *British Political Facts 1688–1760*, Macmillan, London, 1988.

—— and Wroughton, John, *English Historical Facts, 1603–1688*, Macmillan, London, 1980.

Cowley, Philip (ed.), *Conscience and Parliament*, Frank Cass, London, 1998.

—— and Norton, Philip, 'Rebels and rebellions: Conservative MPs in the 1992 Parliament', *British Journal of Politics and International Relations*, 1, 1999, 84–105.

—— and Stuart, Mark, 'Parliament: a few headaches and a dose of modernisation', *Parliamentary Affairs*, 54, 2001, 238–56.

Craig, F. W. S. (ed.), *British Election Results, 1950–70*, Parliamentary Research Services, Chichester, 1971.

—— (ed.), *British Election Results, 1886–1918*, Macmillan, London, 1974.

—— (ed.), *British Election Results, 1832–1885*, Macmillan, London, 1977.

—— (ed.), *British Election Results, 1919–1949*, Parliamentary Research Services, Glasgow,, 3rd. ed. 1983.

—— (ed.), *British Electoral Facts, 1832–1987*, Parliamentary Research Services, Dartmouth, 1989.

Crewe, Ivor and King, Anthony, *SDP: The Birth, Life and Death of the Social Democratic Party*, Oxford University Press, Oxford, 1995.

Crick, Bernard, *The Reform of the Commons*, Fabian Tract 319, Fabian Society, London, 1959.

—— *In Defence of Politics*, Weidenfeld and Nicolson, London, 1st ed. 1962; 5th ed. Continuum Books, London, 2000.

—— *The Reform of Parliament: The Crisis of British Government*, Weidenfeld and Nicolson, London, 1st ed. 1964, 2nd rev. ed. 1968.

Crossman, Richard H. S., 'Introduction', to Walter Bagehot, *The English Constitution*, C. A. Watts, London, 1964, 1–57.

Douglas, Roy, *The History of the Liberal Party, 1895–1970*, Sidgwick and Jackson, London 1971.

Dowse, Robert E., 'The MP and his surgery', *Political Studies*, 11, 1963, 333–41.

—— and Smith, Trevor, 'Party discipline in the House of Commons—a comment', *Parliamentary Affairs*, 16, 1962–3, 159–64.

Drewry, Gavin (ed.), *The New Select Committees: A Study of the 1979 Reforms*, Clarendon Press, Oxford, 2nd ed. 1989.

—— and Butcher, Tony, *The Civil Service Today*, Basil Blackwell, Oxford, 2nd ed. 1991.

Ellis, R. J., *He Walks Alone* [biography of A. S. Cunningham-Reid MP], W. H. Allen, London, 1945.

Ensor, Sir Robert, *England, 1870–1914*, Clarendon Press, Oxford, 1936.

Escott, T. H. S., *Clubs Makers and Club Members*, T. Fisher Unwin, London, 1914.

Fair, John D., 'Party voting behaviour in the British House of Commons 1886–1918', *Parliamentary History*, 5, 1986, 65–82.

Farrell, David, *Comparing Electoral Systems*, Macmillan, London, 1997.

Fellowes, Sir Edward, 'Changes in parliamentary life', *Political Quarterly*, 36, 1965, 256–65.

Finer, Samuel E., 'The individual responsibility of ministers', *Public Administration*, 34, 1956, 377–96.

—— Berrington, Hugh B., and Bartholomew, D., *Backbench Opinion in the House of Commons, 1955–59*, Pergamon Press, London, 1961.

Flynn, Paul, *Commons Knowledge: How to be a Backbencher*, Seren, Bridgend, 1997.

Franklin, Mark, *The Decline of Class Voting in Britain: Changes in the Basis of Electoral Choice, 1964–83*, Oxford University Press, Oxford, 1985.

—— and Norton, Philip (eds.), *Parliamentary Questions*, Clarendon Press, Oxford, 1993.

—— Baxter, Alison, and Jordan, Margaret, 'Who are the rebels? Dissent in the British House of Commons, 1970–74', *Legislative Studies Quarterly*, 11, 1986, 143–59.

Fry, Geoffrey K., *The Growth of Government: The Development of Ideas about the Role of the State and the Machinery of Government in Britain since 1780*, Frank Cass, London, 1979.

Gallagher, Michael, and Marsh, Michael (eds.), *Candidate Selection in Comparative Perspective: The Secret Garden of Politics*, Sage, London, 1988.

Garrett, John, *Does Parliament Work?*, Gollanz, London, 1992.

Giddings, Philip, 'Select committees and parliamentary scrutiny: plus ça change', *Parliamentary Affairs*, 47, 1994, 669–704.

Gordon, Strathearn, *Our Parliament*, Cassell for the Hansard Society, London, 6th rev. and enlarged ed. 1964.

Gorst, H. E., *The Fourth Party*, Smith, Elder and Co., London, 1906.

Greenleaf, W. H., *The British Political Tradition: I The Rise of Collectivism; II The Ideological Heritage; III A Much-Governed Nation; IV The World Outside*, Routledge/Methuen, London, 4 vols., 1983–7.

Griffith, John A. G., *The Parliamentary Scrutiny of Government Bills*, Allen and Unwin, London, 1974.

—— and Ryle, Michael, *Parliament: Functions, Practice and Procedures*, Sweet and Maxwell, London, 1989.

Guttsman, W. L., *The British Political Elite*, MacGibbon and Kee, London, 1963.

Gwyn, William B., *Democracy and the Cost of Politics in Britain*, Athlone Press, London, 1962.

Hanham, H. J., *Elections and Party Management in the Age of Disraeli*, Harvester Press, Hemel Hampstead, 2nd ed. 1978.

The Hansard Society, *Parliamentary Reform: A Survey of Recent Proposals for the Commons*, Cassell, London, 1st ed. 1961, 2nd ed. 1967.

—— *Making the Law: Report of the Hansard Society Commission on the Legislative Process*, The Hansard Society, London, 1992.

Harrison, Brian, 'Women in a men's House: the women MPs, 1919–1945', *The Historical Journal*, 29, 1986, 623–54.

Hawkins, Angus, *Parliament, Party and the Art of Politics in Britain, 1855–59*, Macmillan, London, 1987.

Heath, Anthony, Jowell, Roger, and Curtice, John, *How Britain Votes*, Oxford University Press, Oxford, 1985.

—— Curtice John, Jowell, Roger, Evans, Geoff, Field, Julia, and Witherspoon, Sharon, *Understanding Political Change: The British Voter, 1964–87*, Pergamon, London, 1991.

Held, David, *Models of Democracy*, Polity Press, Cambridge, 2nd ed. 1996.

Hill, B. W., *The Growth of Parliamentary Parties 1689–1742*, Allen and Unwin, London, 1976.

—— *British Parliamentary Parties 1742–1832: From the Fall of Walpole to the First Reform Act*, Allen and Unwin, London, 1985.

Holden, Barry, *The Nature of Democracy*, Nelson, London, 1974.

Hollis, Patricia, *Jennie Lee: A Life*, Oxford University Press, Oxford, 1997.

Hosking, Geoffrey and King, Anthony, 'Radicals and Whigs in the British Liberal Party, 1906–14', in William O. Aydelotte (ed.), *The History of Parliamentary Behaviour*, Princeton University Press, Princeton, NJ, 1977, 136–56.

Howarth, Patrick, *Questions in the House: The History of a Unique British Institution*, The Bodley Head, London, 1956.

Jackson, Robert J., *Rebels and Whips: Discipline and Cohesion in British Political Parties since 1945*, Macmillan, London, 1968.

Jay, Anthony (ed.), *The Oxford Dictionary of Political Quotations*, Oxford University Press, Oxford, 1996.

Jenkins, T. A., *Parliament, Party and Politics in Victorian Britain*, Manchester University Press, 1996.

—— 'The whips in the early Victorian House of Commons', *Parliamentary History*, 19, 2000, 259–86.

Judge, David, *Backbench Specialisation*, Heinemann, London, 1981.

—— *The Parliamentary State*, Sage, London, 1983.

—— (ed.) *The Politics of Parliamentary Reform*, Heinemann, London, 1983.

—— 'The politics of MPs' pay', *Parliamentary Affairs*, 37, 1984, 59–75.

—— 'Representation in Westminster in the 1990s: the ghost of Edmund Burke', *Journal of Legislative Studies*, 5, 1999, 12–34.

Kee, Robert, *The Laurel and the Ivy: The Story of Charles Stewart Parnell and Irish Nationalism*, Penguin, London, 1994 (first published by Hamish Hamilton 1993).

King, Anthony, 'The Rise of the career politician in Britain—and its consequences', *British Journal of Political Science*, 2, 1981, 249–85.

Lowell, A. Lawrence, 'The influence of party on legislatures in England and America', *Annual Report of the American Historical Association*, 1, 1901, 321–542.

—— *The Government of England*, Macmillan, New York, NY, new ed. 1920 (originally published 1908).

Laundy, Philip, *The Office of Speaker*, Cassell, London, 1964.

Law, William, *Our Hansard*, Pitman, London, 1950.

Lubenow, William C., *The Politics of Government Growth: Early Victorian Attitudes Towards State Intervention, 1833–1848*, David and Charles, Newton Abbot, 1971.

Mackenzie, K. R., *The English Parliament*, Penguin, London, 1951.

Mackenzie, W. J. M., and Grove, J. W., *Central Administration in Britain*, Longman, London, 1957.

Mackintosh, John P., (ed.), *People and Parliament*, Saxon House, Farnborough, 1978.

Mancuso, Maureen, *The Ethical World of British MPs*, McGill-Queen's University Press, Montreal, 1995.

Marsden, Philip, *The Officers of the Commons 1363–1965*, Barrie and Rockcliff, London, 1966.

Marsh, David, and Read, Melvyn, *Private Members' Bills*, Cambridge University Press, Cambridge, 1988.

May, Thomas Erskine, *Treatise on the Law, Privileges, Proceedings and Usage of Parliament*, 22nd ed. edited by Sir Donald Limon and W. R. Mackay, Butterworths, London, 1997.

McKenzie, Robert T., *British Political Parties: The Distribution of Power within the Conservative and Labour Parties*, Heinemann, London, 1st ed.,1955.

Miller, William L., Timpson, Annis May, and Lessnoff, Michael, *Political Culture in Contemporary Britain: People and Politicians, Principles and Practice*, Clarendon Press, Oxford, 1996.

Moore, David Cresap, *The Politics of Deference: A Study of the Mid-Nineteenth Century English Political System*, Harvester Press, Hassocks, Sussex, 1976.

Morris, A. J. A. (ed.), *Edwardian Radicalism 1900–14: Some Aspects of British Radicalism*, Routledge and Kegan Paul, London, 1974.

Namier, Sir Lewis, *The Structure of Politics at the Accession of George III*, Macmillan, London, 2nd ed. 1958.

—— *Crossroads of Power: Essays in Eighteenth Century England*, Hamish Hamilton, London, 1962.

—— and Brooke, John, *The History of Parliament: The House of Commons, 1754–1790*, HMSO for the History of Parliament Trust, London, 1964.

Newton, Robert, *Eighteenth Century Exeter*, University of Exeter Press, Exeter, 1984.

Nichols, David, *The Lost Prime Minister: A Life of Sir Charles Dilke*, The Hambledon Press, London, 1995.

Norris, Pippa, 'Legislative Recruitment', in L. LeDuc, R. G. Niemi, and P. Norris (eds.), *Comparing Democracies: Elections and Voting in Global Perspective*, Sage, London, 1996.

—— 'The puzzle of constituency service', *Journal of Legislative Studies*, 2, 1996, 29–49.

—— and Lovenduski, Joni, *Political Recruitment: Gender, Race and Class in the British Parliament*, Cambridge University Press, Cambridge, 1995.

Norton, Philip, *Dissension in the House of Commons, 1945–74*, Macmillan, London, 1975.

—— *Conservative Dissidents: Dissidence within the Parliamentary Conservative Party, 1970–74*, Temple Smith, London, 1978.

—— 'Government defeats in the House of Commons: myth and reality', *Public Law*, 1978, 360–78.

—— *Dissidence in the House of Commons, 1974–79*, Clarendon Press, Oxford, 1980.

—— *The Commons in Perspective*, Martin Robertson, London, 1981.

—— 'Behavioural Changes' in Philip Norton (ed.), *Parliament in the 1980s*, Blackwell, 1985, 22–47.

—— (ed.), *Parliament in the 1980s*, Blackwell, 1985.

—— 'The growth of the constituency role of the MP', *Parliamentary Affairs*, 47, 1994, 705–20.

—— 'Are MPs Revolting? Dissension in the British House of Commons, 1979–92', Paper presented to the Second Workshop of Parliamentary Scholars and Parliamentarians, Wroxton College, Banbury, August 1996.

—— 'The individual Member in the British House of Commons', *Journal of Legislative Studies*, 5, 1999, 53–74.

—— 'Reforming Parliament in the UK: The Report of the Commission to Strengthen Parliament', *Journal of Legislative Studies*, 6, 2000, 1–14.

—— and Wood, David, *Back From Westminster: British Members of Parliament and Their Constituents*, University of Kentucky Press, Lexington, KY, 1993.

O' Brien, Conor Cruise, *Parnell and His Party, 1880–90*, Clarendon Press, Oxford, 1957.

O'Gorman, Frank, *Voters, Patrons and Parties: The Unreformed Electorate of Hanoverian England, 1734–1832*, Clarendon Press, Oxford, 1989.

O'Leary, Cornelius, *The Elimination of Corrupt Practices in British Elections, 1868–1911*, Oxford University Press, Oxford, 1962.

Oliver, Dawn, and Drewry, Gavin (eds.), *The Law and Parliament*, Butterworths, London, 1998.

Parris, Henry, *Constitutional Bureaucracy*, Allen and Unwin, London, 1969.

Parry, Geraint, Moyser, George, and Day, Neil, *Political Participation and Democracy in Britain*, Cambridge University Press, Cambridge, 1992.

Pinto-Duchinsky, Michael, *British Political Finance 1830–1980*, American Enterprise Institute, Washington, DC, 1981.

Pitkin, Hannah, *The Concept of Representation*, University of California Press, Berkeley, CA, 1967.

Pollard, A. F., *The Evolution of Parliament*, Longman, 1920.

Porritt, Edward, *The Unreformed House of Commons: Parliamentary Representation before 1832*, Cambridge University Press, Cambridge, 1909.

Powell, Ken, and Cook, Chris, *English Historical Facts 1485–1603*, Macmillan, London, 1977.

Power, Greg, *Representatives of the People: The Constituency Role of MPs*, Fabian Society, London, 1998.

Punnett, R. M., *Frontbench Opposition*, Heinemann, London, 1973.

Radice, Lisanne, Vallance, Elizabeth, and Willis, Virginia, *Member of Parliament: The Job of a Backbencher*, Macmillan, London, 1987.

Richards, Peter G., *Honourable Members: A Study of the British Backbencher*, Faber, London, 1959.

—— *Parliament and Conscience*, Allen and Unwin, London, 1970.

—— *The Backbenchers*, Faber, London, 1972.

Riddell, Peter, *Honest Opportunism: the Rise of the Career Politician*, Hamish Hamilton, London, 1993.

—— 'The rise of the career politician', *Journal of Legislative Studies*, 1, 1995, 86–91.

—— *Parliament Under Pressure*, Gollanz, London, 1998.

—— *Parliament Under Blair*, Politico's Books, London, 2000.

Roberts, Andrew, *Salisbury: Victorian Titan*, Weidenfeld and Nicolson, London, 1999.

Rose, Richard, 'Parties, factions and tendencies in Britain', *Political Studies*, 12, 1964, 34–46.

—— and McAllister, Ian, *Voters Begin to Choose: From Closed Class to Open Elections in Britain*, Sage, London, 1986.

Rush, Michael, *The Selection of Parliamentary Candidates*, Nelson, London, 1969.

—— *Parliament and the Public*, Longman, London, 1st ed. 1976, 2nd ed. 1986

—— 'The Members of Parliament', in S. A. Walkland (ed.), *The House of Commons in the Twentieth Century*, Clarendon Press, Oxford, 1979, 69–123.

—— *Parliamentary Government in Britain*, Pitman, London, 1981.

—— (ed.), *The House of Commons: Services and Facilities, 1972–82*, Policy Studies Institute, London, 1983.

—— 'The "Selectorate" Revisited: selecting candidates in the 1980s', in Lynton Robins (ed.), *Political Institutions in Britain: Development and Change*, Longman, Harlow, 1987, 151–65.

—— 'The Education, Science and Arts Committee', and 'The Social Services Committee', in Gavin Drewry (ed.), *The New Select Committees: A Study of the 1979 Reforms*, Clarendon Press, Oxford, 2nd ed., 1989, 88–109 and 239–53.

—— (ed.) *Parliament and Pressure Politics*, Clarendon Press, Oxford, 1990.

—— 'Career patterns in British politics: First choose your party . . .', *Parliamentary Affairs*, 47, 1994, 566–82.

—— 'The pay, allowances, services and facilities of legislators in eighteen countries and the European Parliament', in Senior Salaries Review Body, *Report No. 38*, Cm. 3330-II, July 1996, 38–59.

—— 'The Law Relating to Members' Conduct', in Dawn Oliver and Gavin Drewry (eds.), *The Law and Parliament*, Butterworths, London, 1998, 105–24.

—— and Baldwin, Nicholas, 'Lawyers in Parliament', in Dawn Oliver and Gavin Drewry (eds.), *The Law and Parliament*, Butterworths, London, 1998, 155–73.

—— and Cromwell, Valerie, 'Continuity and Change: Legislative Recruitment in the United Kingdom 1868–1999', in Heinrich Best and Maurizio Cotta (eds.), *Parliamentary Representatives in Europe 1848–2000: Legislative Recruitment and Careers in Eleven European Countries*, Oxford University Press, Oxford, 2000, 461–90.

—— and Shaw, Malcolm (eds.), *The House of Commons: Services and Facilities*, Allen and Unwin, London, 1974.

Russell, A. K., *Liberal Landslide: The General Election of 1906*, David and Charles, Newton Abbot, 1973.

Ryle, Michael, and Richards, Peter G. (eds.), *The Commons Under Scrutiny*, Routledge, London, 1988.

Schwarz, John E., 'Exploring a new role in policy-making in the British

House of Commons in the 1970s', *American Political Science Review*, 74, 1980, 23–37.

Searing, Donald D., *Westminster's World: Understanding Political Roles*, Harvard University Press, Cambridge, MA, 1994.

Sedgwick, Romney, *History of Parliament: The House of Commons 1715–1754*, HMSO (for the History of Parliament Trust), London, 1970.

Shell, Donald, *The House of Lords*, Harvester-Wheatsheaf, Hemel Hampsted, 2nd ed., 1992.

—— and Beamish, David (eds.), *The House of Lords at Work: A Study of the 1988–89 Session*, Clarendon Press, Oxford, 1993.

Silk, Paul and Walters, Rhodri, *How Parliament Works*, Longman, London, 4th ed., 1998.

Stark, Tom, 'International Comparisons of the Remuneration of Members of Parliament', in SSRB, *Report No. 38*, Cm. 3330-II, July 1996, 60–8.

Stenton, Michael, and Lees, Stephen (eds.), *Who's Who of British Members of Parliament: A Biographical Dictionary of the House of Commons, 1832–1979*, Harvester Press, Brighton, 4 vols., 1976–81.

Stewart, Robert, *Party and Politics, 1832–1852*, Macmillan, London, 1989.

Sylvester, Christopher (ed.), *The Literary Companion to Parliament*, Sinclair Stevenson, London, 1996.

Thomas, J. A., *The House of Commons, 1832–1901: A Study of its Economic and Functional Character*, University of Wales Press, Cardiff, 1939.

—— *The House of Commons, 1906–1911: An Analysis of its Economic and Social Character*, University of Wales Press, Cardiff, 1958.

Thorne, R. G., *The History of Parliament: The House of Commons, 1790–1820*, Secker and Warburg for the History of Parliament Trust, London, 1980.

Trevelyan, G. M., *History of England*, Longman, London, 1926.

Walkland, S. A. (ed.), *The House of Commons in the Twentieth Century: Essays by Members of the Study of Parliament Group*, Clarendon Press, Oxford, 1979.

—— and Ryle, Michael (eds.), *The Commons in the Seventies*, Martin Robertson, London, 1977.

Watts, Cedric, and Davies, Laurence, *Cunninghame-Graham: A Critical Biography*, Cambridge University Press, Cambridge, 1979.

Weber, Max, 'Politics as a Vocation', in H. H. Gerth and C. Wright Mills (eds.), *From Max Weber: Essays in Sociology*, Routledge and Kegan Paul, London, 1948, 77–128.

Wheeler-Booth, Michael, 'The House of Lords', in John A. G. Griffith and Michael Ryle, *Parliament: Functions, Practices and Procedures*, Sweet and Maxwell, London, 1989, 455–514.

Woodhouse, A. S. P. (ed.), *Puritanism and Liberty: Being the Army Debates (1647–9)*, J. M. Dent, London, 1938.

Young, Alison, *The Reselection of MPs*, Heinemann, London, 1983.

INDEX